DEMOCRACY IN THE
CONTEMPORARY STATE

By the same author:

LABOUR AND POLITICS, 1900–1906 (*with Henry Pelling*), 1958.
CONSTITUENCY POLITICS (*with J. Blondel and W. P. McCann*),
   1965.
THE SOCIAL AND POLITICAL THOUGHT OF THE BRITISH
   LABOUR PARTY, 1970.
THE POST OFFICE ENGINEERING UNION, 1976.
THE POLITICS OF INDEPENDENCE (*with John Sewel*), 1981.

DEMOCRACY
IN THE
CONTEMPORARY STATE

FRANK BEALEY

CLARENDON PRESS · OXFORD
1988

Oxford University Press, Walton Street, Oxford OX2 6DP

Oxford New York Toronto
Delhi Bombay Calcutta Madras Karachi
Petaling Jaya Singapore Hong Kong Tokyo
Nairobi Dar es Salaam Cape Town
Melbourne Auckland

and associated companies in
Berlin Ibadan

Oxford is a trade mark of Oxford University Press

Published in the United States
by Oxford University Press, New York

British Library Cataloguing in Publication Data
Bealey, Frank, 1922–
Democracy in the contemporary state.
1. Democracy
I. Title
321.8
ISBN 0–19–827573–0

Library of Congress Cataloging in Publication Data
Bealey, Frank.
Democracy in the contemporary state / Frank Bealey.
p. cm.
Bibliography: p.
Includes index.
1. Democracy. 2. Political sociology. 3. Representative
government and representation.   I. Title.
JC423.B29 1988   321.8–dc 19   88–10006
ISBN 0–19–827573–0

Typeset by Litho Link Limited, Welshpool, Powys
Printed in Great Britain
at the University Printing House, Oxford
by David Stanford
Printer to the University

To Sheila

PREFACE

THIS book is not intended comprehensively to cover all the difficulties of contemporary democracy. Such a treatment would have resulted in a much larger volume. Foreign and defence policy, and the implications of new security and surveillance systems, are among problems which are missing. Even so, I believe that those I deal with are salient to the dilemma of maintaining democratic procedures and values in a sound condition in an increasingly complex world.

My main contentions are that it is of little significance to consider the operation of democracy separately from the exercise of power and that it shows a misunderstanding of democratic processes to describe their outcomes as 'undemocratic' merely when we find them unfair, or unjust, or distasteful. Doubtless as a result some readers may find my view of democracy unattractive. Perhaps, therefore, I should make it clear that while democracy, as I see it, is a necessary fundamental for a decent existence, it is, for me, by no means a sufficient one. Others may feel that I paint an unduly gloomy picture of the present state of democracy. To them I would respond that though there is no cause for complacency I do not perceive democracy as being in serious crisis.

Despite the limitations admitted above, the work was wide enough to necessitate wide-ranging criticism. I am especially grateful to Richard Kimber, Franz Lehner, Klaus Schubert, and Palle Svensson, who between them made many suggestions for improvement and drew my attention to errors of judgement and fact. Hugh Berrington and Grant Jordan did the same for separate chapters. Byron Criddle was a great help with details of French political life. Of course, any mistakes that remain in the text are solely my responsibility.

An institution whose help I should also acknowledge is the Nuffield Foundation, not only for awarding me in 1980–1 a fellowship which took me to the Political Science Department at Yale, and paid for teaching support while I was on leave, but also for supporting with a grant my workshop on 'Democracy and Stability' at the European Consortium of Political Research's conference at Barcelona in March 1985. The Nuffield Foundation has long been one of the foremost friends of British political science.

I should also express my deep gratitude for all the secretarial help I received during the years of writing and rewriting. Without typists who are aware of authors' idiosyncrasies of presentation and calligraphy all research publication would be severely handicapped. Hence the importance of not destroying close personal links between secretaries and academics by misconceived schemes of pooling and 'rationalization'. I want particularly to thank Fiona Docherty, Betty Eyres, and Helen Innes of our own department. Jenny Albiston, Lorna Cardno, and Gillian Silver also contributed at times to the typing of this book. The good-humoured tolerance and dedication of all these ladies were inspiring.

Finally, I must thank my dear wife for the support she has given me in the writing of all my books. I have dedicated this one to her.

F.B.

Aberdeen,
August 1987

CONTENTS

INTRODUCTION

AT the popular level much is made of the difficulties of defining 'democracy'. It is certainly true that the term has been abused by politicians and the media; and that there is also an intellectual legacy of confusion as a result of an argument, lasting for a century or more, about what democracy implies for individual behaviour and national policies. Yet among political scientists there is now almost certainly a consensus, if not unanimity, that democracy is essentially a decision-making system, assuming certain absences of restriction on free expression, with a highly developed form of citizenship. Democracy combines freedom of criticism of authority with the rights to organize in opposition to authority and to participate in the making of decisions for the whole community. Democracy is not a guarantee of the good life.

Nevertheless, the word is seldom used in a pejorative sense. Only Aristotle, who saw the rule of the demos as a likely prelude to the confiscation of property, might be credited with that sort of usage. Among politicians of all kinds, even authoritarian leaders, democracy is considered to be 'good'. They want to be seen to be on the same side as democracy, and so they feel the need to make some genuflexion to it. Among academic commentators are those who have dealt with the concept in an abstract and philosophic fashion. They have tended to perceive democracy as providing the basis for free intellectual argument, the pursuit of truth. Other writers have been concerned with an accurate description of the operation of democracy, deriving its fundamental features from a comparative survey of those countries known as 'democracies'. In this book I shall attempt to combine, to some extent, both approaches, though leaning more closely to the latter.

Distinguishing Features of Democracy

Among those recent writers who have adopted a more descriptive and empirical treatment, Robert Dahl has perhaps best summarized the fundamentals of what he calls 'polyarchy'. (Elsewhere he says this is a synonym for democracy.) He believes that the *necessary* though not the *sufficient* conditions for polyarchy are based on opportunities for all citizens to formulate preferences for governmental action, and to communicate these preferences to others and to the government, and for these preferences, at least at the initial stage, to be weighted equally.[1]

What Dahl calls *public contestation* connects the traditional civil liberties with the right of political organization and initiation. Freedom of speech, freedom of the press, freedom of assembly, and freedom of association provide freedom of criticism, organization, and opposition. *Inclusiveness* denotes the right of all adults to be included in the political process. It assumes universal suffrage and freedom to compete for political leadership. Polyarchy, or democracy, exists where both public contestation and inclusiveness obtain. Applying this identikit of democracy to the sovereign states of the world, one can easily ascertain how many are democracies— about 30, 19 per cent of the total. Democracy is thus not the most prevalent of political regimes.

Much of the disenchantment with democracy's operation springs from a misunderstanding of its nature. Public contestation and inclusiveness imply, as we have noted, many freedoms; but these freedoms do not provide an opportunity for all to attain their quite different objectives. Nor do they ensure that everyone's version of the truth will be accepted by everyone else. While democracy enlarges everyone's freedom of expression, it does not necessarily increase people's freedom of action. Indeed, it may well restrict the freedom of action of many. This can be restated in the truism that we cannot all have complete freedom to do what we like without society becoming chaotic. We therefore restrict one another's activity. Democratic freedoms are often used to impose restrictions upon citizens of democracies. 'Stop them!' is a familiar cry in democratic controversy.

Misunderstanding of public contestation may arise from failure to grasp the difference between saying and doing. While freedom of speech and the press allow individuals and groups to propose the most outlandish and eccentric ideas, and to advocate the most unpopular policies, it does not necessarily assist the embodiment of ideas and policies in law. (This may seem an obvious point, but it is

[1] R. A. Dahl, *Polyarchy* (1971), 2 ff.

surprising how often it is overlooked.) In fact, the pursuit of unpopular causes may serve to make them more unpopular. Hence freedom of expression may be liberating at first, but frustration may follow when one's ideas and policies do not find general acceptance.

The distinction between freedom to say and freedom to do is especially significant in relation to freedoms of assembly and association. Freedom of assembly is necessarily less absolute, because crowds, especially at open-air meetings, may obstruct people's freedom of movement. More importantly, what is 'said' at a public meeting may bear much more relation to what is 'done' than what is said in private. Speakers may provoke strong and violent opposition and have to be protected by the police, the freedom to voice minority opinions thus being asserted. Conversely, speakers may excite crowds so that they rampage, breaking windows and attacking people. Hence, when speech is used to incite action, as is invariably the case with political speeches, there is a blurring of the boundary between saying and doing. Meetings have more of an immediate impact than private discussion or editorial persuasion. Larger numbers exercise a certain pressure on authority. Moreover, they imply a relationship between the organizers and speakers on one side and the audience on the other. There is an attempt to persuade and, perhaps, to direct.

The more purposive nature of freedom of assembly reflects its closeness to freedom of association. In fact, regular assemblage becomes association. Of course, a very great deal of association is not political but religious, social, cultural, or recreational. Associations with political objectives are pressure groups and political parties. Non-political associations, however, may sometimes have conscious political goals, or they may on occasion be drawn into politics because the actions of political authority may affect them. (A familar case is that of motoring associations.) Indeed, certain restrictions, beyond ordinary or general rules, on many associations are normal and inevitable in view of their wide-ranging operations. There are laws in all democratic countries regulating trade unions and business firms (see Chapters 6 and 7). In consequence, while freedom of association may allow organized groups to have their 'say', it can never guarantee that they will 'get their way'. Nearly all of them will be minorities, and they can only further their goals by bargaining, coalescing, and compromising their objectives.

The need to distinguish between freedom of expression and freedom of action is clearly implied by the logic of democratic decision-making. It is usual for a majority vote to carry the day, though in some instances, as with the American constitution, a two-thirds or three-quarters vote may be the rule. It is surprisingly difficult to argue with forceful logic for any particular proportion as necessary to achieve an outcome, though it would be an affront to common sense if the rule were that a minority vote won. (Were there such a rule, people would vote against the option they wanted.) Democracy is often wrongly defined as 'majority rule'; but though it may involve the majority getting their way, there is clearly much more to democracy than majoritarianism. Majorities may, and sometimes do, act in a completely undemocratic manner. Democracy might be extinguished by a majority voting for the abolition of public contestation and inclusiveness at a general election or national referendum. The Weimar Republic ended in this way.

Under democratic decision-making, minorities will be guaranteed their say, but they will not get their way. The assertion that democracy guarantees respect for minority rights can mean little more than respect for the minority's freedom of expression, protection under the law, and time to convert enough of the majority to become one themselves. It does not, under my definition of democracy, ensure that the law will not be changed, by due and proper process, to their material disadvantage. All the democratic rights that Dahl calls public contestation cannot prevent even large minorities from being continually frustrated. This will be the result of the majority exercising *its* democratic rights.

Severe deprivation may thus result when democracy cannot provide undiscriminatory treatment for minorities. Usually people will be in a majority for some issues and in a minority for others. But where a certain group, often religious and/or ethnic, is losing every time, their only consolation, and it may well be a small one, is the right to speak their mind freely about the situation and to have access to the courts and the media. Indeed, such a position makes access to the media very important. This may be what Rawls might call a 'thin' theory of democracy, but it does have the advantage of simplicity. It makes it very clear that democracy is no necessary safeguard for a liberal society. The real guarantee that minorities are not persecuted is not democracy, but those involved in it, the politicians and the electorate. There is no logical necessity why, through the right of free expression and participation, fair and just treatment for everyone should emerge.

Inclusiveness may become a similar disappointment if its implications are not properly grasped. Except in a very small community, the rights of all adults both to vote and to compete for political leadership may turn out to be rights more in promise than performance. In some democracies many people do little more than cast votes at election time: it is uncommon to be involved in the decision-making process at a higher level. This stems from two fairly basic factors. Firstly, it is probably a characteristic of human nature to be wary of undertaking leadership (see Chapter 8). Many academic studies have shown that even at local levels it is particularly difficult to recruit political leaders. Aspiration to political leadership seems to be associated with quite exceptional personality-types. Secondly, it would be very difficult anyway, in a country of any considerable size or population, for everyone successfully to undertake leadership at the highest level. Representative institutions are a recognition of this fact (see Chapter 2), and criticism of them is often a reflection of disillusionment with the possession of the suffrage. This disenchantment may be directed at the politicians, or even at the whole system, whereas incapacity to obtain what one wants should rightly be attributed to other citizens.

Responsibility of government to the governed, or 'upward control' as it is sometimes called, is also an essential component of democracy, it is often argued. In non-democratic regimes all control is 'downward'. It is at least possible that responsibility may not automatically prevail where public contestation and inclusiveness exist. Freedom of expression and political organization for all may not always result in governments responsible to peoples. If, for example, an enfranchised and politically free people failed to set up an electoral system with periodic elections, it would be difficult for their government to be held responsible for its actions. This may seem rather hypothetical; but an instance of a polity with manhood suffrage and public contestation, and yet without responsible government, can be quoted. The German Empire from 1870 to 1918 exemplified this situation. There were organized political parties with periodic elections, and considerable (if not absolute) freedom of speech and of the press. Yet the chancellor was responsible only to the Kaiser and neither to the Reichstag nor to the electorate as a whole.² Thus it seems inappropriate to describe Wilhelmine Germany as even half a democracy. Governmental responsibility may usually coincide with public contestation and inclusiveness, but not inevitably so. Therefore it must be recognized as a necessary feature of democracy. (See chapter 2, 45–53).

Freedom of expression and association, participatory rights for all, and governments with responsibility to the governed are the distinguishing features of democracy. But all democracies will have other features in common with other types of regime, because all polities have some characteristics in common.

The State as the Framework for Democracy

A further reason for much of the misunderstanding about democracy is the failure to see how it is related to authority and power. Democratic decision-making is meaningless unless it takes place within some framework: it has to apply to a definable number and category of people within a defined territory. Consequently, it operates within the contemporary state. This is not to maintain that such ideas as 'democracy within the union', or 'democracy in the office', or even 'democracy within the tennis club' have no meaning. There is a very real analogy between the representative and electoral arrangements of such bodies and those of the democratic state. But the latter is different in two important respects. It is not a voluntary association, and therefore its 'members' have little choice about belonging to it. Furthermore, having the ultimate authority in society, it possesses the power to alter the arrangements of voluntary associations. In the case of democratic states this will naturally be done through the democratic process.

A most important point to grasp is that the state preceded democracy by some four or five centuries. Its initial functions were external security, internal law enforcement, and management of the country's finances. Later, control over the nation's communication system was often added. When states became democratic the new regimes inherited these functions; a democratic state, like any other sort of state, cannot escape the exercise of power and authority. If it did it would no longer be a state, and democracy would collapse with it.

The capacity of a state to exercise its functions, both externally

² A. L. Lowell, *Governments and Parties in Continental Europe* (1919), 278.

and internally, is described as its 'sovereignty'. The state can only continue where it can prevent its integrity being impaired by other states. Hence it will usually tend to train and support armed forces and to develop a pattern of relationships with other states. The sovereignty of a state will be limited where it is prevented from acting autonomously in its external relations. (In practice, of course, all contemporary states have some dependency on other states, so absolute sovereignty is unknown today.) Again, if a state is unable to carry out its internal administrative functions then its sovereignty is impaired. This especially applies to the maintenance of law. A state unable to impose its law upon citizens is ceasing to be a state. It is not able to order its affairs in the way it should. The forces of order are no longer maintaining the law—'Law and order' are breaking down.

Because the problems of organizing national defence and administering the law are not new I shall not examine them in this book. Of course, it is true that in spite of being old problems they have contemporary manifestations. New types of crime, such as terrorism, pose particular difficulties for the state today.[3] Nuclear weapons have changed the nature of national security. In their essentials, however, these two fundamental features of the state have not greatly changed with the advent of democracy.

Yet in one respect democracy transforms the fundamental problem of sovereignty, which is complicated by the government becoming more dependent on the governed. If they withdraw their support sovereignty is weakened; it is strengthened if they desire to defend and consolidate it. How much the citizens wish to uphold their state depends on how much legitimacy they accord it. A state is not likely to be viable if its subjects do not regard its rule as legitimate. In the democratic state there are reasons why legitimacy is both more, and less, likely to be granted. Democracy encourages criticism of authority and opposition to government. This situation may commend itself to many who may feel more emancipated under democracy than any other form of government. Consequently, democracy may command more support than any other form of government. (It depends on how much people value democratic freedoms.) On the other hand, freedom to criticize may result in decline in respect and prestige: an unsuccessful democratic government may lose much of its legitimacy as a result of failure.

[3] See P. Wilkinson, *Terrorism and the Liberal State* (1977).

Hence expectations of improvement, self-advancement, national prosperity, etc., if disappointed, may lead to a loss of legitimacy on the part of the state. The efficacy of government in the modern democratic state is bound up with the question of the state's legitimacy. Economic failure may weaken the allegiance of citizens, whose criticisms will become more strident with increasing unemployment and/or rising rates of inflation, especially if successive governments fail to cope with such problems. This is a problem I shall examine in more detail in Chapters 6 and 7.

As we have noted, the need to preserve sovereignty and legitimacy is the concern of all states, democratic and undemocratic. A state's legitimacy, and therefore ultimately its sovereignty, is affected by the problems with which this book is concerned: the increasingly bureaucratic and centralized nature of the modern state—to what extent national leaders allow their administrators to make and shape policy; the increasing demands for social and economic equality—to what degree egalitarianism and socialism impair the working of authority; how authority and leadership can survive under the growing pressures of a better-educated citizenry; and finally, how we can reconcile the authority of the democratic state with the collectivist forces to which modern industrialism and urbanization have given birth. The pluralism of modern society infuses all these problems. We no longer face only the question of how the individual should relate to the state. In modern industrial society our concern is with how collectivities relate to the state, as well as to the individual and each other.

These problems are not, as I have indicated, confined to democratic states. Some of them, perhaps nearly all of them, to a greater or lesser degree, affect all modern industrial states. Even so, the existence of democracy makes for a qualitative as well as a quantitative difference in confronting them. Hence, what democracy implies, and what it does not imply, need to be spelt out carefully at the beginning. Unfortunately the implications of democracy have been misunderstood by two groups of people, its critics and its supporters. It is with the misconceptions of the liberal friends of democracy that I am largely concerned here.

What Democracy Does Not Imply

In the first place, democracy does not guarantee a 'good', 'fair', 'just', society. It is true that it has often been seen, by liberals especially, as a system which embodies the values of truth, right, and goodness. In fact, democracy does not necessarily embody any absolute values at all. Indeed, as a system it may make it difficult for absolute value positions to be asserted. Democratic preconditions, and democratic procedures, allow 'goodness', 'truth', and 'social justice' freely to be debated. They provide the cultural and institutional framework within which people may articulate such values and within which a conflict of values may take place. For clearly what is good, fair, and socially just is a matter of opinion. In a democracy there will be disagreement about social justice. The degree of social and economic inequality to be tolerated is a matter for discussion, and in modern industrial democracies it is likely to be a permanent item on the agenda.

Secondly, it is misleading to associate democracy too closely with freedom, at least with most interpretations of the concept. Of course, what we have above called the 'democratic freedoms'—that is, the freedoms of the person, speech, the press, assembly and organization—are indispensable to democracy. These relatively unrestricted freedoms allow citizens to proclaim what they consider is bad, untrue, and socially unjust in their society. (In societies which are not democratic this may be impossible.) But these democratic freedoms, or civil liberties, do not allow considered wrongs to be righted except by procedures which may be tedious and complicated. Success through such processes is likely to be dependent on persuading a very large number of other people. Hence one does not have freedom to obtain what one wants under a democratic regime. Individuals and minority groups, as we have seen, may have disconsolately to put up with what they do not want. Democracy does not assure satisfaction for everyone: rather, it encourages the expression of dissatisfaction. To repeat, democracy provides us with great freedom for 'saying', but freedom for 'doing' only when the majority of our fellow citizens are prepared to support us.

Thirdly, democracy cannot be too closely associated with 'rationality', a term which covers a large area of thought. Paul Diesing distinguishes five types of rationality.[4] Technical rationality is the efficient achievement of a single goal; economic rationality effects maximum goal achievement through the ability to measure the factors involved and to put them to their most economic use, requiring perfect information about all other economic factors;

---

[4] P. Diesing, *Reason in Society* (Westport, 1973).

legal rationality is concerned with the observance and codification of rules and postulates, the notion of the reasonable man who can be relied upon to act in a normal and predictable way; social rationality exists where shared relationships between people produce understanding and trust; and political rationality is the rationality of decision-making, which David Regan divides into qualitative and quantitative rationality. A qualitative rational decision is an appropriate choice of alternatives and can only apply to the end sought. Quantitative rationality is concerned with choosing a more as opposed to a less rational decision.[5]

Certainly, in any complex decision-making system rationality can never be anything but relative. As Brian Barry and Russell Hardin maintain, too much is expected of the notion.[6] To be rational a man must be able to rank the outcomes which may result from a proposed action.[7] His preferences should be ranked consistently; for example, if he preferred capitalism to socialism, and a mixed economy to capitalism, it would be irrational if he then preferred socialism to a mixed economy. Again, he should be consistent in making the same choice when faced with the same options another time. And he should choose means appropriate to his desired ends. He will also need information, especially about the options with which he is faced and the views of relevant experts capable of analysing the situation. Hence rationality is difficult to attain. No one is fully rational and no political decision can be completely so. Is democracy, however, characterized by more rationality than other types of regime? I shall briefly answer this question in terms of ordinary voters, decision-makers, processes, and outcomes.

In the first place it can be argued that the democratic citizen participates in politics only through irrational motives. Anthony Downs argues that even the act of voting is usually not rational because the costs much outweigh the benefits of voting in nearly all

[5] D. E. Regan, Rationality in Policy Making: Two Concepts Not One, *Long Range Planning,* 11. (Oct. 1978), 85.

[6] B. Barry and R. Hardin, *Rational Man and Irrational Society* (1982), 385.

[7] There is a vast literature about rational choice, e.g. K. J. Arrow, *Social Choice and Individual Values* (Yale, 1951); J. M. Buchanan and G. Tullock, *The Calculus of Consent* (Ann Arbor, 1962); R. D. Luce and H. Raiffa, *Games and Decisions* (New York, 1957); M. Olson, *The Logic of Collective Action* (Cambridge, 1965); A. Rapoport, *Fights, Games and Debates* (Ann Arbor, 1960). A useful short summary is D. H. Blair and R. A. Pollak, Rational Collective Choice, *Scientific American,* 249/2 (1983) 88–95.

cases.[8] This is because the probability of one vote making any difference to the result is remote indeed. Yet most citizens do vote, probably because they feel it is a privilege and an obligation. They want to 'stand up and be counted' even when they know it will not affect the outcome. These motives are nothing to do with economic rationality, which one can only reconcile with observed political behaviour by introducing concepts unknown to economists, such as psychological costs and benefits.

The ordinary voter has another problem, also affecting other democratic actors. There is no possibility of obtaining all the information needed to make a decision. (In fact, the average citizen cannot know what is the necessary, and what the unnecessary, information.) As total information is needed in the market for rational choices to be made, one may likewise argue that voters cannot decide whom to support without full knowledge of all the issues. This they clearly do not possess. Indeed, if they tried to obtain all the information they would probably not have time to process it. In other words, it is not rational, in the sense of reasonable, to attempt to attain perfect rationality. As Anthony Heath argues, it would take so much time and trouble that our lives would be disrupted.[9] The democratic voter is regaled with far more information than is the citizen of a non-democratic state; but this does not ensure great political rationality. It merely provides an *opportunity* for more rational choice.

Moreover, there are vast inequalities in the amount of knowledge which people possess, as well as in skills and resources for processing and organizing it. Democracy has not eliminated these differences, though it may have slightly mitigated them. Knowledge about public affairs is roughly proportionate to political power. Furthermore, in the exercise of power information, and therefore people's opinions, are inevitably manipulated.[10] All rulers misinform. In democracies, however, free self-expression and competition for power lead to a proliferation of misinformation. Democratic citizens are aware that professional politicians know much more about the issues than they do; but the conflicting facts and assessments assailing them can bewilder and intimidate. Often

---

[8] A. Downs, *An Economic Theory of Democracy* (New York, 1957). It is criticized in B. Barry, *Sociologists, Economists and Democracy* (1970), 15–46.

[9] A. Heath, *Rational Choice and Social Exchange* (Cambridge, 1976), 76.

[10] See R. E. Goodin, *Manipulatory Politics* (New Haven, 1980), esp. ch. 2, The Politics of Lying.

the reaction will be great scepticism about democratic politicians. Hence even quantitative rationality—more as opposed to less—will not be easy to attain.

At other times the rhetoric of the politicians, for example about foreign policy issues, may influence the voters. Unreason may well sway the majority. Consequently, some democratic decisions are characterized by irrationality. Others are more rational because they arouse less emotion and because there is more time to make sound and systematic analyses of the different options. Even in these instances, however, where much briefing from bureaucrats and other experts may take place, the complexities of democratic decision-making will not greatly facilitate rationality. Like voters, democratic leaders may be overwhelmed by the flood of information. They will be aware that interest groups and bureaucrats, who are better informed, will have their own biases; but they may not know to what extent they should discount them. They can only do their best. Thus, such models of decision-making as Herbert Simon's—(1) list the options, (2) determine the consequences of each, and (3) estimate each consequence in order to discover the best option[11]—may be useful as guides, but in practice 'satisficing' rather than 'optimizing' will be the philosophy of action. Ed Lindblom comes to the conclusion that comprehensive or 'synoptic' problem-solving is impossible because of man's limited intellectual capacity, inadequacy of information, the costliness of analysis, and the difficulty of defining complex problems. Strategies can be devised but not solutions.[12] Gunnel Gustaffson and Jeremy Richardson write: 'The difficulty in trying to increase rationality is that western democracies have a policy style which is positively hostile to greater rationality.'[13] Many democratic decisions are characterized by irrationality and inefficiency.

It is thus hardly surprising that economic rationality is not likely to emerge from the democratic political process. The assumption of individual awareness of self-interest is only a little less credible than group awareness of collective self-interest. Moreover, economic rationality can scarcely be expected from democratic politicians,

[11] H. A. Simon, *Administrative Behavior* (New York, 1958). A simple model, What is the Goal? What are the Alternatives? Which is the Best?, appears in J. Dewey, *Studies in Logical Theory* (Chicago, 1909).

[12] C. E. Lindblom, *The Intelligence of Democracy* (New York, 1965).

[13] G. Gustaffson and J. J. Richardson, Concepts of Rationality and the Policy Process, *European Journal of Political Research*, 7. (1979), 450.

who will be calculating in votes rather than monetary profit and loss. For instance, it may be much more rewarding for politicians to keep uneconomic shipyards open, maintaining voters' jobs and therefore their support, than to close them, even if that is more efficient in terms of pounds and pence. Indeed, the normal three to five years between elections does not encourage rational economic policy. Hence political rationality may drive out economic rationality.

This brief and inadequate treatment of rationality will at least (I hope) demonstrate that reason, so much desired by intellectuals, should not be expected from democratic regimes. It must be remembered, however, that absolute rationality is not a characteristic of any type of political regime. Democracies at least provide the opportunity of being *more* rational than other polities. Free discussion and a free press offer much more chance of arriving at a rational decision than oppression and censorship. Freedom of information will naturally improve the situation even further.

Finally, democracy is not based on a broad agreement or consensus about the values or goals of society. As we have seen, democracy stimulates disagreement and dissent. It is argued by some, however, that for democracy to emerge and to be maintained there must be an underlying consensus about certain fundamentals. These may be basic values, probably of a liberal kind, or they may be cultural characteristics, or they may be both. The implication is that in a democratic country the regime markedly rests on respect for the individual, or a belief in human dignity, or Judaeo-Christian ethics. These are very widely accepted values to which people will instinctively respond. Similarly, it is implied that in democracies there is a way of life, embodying certain cultural norms, about which there is a general consensus. Contravene these fundamental values, show lack of respect for these ways of life, it is argued, and the consensus will be breached. Democracy will be in danger because it rests on a stable equilibrium which must not be disturbed.

So strongly has this view been canvassed in the years since World War II that many thinkers (perhaps we should call them the 'consensualists') have tended to equate democracy and stability. The equation stems from the premises that both democracy and stability are 'good' and that therefore they tend to support each other. Stability, by definition, helps democracy to survive: the maintenance of democracy enhances the stability of democratic regimes. The propositions are confusing and, basically, tautological.[14] Stability, as applied to any type of regime, is likely to be synonymous with the status quo. Many authoritarian regimes have been among the most stable. Hence stability by itself can hardly be a sufficient basis for democracy. What the consensualists applaud is stable democracy. On the other hand they fear unstable democracy, a situation where political, social, economic, and industrial conflict occurs. Democracy, to them, is most important as a device for defending the status quo. Indeed, it sometimes seems that a set of political arrangements described as 'democracy' are used to confer legitimacy on social and economic institutions whose existence the consensualists wish to maintain. Thus, the effectiveness and legitimacy of the state are associated with the stability of the society and the economy.

In this vein Seymour Lipset writes:

The stability of any given democracy depends not only on economic developments but also upon the effectiveness and the legitimacy of its political system ... Effectiveness means actual performance, the extent to which the system satisfies the basic functions of government as most of the population and such powerful groups within it as big business or the armed forces *see them*. Legitimacy involves the capacity of the system to engender and maintain the belief that the existing political institutions are the most appropriate ones for the society.[15]

The basic argument seems to be that where the citizens and other important groups perceive a democracy as functioning successfully they feel it is appropriate. Its successful functioning depends upon the way it deals with divisive questions. Lipset continues: 'The extent to which contemporary democratic political systems are legitimate depends in large measure upon the ways in which the key issues which have historically divided the society have been resolved.'[16] Of these major social divisions he writes:

The character and extent of the major cleavages affecting the political stability of a society are largely determined by historical factors which have affected the way in which major issues dividing society have been solved or left unresolved over time ... Where a number of historical cleavages inter-

---

[14] For further discussion of stability as a concept see K. M. Dowding and R. Kimber, The Meaning and Use of Political Stability, *European Journal of Political Research*, 11/3 (1983), 229–44, and U. Rosenthal, *Political Order* (Alphen aan den Rijn, 1978).

[15] S. M. Lipset, *Political Man* (1960), 77 (my italics).   [16] Ibid. 77.

mix and create the basis for ideological politics, democracy will be unstable and weak, for by definition such politics does not include the concept of tolerance.[17]

The inference must be that where a country has been unstable and divided before democracy it is likely to remain so afterwards (for a sociologist, Lipset attaches great importance to historical factors). Furthermore, social and economic stability are closely linked to political stability. All three tend to support each other. Where there are few major divisions in society people are more tolerant and less likely to disagree. Where these cleavages have been less deep, so that disagreements have been debated civilly, leaving no festering wounds in the body politic, political conflict will be relatively undisturbing.

One could ridicule too much these evident truths. It is not foolish to assert that stability in the present tends to beget stability in the future; and that stability in one area of a nation's life will encourage stability in others. This is often the case. Unfortunately, however, the statement that where consensus obtains will be where it will continue to obtain, though largely true, does not help the political analyst who wishes to know when and where consensus may break down, and whether and to what extent its collapse will endanger democracy. While the consensualists seem to conclude that as little conflict as possible is needed in order to ensure the continuance of democracy, the important question for us is, how much dissent about goals can take place, and in what ways, before consensus about rules disintegrates? The consensualist model assumes more agreement about goals in society than actually exists. The ultimate implication must be to emphasize stability even at the expense of democracy. It is no coincidence that the construction of such models occurred at a time when world communism seemed poised to prey on unstable polities.

Hence overall harmony was stressed even where cleavages were identified; and where there was conflict its impact was played down. It was argued by Daniel Bell that we have reached 'the end of ideology' and by certain French political scientists that political life had been 'depoliticized'—the ideological heat had been taken out of the debate on issues. Lipset argued:

The characteristic pattern of stable Western democracies in the mid-twentieth century is that they are in a post-politics phase i.e. there is

[17] Ibid. 83, 85.

relatively little difference between the democratic left and right. In large measure this situation reflects the fact that in those countries the workers have won their fight for full citizenship.[18]

However, 'full citizenship' (presumably, universal suffrage) is by our definition, one of the ingredients of democracy. Hence Lipset's statement seems to mean that because democracy has been attained, class conflict and ideological polarization have ceased. And this inference is borne out by another argument of Lipset nearly a decade later:

A number of answers have been suggested to account for the ability of conservative political groupings to win significant lower-class support. This support is a requirement for political stability. For the legitimacy of a democratic polity rests on the opportunity of all significant actors to have access to power. If the conservatives were deprived of such opportunities they would lose their commitment to the democratic rules of the game . . . No one wants to keep playing in a game that he can never hope to win.[19]

Here the emphasis is on a balance of social forces enabling the upper class to share in power at the same time that it deprives the more numerous lower class of permanent power.

Indeed, there are two separate though frequently conflated positions advanced by those who are anxious for stability. One is that the advent of democracy has lessened political divisions and made social relations very much more harmonious. The other is that within democracy harmony needs to be cultivated if a felicitous balance of social and political relationships is to be maintained. The former position, characterized by the first quotation in the paragraph immediately above, perceived democracy as an aid to stability. The latter, contained in the second quotation, perceived that instability of social forces may result from democracy, but hopes that a happy concatenation of outcomes may bring about a constant restoration of equilibrium. One position sees democracy as a safeguard of stability: the other is less sure about it.

What Democracy Does Imply: Rules

It is often said that democracy is based not on consensus about values but on observance of the rules of the game. There is some truth in this. Decision-making in democracies is initially based on

---

[18] Ibid. 92.
[19] S. M. Lipset, *Revolution and Counter-Revolution* (1968), 159, 160.

adherence to procedures which cannot easily be broken without democracy foundering. Observance of these rules, however, does assume certain values, and the metaphor of politics as a game does have merit if it is not overworked. Games may not be worth playing if the rules are broken too often. Their enjoyment is enhanced if the participants compete in a spirit of fair play, accept refereeing decisions without question, and approach defeat or victory with an attitude of good sportsmanship. There *are* values associated with democratic decision-making, though they may not be dramatic values like truth and justice. Rather are they humdrum values like trust, tolerance, and the merits of compromise. These may precede the inauguration of democracy in a polity. If they do not, they may be engendered by the operation of democracy.

The need to observe the rules follows from the fact that in a democracy the rules and the laws have been made, and/or can be repealed or amended, through democratic processes. Consequently every citizen who wishes to maintain democracy should be concerned to obey even uncongenial laws, because every citizen possesses the right to attempt to change them. Breaches of the law are thus breaches of democracy. But the obligation to support the law extends beyond the citizen to the government and its servants. They should apply the law consistently and without arbitrary dispensation. In particular, the guardians of law and order must respect the democratically determined laws. The maintenance of order is essential to the rule of law.

The 'rule of law' is said to be in operation where the law is being obeyed and administered in a consistent fashion. Joseph Raz perceives the concept in two aspects:[20]

(1) that people should be ruled by the law and obey it, and (2) that the law should be such that people will be able to be guided by it . . . if the law is to be obeyed *it must be capable of guiding the behaviour of its subjects*. It must be such that they can find out what it is and act on it.

He selects eight important principles[21] to be derived from the idea of the rule of law. Five of them relate to law enforcement:

1. The independence of the judiciary must be guaranteed.
2. The principles of natural justice must be observed.
3. The courts should have review powers over administrative action and all legislation and subordinate law- and rule-making.

[20] J. Raz, *The Authority of Law* (Oxford, 1979), 213.
[21] Ibid. 214–18. This is not his order.

4. The courts should be easily accessible.
5. The discretion of the crime-preventing agencies should not be allowed to pervert the law.

Three of the principles require that the law should conform to standards designed to enable it effectively to guide action. These are:

6. All laws should be prospective, open, and clear. They should not be retroactive, ambiguous, obscure, and imprecise.
7. The making of particular laws (particular legal orders) should be guided by open, stable, clear, and general rules.
8. Laws should be relatively stable. If they are changed too often people may find it difficult to be guided by law in their long-term decisions.

What is the relationship of this characterization of the rule of law to democracy? Here it is not difficult to agree with Raz:

The rule of law is just one of the virtues which a legal system may possess and by which it is to be judged. It is not to be confused with democracy, justice, equality (before the law or otherwise), human rights of any kind or respect for persons or for the dignity of man.[22]

A state which decreed that the first-born should be slaughtered would be observing the rule of law if it ensured that no exceptions were permitted. Totalitarian governments may observe the rule of law quite conscientiously in some respects. The rule of law has no necessarily moral significance. Yet, as we have noted, it is essential to a democratic society because decisions made by democratic processes, democratic citizens must insist, are legitimate. Laws enacted under such processes must be obeyed unless and until they are amended or repealed by the same processes, or by some supreme legal body set up by a democratic constitution. The rule of law is independent of democracy and is not, therefore, a *distinguishing* feature; but democracy cannot operate without the rule of law, which is thus a *necessary* feature.

The rule of law has also been cited as a principle restricting governmental power. Governments should conceive the laws as defining and limiting their own actions in the same ways that laws confine the activities of their subject. F. A. Hayek's formulation is that

government in all its actions is bound by rules fixed and announced beforehand—rules which make it possible to foresee with fair certainty

[22] Ibid. 211.

how the authority will use its coercive powers in given circumstances, and to plan one's individual affairs on the basis of their knowledge.[23]

The precept that government power is restrained by clear rules already promulgated will commend itself to many. Like Raz's eighth principle, however, it is not ultimately reconcilable with democratic practice. Democratic majorities may decide to alter the extent of governmental power on occasion, so that there is always uncertainty, at any given time, about what the position will be in a few years. Moreover, at times, perhaps for entirely appropriate reasons—war or the threat of war, economic crisis, etc.—the speed with which a democratic country decides to allocate more power to its government may change considerably. It is when a democratic government expands its area of action without proper democratic consent that democracy is threatened. Consequently, I would place the emphasis on knowledge and control of the scope of government power, rather than on the exact extent of that scope.

Thus, while a greater or less degree of relative stability in laws is probably in accordance with the desires of most human beings, it cannot be assumed, as I have argued earlier, that people will always opt for no instability. Democracy encourages a certain amount of instability. How much relative stability people want will vary in time and place. Raz rightly says that stability is essential if people are to be guided by laws in their long-term decisions.[24] Unfortunately most of the inhabitants of the industrialized nations are not in a position to make long-term decisions: they have much less control over their individual destinies than the business and professional classes. With medium-term, or short-term, horizons they may use their majority position to change the laws and the powers of authority with comparative sang-froid.

To sum up: all of Raz's principles of rule of law are wholly consistent with democracy, but with regard to the eighth—the requirement that laws should be relatively stable—much will depend on how relative is 'relative'. Hayek and others who want to stretch the rule of law so that government action is very restricted see the concept as a bulwark against change, especially in the economic sphere. Democracy they perceive as a recipe for harmony. But democracy may well be expressed in adversarial politics, with wounding conflict over legislation. This makes the rules which

---

[23] F. A. Hayek, *The Road to Serfdom* (1944), 54.
[24] Raz, *The Authority of Law*, 215.

apply to the policy-making and legislative processes—indeed, to the whole of the political 'game'—very important.

The rules of the political game may be embodied in constitutions and constitutional laws, and in conventions. If democracy is to be maintained these rules must be observed by all the entities involved. They may relate to matters as important as the transfer of power from one set of leaders to another—one of the crucial tests of democratic validity. In Britain, for example, it is a convention that when a government is defeated at the polls it resigns and is succeeded by the leaders of the successful party. Thus the alternation of Government and Opposition in Britain is a very important democratic rule founded on constitutional convention. If a British government refused to resign in these circumstances it would be breaking the rules and would be repudiating democracy. Yet so far Britain's leaders, who like all politicians vastly prefer holding power, have notwithstanding resisted any temptation to break the rules and have acted within the terms of this constitutional convention, relinquishing power when the verdict of the electorate has gone against them. The behaviour of leaders in a democracy is most important for the prestige of the rules of the game.

The analogy with a game breaks down when rules are in dispute. In a real game the referee interprets the rules; but in a democratic society there is no such authoritative arbiter. (A Supreme Court may rule on laws but will not recognize conventions.) The government cannot be analogous to a referee: indeed, its political leader is analogous to the captain of a winning team. Moreover, much more is at stake in competitive politics than merely losing the match. Consequently, when the rules are not clear, different interpretations are claimed. Of course, where laws are disputed, rulings can be obtained in the courts; but with conventions there can be no such recourse and the matter may simply be argued about until a law enforcing the convention is passed. An example of this occurred in Britain when the House of Lords breached the convention that it did not interfere with financial bills and began to amend Lloyd George's Budget. The result was the embodiment of the convention in a law, the Parliament Act, 1911.

The tendency to observe the rules of the game has been described as 'constitutionalism'. Where the rules have long been followed constitutionalism flourishes. Political leadership, especially, has the responsibility for observance of the rules: constitutionalism is dependent on the relationship of competing political leaders with each other. But comprehension of the significance of democratic processes may be found among non-élites. Harry Eckstein contrasts the scepticism with which the average Norwegian voter regards politicians with the great respect held for the democratic political process.[25] Constitutionalism has become a value in itself.

What Democracy Does Imply: Values

We have already noted that democracy is likely to encourage relativist rather than absolute values. It puts more emphasis on means than ends. Consequently, it is likely to be most suitable for people who are less than adamant about obtaining what they want. Those who would stop at nothing will not make good democrats. The whole process of decision-making, in which everyone can participate and criticize, makes it difficult for governments and other collectivities to attain their goals. Freedom of expression (though information may not always be as available as it should be) produces an atmosphere in which people can be persuaded to change their views, so that even elected governments cannot be sure of support. The complexity of the pressures, in consequence, usually leads to compromise between the goals of different groups. An ability to make compromises is bound to be a help to democratic political leaders. They do not have to compromise on every issue, but it is likely that they will be doing so on most.

It follows from this that democratic nations find it difficult to proclaim national purposes. What policies and leaders the majority of the people want at one time may well be those they do *not* want a year later. Furthermore, those who agree on some ends may well disagree on others. Consequently, among voters there are likely to be shifting potential alliances about policies; and for leaders the decision-making context is one of political insecurity. It is not a situation in which ideologies and ideologues can flourish. Only on some highly specific end—such as winning a war—can a sense of national purpose be inculcated. At other times a democratic country's decision-making is likely to proceed rather haphazardly as contending politicians pragmatically adjust themselves to varying political pressures. It is in authoritarian states that national

[25] H. Eckstein, *Division and Cohesion in Democracy: A Study of Norway* (Princeton, 1966), 19.

goals can be promulgated and citizens easily mobilized to pursue them.

Hence, although democracy may not guarantee a just or good society, it will probably provide one in which people tend to be temperate in their approaches to their goals. Usually the latter cannot be attained quickly and wholly. A great deal of discussion and argument must be endured and certain aspirations relinquished in order to persuade opponents to concede others. A process of give and take is almost inevitable, putting a premium on political leaders who are brokers and bargainers. One important implication of democracy is that freedom of expression makes it almost impossible to avoid knowing the aims of groups other than one's own, and frequently they have to be taken into account.

A political market-place in which highly unpopular groups are allowed to broadcast their ideas and aims can flourish only in an atmosphere of tolerance. Large majorities may wish to impose their wills on small minorities; but a premiss of democracy is that they must not do this except by legal and constitutional processes. So, for democracy to be assured, the authority of the state may have to be deployed, through the forces of law and order ensuring that small unpopular minorities can exercise without impediment their democratic rights. Thus democracy is guaranteed by the coercion, if necessary, of the intolerant among the majority; and in Britain such an organization as the National Front, whose aims are to overthrow democracy, has its democratic freedom of expression safeguarded by police cordons.

Competition between large organized groups with mutually exclusive goals, if it is not to involve the destruction of democracy, must be conducted with tolerance of each other's democratic rights. But, as such groups as major political parties are likely to wield power, more than tolerance is needed. A large governing political party in a democracy, using the apparatus of the state, could deprive opposing parties of their freedom to organize opposition. Fear that this might happen if it loses power to its opponents might encourage a governing party to do this. On the other hand, the opposition, suspicious of the governing party, might forestall its expected repression and seize power undemocratically. Consequently, trust is essential for the working of any democratic polity.[26]

[26] For a discussion of trust, see N. Luhmann, *Trust* (Stuttgart, 1973).

Hence democracy is dependent on the trust of both élites and non-élites. The leaders of the largest and most powerful groups, especially, must trust each other or democracy cannot flourish; and confidence in one's political opponents very much depends on their continuing observance of the political conventions. Hence political leadership must refrain from flirting with those groups and blocs of opinion who are disloyal to democratic procedures. If trust is shaken and suspicions rapidly accelerate, the rules of the game may be flouted on all sides. Leaders must trust not only other leaders, however: they must trust the non-élite. Particularly where an aristocratic tradition preceded the inauguration of democracy—that is almost everywhere in Europe—an élitist suspicion of 'the masses' lingers on among Right and Centrist leaders. Conversely, in such countries the citizens themselves, especially the under-privileged may distrust the élite. Veronica Hart writes that in late Victorian Britain political distrust may have been a well-established cultural tradition,[27] but remarks that the distrustful in democracies may be integrated into the norms of the regime, even when resentful of its current condition.[28] What degree of distrust of leaders will lead to alienation from democracy itself is not known: much will depend on cultural and traditional factors. In general, it can be said that, however strong and apparently enduring, trust may be quickly dissipated.

Although tolerance is important, trust is a more essential ingredient of a democratic polity. Trust relates to our expectations of other people's behaviour. We trust our political opponents to honour our democratic freedoms—including our right to organize to deprive them of their political power by democratic processes—for two main reasons, I believe. In the first place, in some democracies it is a situation which has persisted for a very long time. For example, the procedures for the succession of power have been accepted over a long period and the habit of obeying them has become a tradition. Secondly, if we want our political opponents to respect democratic procedures, and our privileges in relation to them, then we shall be concerned to obey and defend them ourselves. In the ultimate analysis, the rules of the game are likely to be more observed the longer people observe them and the more strongly all players feel that they ought to continue to be observed. But as 'all the players' in the democratic game may be, literally, all

[27] V. Hart, *Distrust and Democracy* (Cambridge, 1978), 79.   [28] Ibid. 29.

the country's adults, the implication must be that democracy can only be safe when all citizens have some awareness of what democracy requires; and as relatively few in some countries participate in political life, democracy may be based on comparatively weak foundations. In no democracy is there widespread and conscious awareness of all implications of the game rules.

Tolerance and trust may be the primary values which both support and are engendered by democracy, but there are secondary values which characterize what we may call 'democratic society'. Foremost among these is civility, or procedural good manners. The right of self-expression may be worthless where people who disagree are not prepared to listen to each other. Thus, abusing one's opponents personally in discussion will not assist tolerance and trust, and shouting them down will be even less helpful. People who insist 'Give them a fair hearing!' are nurturing democracy. Those bawling 'Out! Out! Out!' at speakers whose views they deplore are enemies of democracy, even though they are not aware of it. Here again a sense of fair play contributes to civility. Civic courage is enhanced by the presence of such values, for democracy is characterized by the absence of the degree of fear that is typical of authoritarian regimes. Non-conformity, even eccentricity, can flourish where individuals can speak up and act within the law, even when in a minority of one. Democracy cannot in itself protect minorities against discrimination, but it is likely to produce a society in which the act of listening courteously to others' views leads to respect for their social and human needs. Democratic societies may not be able to eradicate racialism; but they are likely to be less racialist than non-democratic societies. This may be for liberals a disappointing statement, but then democracy *is* a disappointment for liberals (and for conservatives and socialists too!)

The values associated with democracy, therefore, are pedestrian rather than dramatic. What we regard as fair, just, good, and rational will be disputed by others using their freedoms of self-expression and organization. These values arouse much passion and controversy, and are demonstratively capable of provoking undemocratic behaviour. On the other hand, those values relating to relationships between people, such as tolerance and trust—what Dahrendorf calls 'public virtues'[29]—are the values important for democracy.

[29] R. Dahrendorf, *The Tradition of Authority, Democracy and Social Structure in Germany* (1965), 14.

Conclusion

Democracy can clearly be a very disappointing experience for those with pressing social and political objectives. It can guarantee neither the attainment of 'progressive' goals such as socialism, nor the maintenance of 'conservative' or 'pragmatic' ends such as capitalism. Nor does democracy necessarily stand for 'liberalism' in all the aspects, at least, of that overworked concept. For this reason I have eschewed the term 'liberal democracy',[30] which to me seems most misleading. Democracy is liberal in the sense that freedom of expression and political rights for all citizens are necessary preconditions. On the other hand, it does not guarantee full development for the individual personality in all social and economic spheres. Democratic states restrict individuals, and groups of individuals, as do all states.

Indeed, liberal values are open to attack in democracies, as well as other accepted values. As Justice Jackson said:

The freedom to differ is not limited to things that do not matter too much. That would be a mere shadow of freedom. The test of its substance is the right to differ as to things that touch the heart of the existing order.[31]

Democracy only safeguards the status quo, liberal or otherwise, if the majority of citizens wish it. Frequently, in modern democracies many citizens desire change because society changes rapidly in responding to technological advance. Adaptation to change can be accomplished by various decision-making systems and one of these—the best, many would argue—is, democracy. Authoritarian regimes may resolve problems with more speed and despatch because few participants and critics are involved in their decision-making; but the outcomes may be sustained with more difficulty, and often with repression. In democratic regimes decision-making will proceed more slowly, but consent should be assured because, though not everyone agrees with the outcomes, everyone has had the right to participate. Implementation, therefore, will be less of a problem. All contemporary regimes have to adapt to change, but democracy is the type which permits change to take place most successfully.

The attainment of democracy by a formerly non-democratic state, however, does not imply that problems, especially initially,

[30] The term arose, I believe, as a result of J. L. Talmon, *The Origins of Totalitarian Democracy* (1952).
[31] C. Cohen, *Democracy*, (Athens, Ga., 1971), 153.

are more easily resolved. The inauguration of democracy does not abolish the exercise of power and the structures of hierarchy: it only results in greater precision in the definition of power and more supervision of the activities of the hierarchs. Democracy cannot be divorced from political authority and in the contemporary world this means the organization we call the state. As Robert Lynd writes, there is no fundamental incompatibility between democracy and power.[32] Yet the exercise of any sort of power, including governmental power, is much less likely to escape criticism and dissent within democratic polities; and among the allegations that are made will almost inevitably be some claiming that the actions in question are undemocratic. A necessary question which I shall attempt to answer is, how can we determine whether the exercise of power in modern industrial societies endangers democracy? How can we distinguish the forces which seek change in ways which are undemocratic from those which seek change in ways which are not?

From the preceding discussion it would follow that any threat to the fabric of the state and the rule of law endangers democracy. Foreign aggressors, internal revolutionaries, deliberate and collective breaches of the law all threaten these necessary conditions for democracy. Inclusiveness would be threatened by groups attempting to disenfranchise blacks, or Jews, or women (or men), or by any limitation of people's rights to be representatives. Public contestation will be threatened by any attempt to limit freedom of expression, or any restriction on the right of opposition. Above all, individuals and groups who place a higher value on attaining their goals than they do on the maintenance of democracy, will endanger it. They will be willing to break the rules in order to attain their objectives.

'Breaking the rules', however, does not mean attempting to change the social and economic system, or the 'underlying values', or the 'way of life' (whatever these mean) in any particular society. The obsession of the 'consensualists' with stability misses the point. What endangers democracy is not the propagation of radical ends (or, for that matter, reactionary ends) but the pursuit of *any* ends by methods which break the law or the constitutional rules and conventions. A democratic society full of vigorous and conflicting forces may be in less danger, if these forces respect the rules, than

[32] R. S. Lynd, Power in American Society, in A. Kornhauser (ed.), *Problems of Power in American Democracy* (Detroit, 1959), 38.

one with little conflict in which the few contending parties break them.

These answers, however, simplify the problems, because the survival of democracy in the last resort depends upon the reactions of ordinary citizens to the legal and democratic exercise of power. This may be especially the case where a sudden shift of power installs a new party, or the representatives of a new class, in power. There may be less than total acceptance of the change and the legitimacy of the new government's right to power may be challenged. A new type of democratically elected government—e.g. a country's first socialist government—may behave in unfamiliar ways. Even when its actions are perfectly legal, surprise and shock may be expressed, probably in relation to its intervention in the economy. Much of the controversy about the exercise of power in democracies rages round the validity of governments as economic actors. In many countries governmental powers of economic management are not enshrined in law, so that the exact legality of government actions may be difficult to determine, and this may also apply to individuals and groups attempting to obstruct national economic policy.

Thus in contemporary democracies the right to act of governments, and for that matter of other collectivities, may be a complex question. The simple contention that a government should be obeyed because it has been elected by a majority at the last election is not very satisfactory, because democratic governments may behave undemocratically. Hence a very important relationship to examine is that between governments and the governed. To what degree, and in what ways, are elected governments responsible to the people? This I shall try to answer in the next chapter, bearing in mind that the relationship is affected by the decision-making structures of democracy.

2

DIRECT AND REPRESENTATIVE DEMOCRACY AND RESPONSIBLE GOVERNMENT

DEMOCRACY, a political regime found in some modern states, is a decision-making process which can only exist when public contestation, inclusiveness, and responsible government are present; and which can only be maintained when there is a rule of law. I stated the circumstances and implications of democracy in somewhat abstract terms in Chapter 1 but did not discuss there its practical operations. How does it work? Does it work well? What are the problems of its workings?

Some questions immediately arise. How can one take a vote about an issue if the voters are numerous? Where are decisions to be made? How is decision-making to be phased—for example, how long should discussion last and what structures should be imposed upon it? How are the citizens to know what is being discussed? Are the decision-making agenda and the discussion public, and how should reports of them be disseminated? How do the citizens make up their minds: do they vote according to what they conceive as the public good, or are they motivated by self-interest? When the decisions are made, how are they to be implemented? In sum, when democratic decision-making is embodied in institutional processes, to what extent do they affect democratic theory and practice?

Direct Democracy

Direct democracy and representative democracy are the two alternative mechanisms for democratic decision-making. Direct democracy is a good deal rarer than representative democracy, but both can be found in all democratic countries. The two variants provide different answers to the fundamental question. Who will make the decisions?

The components of direct democracy are three: the recall, the initiative, and the referendum. The recall, not widely used, allows constituents to force an elected person to resign, or to fight a by-election, and so to reaffirm (or otherwise) his/her majority support. It assumes that representatives have a duty to pay close attention to local opinion. A. L. Lowell said that the advocates of the recall saw the device as 'a method of getting rid of a man who has proved himself unworthy';[1] but he added that this was 'an acknowledgment of popular incapacity to choose trustworthy men'. Clearly the recall springs from a feeling that representatives are not to be trusted, a reflection of its populist origins in the American Midwest. The initiative allows a certain number of citizens (say 5 per cent of the voters) to introduce proposals for legislation, so bypassing legislative procedure. Such a proposal becomes law when passed by a majority vote of the total electorate. This involves a nation-wide poll or referendum.

The referendum is so obviously the most used of the tools of direct democracy that the two terms are often regarded as synonymous. Its origins and history explain much of its significance. The earliest record of a formal popular vote on a particular measure seems to be for fifteenth-century Berne.[2] By the eighteenth century it was widely practised in the Swiss cantons as an instrument of local democracy. Writing in the eighteenth century, the Swiss philosopher Jean Jacques Rousseau, who had seen its operation in his native Geneva, conceived the referendum or plebiscite as the institutional instrument of his idea of popular sovereignty. It was the only practical way in which the will of the people, or what Rousseau called the General Will, could be registered.[3] It permitted a relationship between the law-making authority, the 'Legislator' as Rousseau called him, and the people, without any intermediate groupings. Like all advocates of direct democracy, Rousseau disliked political parties and pressure groups, sectional wills subverting the General Will. The American Revolution borrowed the institution, and in 1778 it found a place in the new constitution of Massachusetts. Condorcet extolled the referendum in his writings.[4] The French Revolutionaries used it for ratifying constitutions in 1793, 1795, and 1799; and Napoleon in 1800, 1802, and

[1] A. L. Lowell, *Public Opinion and Popular Government* (New York, 1914), 148.
[2] Id., *Governments and Parties in Continental Europe* (1919), ii. 243.
[3] E. Barker (ed.), *Social Contract: Essays by Locke, Hume and Rousseau* (1947), 274. Typically, however, Rousseau was not very clear about it.
[4] M. Crampe-Casnabet, *Condorcet lecteur des lumières* (Paris, 1985), 45.

1804.[5] Thus, at the end of the eighteenth century the referendum, hitherto used essentially in small political units, was adapted to large states.

Several purposes are claimed for the use of referendums. Most generally it is claimed that the actions of representatives can never be necessarily in accord with their constituents (I shall expand this below). Consequently only popular votes of whole electorates can confer legitimacy on governmental acts. Oswald Mosley, leader of the British Union of Fascists, anticipated governing Britain by legitimating the acts of a Fascist government through 'the direct will of the people directly expressed'.[6] Advocacy of the referendum stems from great distrust of legislators and legislatures.

Another argument is that important national options, if not everything, should finally be decided by national vote. This envisages the nation at a cross roads where an important decision has to be taken about national direction, a use of the referendum easy to support, because it associates citizens with national decisions, making implementation therefore much less difficult. Thus, Norway and Denmark put the decision of whether or not to join the European Economic Community to the popular vote, with differing results.[7] Other national choices such as, for example, whether to declare war or not, may not be so appropriate if decided by referendum because, with an enemy at the gates, a long, agonizing debate is not advisable. It is the spectacle of the nation involved in a long campaign, educating itself about an issue, which recommends the referendum to many.

This holds for the third declared purpose of referendums, the need to put constitutions and constitutional amendments to the whole people. It is common for constitutions, like the American and the French, to include provisions for reference of amendments to the electorate in certain circumstances. In France the early republican constitutions, as we have noted, were referred in this way, and this has continued with the Fourth and Fifth republics.[8] Again the

[5] J. Godechot, *Les Institutions de la France sous la révolution et l'empire* (Paris, 1968), 279 ff, 467 ff.

[6] O. Mosley, *The Greater Britain* (1934 edn.) 189, quoted in R. Bassett, *The Essentials of Parliamentary Democracy* (1937), 243.

[7] S. S. Nilson, Scandinavia, in D. Butler and A. Ranney, *Referendums* (Washington, D. C., 1978), 184.

[8] G. Wright, *The Reshaping of French Democracy* (1950) for the Fourth Republic referendums, 94, 176 ff, and for the Fifth Republic, P. M. Williams and M. Harrison, *De Gaulle's Republic* (1960), 88 ff.

view is that something so fundamental must be legitimated by popular consent. With federal constitutions it is common for the consent to be in terms of a majority of the units making up the state. Article V of the American Constitution stipulates that three-quarters of the states must assent before a constitutional amendment is passed. For the Australian Constitution to be amended there must be not only a majority of the total electorate but also a majority in four out of the six states. Denmark's constitution can only be amended if, as well as 50 per cent of those who vote, 40 per cent of those on the electoral roll agree.[9] The purpose of these provisions is to ensure that more than an ordinary majority is needed for a constitutional amendment. It envisages the original document, inaugurating the nation-state, as so sacred that extraordinary majorities are required.

Fourthly, and especially prevalent in certain American states, has been the presentation of financial measures to the voters for ratification. Even contracts between the state and developers have in some instances been referred to the electorate. This usage springs from great distrust of state legislatures and executives. Early in their history, the Midwest and Western states experienced much corruption. Cattle barons, oil barons, and railroad kings bribed enough legislators to obtain what they wanted. This failure of representative government led to a reaction towards direct democracy, inspiring the introduction of the initiative first devised by the Swiss. (In Switzerland the initiative can also be used to amend the federal constitution.) The use of direct democracy in this way was intended to defeat selfish interests and pressure groups, but the latter may be as likely to organize an initiative and to win a subsequent referendum campaign as to control a legislature if there is considerable public apathy about the issue in question.

Finally, the referendum has to be used where legislatures are fractious and/or national decision-making becomes deadlocked. In these circumstances a national referendum becomes a sharp sword to slash the Gordian knot of political impasse. There are two classic instances of this resolution of decision-making dilemmas. In the first case, a legislature may be able to produce no clear majority. This was alleged to be the reason for the use of the referendum in the multi-party Weimar Republic. The German coalition governments of the 1920s were 'embarrassed and confused', their policy-making

[9] Nilson, *Scandinavia*, 171.

spasmodic, and their instability accentuated by the use of referendums.[10] The British referendum on the EEC in 1975 resolved an impasse for the governing Labour Party which did not have enough pro-EEC MPs to carry a majority for it in the House of Commons. Agreeing to a referendum on whether to withdraw from the EEC or not, and allowing all members, including MPs and ministers, to differ publicly and to campaign either for or against, was Labour's way of dealing with its own internal division.[11] Here was an example of a government and governing party unable to make up its mind and so passing the buck to the people.

The second instance of legislative impasse occurs when the two chambers disagree. Arthur Balfour, leader of the Opposition, suggested a national referendum to resolve the constitutional crisis of 1911 when the House of Lords appeared to be going to refuse to limit its own powers.[12] The Australian Constitution, however, has a special clause relating to disagreement between the two houses. When, after an interval of three months, a measure passed by one House is rejected or amended by the other, the governor-general may submit the proposal to the electors in each state.[13] This procedure resolves the problem at the expense of lowering the status of the legislature.

Underlying these alleged functions of direct democracy are numerous attitudes and values which imply criticisms of representative democracy. Let us examine these in turn.

One virtue ascribed to the referendum is clarity. As compared with public discussion and election campaigns when issues become blurred are not put to the voters properly and explicitly, the referendum sets the issue down on paper so it can be settled in a unambiguous manner. In other words, the politicians are eliminated from the process. In practice, however, it is not so easy. In the first place, someone has to phrase the question and, if he/she is a politician, it may be far from clear. (Sometimes simplicity, which may pass for clarity, can be very confusing.) If the government phrases the question, it will probably do so to its own advantage. Sometimes the questions may be deliberately misleading. There are

[10] H. Finer, *Theory and Practice of Modern Government* revised edn., (1949), 566.

[11] D. Butler and V. Kitzinger, *The 1975 Referendum* (1976), 18 ff.

[12] B. E. C. Dugdale, *A. J. Balfour*, ii. (1939), 44.

[13] L. F. Crisp, *The Parliamentary Government of the Commonwealth of Australia* (1949).

many political questions to which the answers 'Yes' or 'No' cannot easily be given. Some referendum questions may be long and technical—this may be the case where legislative proposals are submitted—and there may be many 'Don't knows'. But when many abstain, the whole purpose of legitimation, either one way or the other, will be defeated. This may be mitigated by lengthy referendum campaigns in which all sides of complex questions will be aired. One result may then be that the electorate may feel such a poll is like a general election and vote not on the question but on the government's popularity. Indeed, General de Gaulle used his referendums, among other purposes, as votes of confidence in his presidency.[14] When he was at last defeated, in 1969, he resigned.

Another quality of direct democracy, it is claimed, is specificity. Referendums isolate issues and place them before the electorate, to be judged on their merits. In representative democracy the interplay of political forces mixes up the issues and, in the cross-fire of political debate, it becomes very difficult for the voters to make proper judgements. The confusion may indeed be deliberately stimulated by politicians who want to avoid responsibility. Sometimes the voters may not be aware of what they are voting for. None of this, it is argued, can happen when issues are taken separately. Unfortunately, the separation of policies may be very artificial. Most issues are interdependent and interconnected, and in one important way nearly all policies are related—they depend on money for their implementation, so more of one policy may mean less of another. Thus specificity may be little more than unrealistic simplicity.

A third advantage claimed for the referendum is that of immediacy. With representative institutions, proper approval or disapproval of measures may have to wait until the next general election. The British are only free, Rousseau said, at election time.[15] Immediate mandates allow questions to be dealt with as they arise, and public opinion may make its impact on governments in between elections. The objection to immediate mandates is that they may permit little time for reflection and discussion and that policies may become uncoordinated as a result. Taken to the extreme, one could envisage an electorate continually visiting the voting booth, a situation in which democracy might become breathless and erratic.

[14] V. Wright, France, in Butler and Ranney, *Referendums*, 146.
[15] Barker, *Social Contract*, 373.

Fourthly, the referendum's decisiveness is supposed to contrast with the indecisiveness of representative democracy. The difficulty of making decisions on important issues may have many causes: the complexity and many-sidedness of the problem, for example, or the division of opinion into several sections with an uneasy balance between them. Sometimes making no decisions may be the result of this pluralistic stagnancy, and no decision may be the proper democratic outcome. Indeed, no decision *is* a decision—the decision to maintain the status quo. Trying to force everyone into two camps, 'Yes' or 'No', when in fact there are numerous camps may be distorting the wishes of the voters. Fractiousness in the legislature probably reflects the division of political forces in the country and doing nothing may provide the equilibrium between them.

The mechanism of direct democracy, therefore, may be open to many of the same criticisms as representative democracy (see below). It may disappoint reformers and disillusion the voters. In fact, as I hope the above argument demonstrates, the claim that direct democracy is more legitimating may be highly dubious. While values such as clarity and specificity can hardly be associated with undemocratic attitudes (however unrealistic they may be), immediacy and decisiveness may sometimes be part of the vocabulary of authoritarianism. Over much of Europe, plebiscitary democracy has incurred a reputation as a tool of dictatorship. Napoleon I and Louis Napoleon used it arbitrarily to obtain the results they desired.[16] Boulanger intended to govern by it.[17] Above all, Adolf Hitler used it to come to power. In his referendum of August 1934, calling for a fusion of the presidency and the chancellorship, the question began 'Do you German man or woman agree that . . . '[18] implying that no true German could answer 'No'.

Yet while European left-wing parties have distrusted the referendum because of its association with a populist, nationalistic right, in Australia and the United States it has been one of the nostrums of populist radicalism. Indeed in Australia, the Labour Party espoused direct democracy at the beginning of the Commonwealth. In 1897 the New South Wales Labour Party's programme for the constitutional convention was a one-chambered Parliament, elected on the

---

[16] A. Aulard, *Histoire politique de la révolution française* (Paris, 1926), 752; W. Smith, *Napoleon III* (Paris, 1982), 164.

[17] D. W. Brogan, *The Development of Modern France* (1949), 200 ff.

[18] Finer, *Theory and Practice of Modern Government*, 568.

basis of one adult, one vote, and restrained by the initiative and referendum. The Conservative Party, on the other hand, feared and fought direct democracy. Sir Henry Parkes, prime minister of New South Wales, deprecated the reference of issues to the electorate, saying 'the uninformed and reckless are always ready to denounce any work which they cannot comprehend'.[19] Today these positions are reversed. The referendum has not been widely used at the federal level in Australia, but when it has the voters have displayed a marked disposition to reject innovation. In the first seventy-four years of the Australian Commonwealth only five out of thirty-two constitutional amendments have been passed.[20] Consequently, the Labour Party has come to dislike the referendum, whereas the Liberal-Country Party, the heirs of the Conservatives, tend to regard it as a bulwark against change.

Ideological attribution of direct democracy, therefore, may be somewhat misleading. A recent empirical study of referendums cautiously concludes: '. . . our preliminary verdict would be that the referendum is a politically neutral device that generally produces outcomes favoured by the current state of public opinion'.[21] In different contexts (of time and place) it has assumed differing implications of fascism, radicalism, and conservatism. Its origins lie in micro-polities like the Greek polis, the New England town meeting, and the Swiss canton. The support for it for large states in modern times springs from discontent with representative institutions and distrust of legislators. Combined with these feelings are suspicions about political parties, rooted in the belief that the nation's politicians are remote, corrupt, and fractious, and are therefore failing in their obligations to those who elected them. Direct democracy is suggested as a 'more democratic' system of decision-making than representative democracy.

Representative Democracy

As opposed to direct democracy, representative institutions provide an indirect way for people to be involved in decision-making. The voters elect representatives who make the decisions for them. The people making the laws, therefore, stand as intermediaries between the people and the government implementing them. Representative

---

[19] Crisp, *Parliamentary Government of Australia*, 14.
[20] Id., *The Australian National Government* 4th edn. (1978), 42.
[21] Butler and Ranney, *Referendums*, 244.

democracy complicates democracy in numerous ways. What are its supposed advantages?

The first and obvious advantage is a practical one. With vast numbers of people in the modern nation-state, total participation in decision-making is impossible. Discussion of issues may take place everywhere, but for laws binding the whole nation the debate must be organized at the centre, usually in the capital city, and in a chamber small enough for every legislator to be heard by every other. The restriction of the final stages of discussion to a few hundred people, or even in legislative committees to many fewer, does not prevent its circulation through the media to many millions. On the other hand, it does allow for a more structured, more civil, and more considered law-making. Those crictical of representative democracy, however, regard legislatures with disapproval as assemblages of unrepresentative (in the sense of not reflecting the average) people, remote both geographically and mentally from the country as a whole.

Secondly, representative democracy, in permitting the conduct of affairs to be handed over to the few, allows the many to have more time for other activities. This purpose assumes that not too many citizens want to be political leaders. Those who do allow all the others to undertake instead other occupational and recreational pursuits, such as becoming stockbrokers or bricklayers, collecting moths or playing darts. In other words, the specialization of modern society includes the drafting of laws and the making of decisions by those who have the time and inclination to specialize in it. Hence a new specialization, that of the paid legislator, the 'professional politician', has emerged during the twentieth century. This has some obvious disadvantages which have been emphasized by critics of representative democracy. It may produce a group of specialized people with corporate interests conflicting, it is argued, with the public interest and contributing to an even larger gap between leaders and people.

Representative democracy also permits a further selection of leaders to take place from among the legislators. In many countries the government is selected from the representatives, a further specialization of function. Hence in a modern democracy there is training and recruitment for leaders at all levels—local government, Parliament, and government. Critics allege, however, that this complexity makes representative democracy Byzantine.

Moreover, the fact that government cannot normally be shifted from power until the next election renders it insensitive to the promptings of the electorate.

The centralization of decision-making facilitates its rationalization. Decisions are not only centralized geographically, they are also easily related to other decisions. Hence agendas can be drawn up and priorities accorded, giving the democratic process a rational direction that would not be possible under direct democracy. A policy-making executive may be one likely result of the institution of a legislature. Opponents of representative democracy, however, will usually be opponents of centralization and rationalization. They will prefer issues to be dealt with on their merits and will resent the drafting of programmes in which one issue—so they will argue—is traded off against another. Bargaining and compromising will be a 'wheeling and dealing' from which most people will be excluded.

Representative democracy, therefore, almost inevitably implies the formation of political parties. Parties are needed to inform electorates, articulate programmes, and aggregate voters; they are needed to select candidates to contest elections; and they are usually needed for governing. Parties are needed for bargaining with other parties. Consequently, polictical parties have become a conspicuous and important part of contemporary democracy. As Ramsay MacDonald said, 'Democracy without party is like a crowd without a purpose'.[22] But parties have their detractors. They mediate between the public and the government, and they may make it more difficult for some to attain their objectives. Democratic political parties have developed vast decision-making systems of their own and large bureaucracies, adding to the complexity of contemporary politics. In their attempts to win elections they have so tended to blur policies that their role of informing the electorate and presenting it with clear options may be very much exaggerated. Clarity and specificity, the alleged hallmarks of direct democracy, cannot be claimed as distinguishing features of party-dominated representative democracy; indeed, critics might assert that obscurity and generality are its main characteristics. Certainly, representative democracy is more attuned to the activity of centralized policy-making and administration, two essential characteristics of the contemporary industrialized state.

[22] J. R. MacDonald, *Socialism and Government* (1909), 13.

The representative in a democratic state is confronted by a number of different pressures. There is pressure from the voters who have the power of dismissal at the ensuing election. There is pressure from the 'selectorate', the people who choose the candidates. (Selection and reselection are indispensible where parties are involved, and often the local party activists will exert power in these procedures.) There is pressure from people who provide parties with funds. There is pressure from the central party organization and from the party group in the legislature. The pressures will be support for, or opposition to, various measures that may be local or national, specific or general, self-seeking or altruistic. The representative has to decide how to react to these pressures, attempting to balance some, withstand some, and give way to others. Depending on circumstances, tastes, dispositions, and values, different types of representative emerge.

A common way to understand the relationship between representative and electorate is to examine the amount of control the latter exerts. One can envisage a spectrum stretching from complete control over speech and action to a position where the representative has complete freedom, conditional upon undergoing periodical re-election. Where the representative is closely controlled it is usual to say he/she is 'mandated' or 'delegated'. 'Delegates' are supposed to carry out instructions. One can imagine hypothetically a legislature full of delegates in which no debate is necessary, only votes need to be taken because positions have been taken up at election time and cannot be changed. Extreme delegation thus produces great legislative weakness, but voters' strength: a situation not unlike direct democracy. Voters' control may be strengthened by factors such as the 'locality rule', some form of which can be found in all American states. This limits candidatures to local people, who are more likely to be subject to local pressures. American congressmen and senators, however, are by no means supine people, and few of them would perceive themselves in a delegate role. The pressures of party do not bear down on them in the way they do on many European representatives, and many American legislators would claim relative autonomy.

Some American political scientists have concluded that representatives can be divided into three groups: delegates, trustees, and politicos.[23] The trustee stands at the opposite end of the spectrum to

[23] H. Eulau, J. C. Wahlke, W. Buchanan, and L. C. Ferguson, The Role of the Representative: Some Empirical Observations on the Theory of Edmund Burke,

the delegate in a stance made famous by Burke, who saw the trustee's relationship with his constituents as follows:

> Their wishes ought to have great weight with him; their opinion high respect; their business unremitted attention . . . But his unbiased opinion, his mature judgement, his enlightened conscience, he ought not to sacrifice to you; to any man, or to any set of men living . . . Your representative owes you, not his industry only, but his judgement; and he betrays you, instead of serving you, if he sacrifices it to your opinion . . . government and legislation are matters of reason and judgement and not of inclination and, what sort of reason is that, in which determination precedes the discussion; in which one set of men deliberate, and another decides. Parliament is not a congress of ambassadors from different and hostile interests . . . but . . . a deliberative assembly of one nation . . . where, not local purposes, not local prejudices ought to guide, but the general good, resulting from the general reason of the whole.

Extreme trusteeship thus places the voters in a weak position, able only to influence their representative at election time. Even then, Burke considered, the voters had no right to demand pledges. He affirmed:

> . . . authoritative instructions; mandates issued which the member is bound blindly and implicitly to obey, to vote, and to argue for, though contrary to the clearest conviction of his judgement and conscience: these are things entirely unknown to the laws of this land, and which arise from a fundamental mistake of the whole order and tenor of our constitution.[24]

The trustee acts independently of pressures, and the voters must, depend on his judgement which, it is implied, is far superior to theirs. If they do not like the results of the trustee's judgement they can dismiss him. The implication of this for the legislature is that it will be composed of strong, independently minded representatives who perceive their role not as pursuing local or sectional interests but as participating responsibly in the formation of national policy.

Of course, in modern democratic legislatures there are few delegates or trustees, though some representatives may be nearer one or other role and some may wax rhetorical about their country's traditions in this respect. British MPs, when under pressure from outside bodies, sometimes quote Burke and proclaim their duty to

---

American Political Science Review, 53 (1959), 742 ff. Reprinted in H. Eulau (ed.), *Political Behaviour in America* (New York, 1966), 24 ff.

[24] Speech to the Electors of Bristol, in B. W. Hill (ed.), *Edmund Burke on Government Politics and Society* (1975), 157–8.

be guided by their consciences. (Burke is largely irrelevant, for he lived in the era of limited suffrage before there were mass parties.) In practice, however, modern representatives have to balance both roles, that is, they are politicos. This is partly the result of commonsense: assuming that one wants to be a representative, it is foolish to ignore the views of local constituents. And the rise of political parties has made it very difficult for a representative to act autonomously. The voters have come to vote for 'the party' much more than for 'the man'.

Hence in contemporary democracies the relationship of the representative to his/her national party is very important. In many legislatures, fairly strong party discipline will be employed to keep the party group to the party line. Representatives' support will be needed for the policies of the party, or parties, which form the government. Thus the relationship of the representative to party is closely associated with the relationship of the representative to government. The rise of disciplined parties has in many countries changed the nature of legislative–executive relations. An important function of representatives in most democracies is either retaining their party in governmental power by upholding its majority in the legislature, or supporting opposition policies faithfully when their party is not in power, in the hope that the governmental majority will falter and collapse. Naturally this system does not appertain in such countries as the United States where a presidential executive is not part of the legislature, and as a result the national parties (such as they are) have not forged firm links between the legislature and executive policy-making. In Britain, on the other hand, Cabinet government has been virtually majority-party government for a hundred years or more. The House of Commons has become a sort of electoral college to which the return of members of Parliament at general elections determines the political colour of the executive. In most representative democracies, therefore, if not all, it is usual to declare that the role of the representative is in decline.

This is in keeping with the 'decline of legislatures', a familiar theme with those who study contemporary political institutions.[25]

---

[25] See F. W. Bealey, The Relationship Between the Decline of Legislatures and the Growing Interdependence of Polity and Economy: A Comparison between France, USA and Britain, Workshop paper PEIHID 2 for Freiburg Joint Sessions of ECPR, March 1983.

The classical position was that legislatures made laws and executives implemented them. (This was consistent, as we have noted,
with trustees as representatives.) The roles normally imputed to
legislatures were law-making, controlling financial policy, criticizing and exercising surveillance over the government by supplying a
majority.[26] Even in the nineteenth century, however, executives
often exercised prerogatives over foreign policy decisions without
consulting legislatures. (This was especially so with the British
government.) Urgency and secrecy ease diplomacy, while public
discussion may be an embarrassment. Thus the Parliament of the
Third French Republic, *par excellence* the reflection of popular
sovereignty, did not in 1938 discuss the Munich crisis.[27] Two world
wars in the twentieth century have further eroded legislative power,
one important reason being that 'total war' involves some control
of the economy. War efforts require coherent direction and legislatures are not good at it. Economic depression has also contributed
greatly to increased governmental power, and voters have contributed by expecting governments to improve their material situation
and by punishing those who do not. Political leaders have therefore
found it difficult to escape blame for the economic situation even
when not responsible for it. Keynesian ideas of economic management have been used in all democracies since the 1940s as a result
of electoral pressure. But urgency and secrecy may also characterize
such measures. Hence much of the economic activity of modern
government,[28] as David Coombes and Stuart Walkland suggest,
resembles foreign policy decision-making.[28] Consequently, democratic legislatures have declined in all roles except that of supporting executives. Policies are often made by party conferences and
transformed into legislation by executives; financial policy has been
complex and difficult to follow; general supervision has been a
great problem for parliaments because of the enormous growth in
the volume of business; and television and party conferences have
detracted from legislatures as arenas for the discussion of national
issues.

Therefore, to a greater or lesser degree in all democracies, the
relationship that has become most important is that between

[26] See K. C. Wheare, *Legislatures* (1962), 2 ff.
[27] P. Williams, *Politics in Post-war France* (1954), 196.
[28] D. Coombes and S. A. Walkland, *Parliaments and Economic Affairs*
(1980), 12.

electorate and ministers or opposition leaders. On the other hand, the relationship of the average voter with the legislature, if one exists at all, is still likely to be with his own representative, who may be petitioned to obtain redress or favours from the government. This puts an emphasis on elections as the only occasions on which voters directly participate in the distribution of power. Between elections they take part indirectly through legislators, political parties, and pressure groups. Is the general implication of this for democracy, as Giovanni Sartori says, an altogether different formula?[29]

Micro and Macro-democracy

Direct and representative democracy are two different ways of operating a democratic polity. The operation of democracy may vary, however, according to size. Within a small political unit such as a city-state, the implications for democratic relationships will be quite different for those in the nation-state. Aristotle's description of the workings of the Greek polis, and other information we have about New England towns, Swiss cantons, and small Scottish burghs bears this out. I shall call democracy on the small scale 'micro-democracy' to distinguish it from macro or large-scale democracy. This book is largely concerned with 'macro-democracy'; but an understanding of the situation in micro-democracy helps not only the exposition of the main theme but also the centralization/decentralization discussion in Chapter 4.

In the first place, however, the connection (if any) between this dichotomy and that between direct and representative democracy needs clarification. Direct democracy is clearly more appropriate to small polities, whereas representative democracy is much more suitable for large. But there is no clear correspondence between direct democracy and micro-democracy. The division between direct and representative refers to institutional methods of making decisions. The division between micro and macro refers to size and to how size affects relationships betwen leaders and followers. By 'size' I refer particularly to numbers of citizens, though geographic extent is another criterion.

In micro-democracy citizens can communicate easily with each other and their leaders. The result of this is likely to be that the

[29] J. Plamenatz and G. Sartori, 'Electoral Studies and Democratic Theory', *Political Studies*, 6/1 (1958), 13.

history of issues, their backgrounds (as people often put it), will be widely known. Consequently, the motives of people who support or oppose certain lines of action are often correctly assessed. Moreover, it is much easier in a face-to-face society (or something approaching it) to judge the gap between promise and performance. It should be much clearer what policies are being advocated and later implemented (they will be much slighter in scope anyway), and therefore judgements about the competence of those who support and execute policies can be made without great doubt. In this decision-making context it will be much easier for each individual to relate his/her values and interests to those of other people. It should be widely known where everyone stands and what they stand for. If the rules are accepted, people know to what they have consented, once a decision is made, even if they are in the minority. Majorities for certain courses of action will clearly have the responsibility for the outcomes. Citizen control appears to be maximized and 'government by the consent of the governed' is visibly in operation.

This model does not, however, assume altruistic action. The citizens, it is presumed, will be seeking the maximization of self-interest, not opting for what they believe to be the general will or the public good. Like all democracies, micro-democracies can be conflict-ridden; indeed, there is much evidence to suggest that where conflict arises in small communities, largely because personalities intrude, it will be more severe.[30] In most, however, an ideology of harmony may well hold sway,[31] if it is widely accepted that a small community cannot withstand discord and conflict. And so those who show signs of rocking the boat will be unpopular, resulting in a tendency to maintain the status quo. In a democracy where many citizens place great value on harmony, peace and quiet are more likely to prevail; on the other hand, dissent may be stifled.

Micro-democracy, by many criteria, may be judged more rational than macro-democracy. Information in the former is much easier to come by, and therefore rational policy-making is much more attainable. Participation by the individual citizen, as J. S. Mill argued, educates in the policy-making process. Where all are

---

[30] G. S. Black, 'Conflict in the Community: A Theory of the Effects of Community Size', *American Political Science Review*, 68 (1974), 1245 ff.

[31] See F. W. Bealey and J. Sewel, *The Politics of Independence* (Aberdeen, 1981), 82 ff.

supposed to participate, and all are aware of the histories of issues and policies, understanding will be much greater. Individuals can propose action and act more rationally. Responsibility can be attributed with relative clarity, and voters should be aware of both promises and performances. People's words and actions will be more intelligible and less unexpected, giving less grounds for suspicion. Rulers will not be remote and they can continually be checked and easily made accountable. Consequently, there should be much more trust in this type of society.

The quality and competence of leadership in micro-democracy may, however, not measure up to modern standards of rationality. Leaders will be part-time, unspecialized, and barely distinguishable from ordinary citizens. As Robert Dahl and Edward Tufte write: 'Only in smaller-scale polities can differences in power, knowledge and directness of communication between citizens and top leaders be reduced to a minimum.[32] The lack of specialization and training may not matter in very small communities where issues are very local and very simple, and where the scope of the political unit's decision-making power is small. One does not have to ascend far, however, to reach a size of polity that needs more expert, less part-time decision-makers. The nation state could hardly be run by part-time politicians.

In modern industrialized democracies the scope of decision-making is extensive. Great specialization of role has produces a highly complex society, difficult for anyone to grasp in its entirety. Most people, including very well-educated people, will not be very well informed about the backgrounds to most issues. They will therefore not understand the motives, statements, and actions of others, including the professional politicians, the only people highly involved in politics. It will accordingly be difficult to make any assessment of the politicians' promises, and likewise to assess their performances and to decide how one's interests are affected if one is not closely involved. Hence much may be decided without citizens being aware of the implications of decisions. Information will not be readily available and even policy outcomes may be unclear. (For example, every election campaign may be the occasion for disputes about the success or failure of the government's economic policies, in most cases leaving voters no wiser and in no better position to vote.) It will not be easy for the average citizen to remember

[32] R. Dahl and E. R. Tufte, *Size and Democracy* (1974), 88.

whether policies were consented to or not. Most people, being non-political, will feel that it is for the political leaders to propose and carry out policies. As John Plamenatz said, 'the role of the people in government is negative'.[33] This presumes a quite different atmosphere for macro-democracy.

The problem for the citizen in macro-democracy will be that of evaluating performances in terms of promises which lacked clarity when they were given. Rationality in its academic sense, therefore, will not be a marked feature of political life. People will not find it easy to explain, for instance, their voting behaviour, and much may depend on habit, cultural tradition, and even fortuitous circumstances such as the candidate's place on the ballot paper. Robert Lane and David Sears write:

> The indignant citizen often manipulates his cognitions in the service of some compelling emotional need, such as an embracing hostility towards authority . . . On the other hand, the rational citizen must in fact be able to relate incoming information to personal interests about which he feels deeply. The individual who forms opinions in ignorance of his short-term and long-term personal interests is not acting rationally either.[34]

Long-term interests are especially difficult for a citizen to perceive in contemporary democratic society. The unpolitical individual (and such people comprise perhaps a quarter of the electorate) faces solicitations from the leaderships of contesting political parties whose promises he does not understand and whose performances have made him suspicious. The information from the media about politics he distrusts. Hence, when the unpolitical man acts politically—which means when he votes (if he votes)—his rationality is not of a high order. He will be likely to proceed largely by impression and intuition.

Responsibility of Government

In macro-democracy, I have argued, mass electorates and elaborate institutions make the responsibility of governments to the governed a major problem. The term 'responsible' seems to be used in relation to government in four ways. Often it is a synonym for 'sensible' or 'prudent'. With this meaning one can detect responsible government by the same criteria as one identifies a responsible

[33] Plamenatz and Sartori, *Electoral Studies*, I.
[34] R. E. Lane and D. O. Sears, *Public Opinion* (Englewood Cliffs, 1964), 74.

person—someone in authority who takes especial care when making statements of intent and who worries about how present actions will affect other people now and in the future. In practice this usage is not far removed from the other three; but the others all have implications for democratic theory. A non-democratic government could, in this first sense, be as responsible as a democratic government.

The three other meanings are more technical. Responsible government often means government dependent on a majority in the legislature. Thus it means 'dismissable' government, and this could also be taken to apply to defeat at general elections. A government which can lose its majority at the polls, or as a result of a successful vote of censure or unsuccessful vote of confidence in Parliament, is responsible.

Another meaning of the term denotes government which is 'answerable' or 'accountable'. It has to give an account of itself to the governed or their representatives, to be prepared to listen to, and deal with, criticism and complaint, and to answer questions in the legislature about its activities. Clearly, accountability is linked with dismissability because the investigation and criticism of a government may result in its loss of office. On the other hand, giving a good account of oneself to the governed, or their representatives, helps to keep one in power.

Both dismissability and accountability are concerned with 'responsiveness', the quality of responding to citizens' political preferences. This may merely imply a disposition to answer questions and explain and justify policy; but it may result in the revision, or even the withdrawal, of policy. The threat of dismissal, or the experience of being accountable, should dispose governments to be responsive. Responsiveness derives from the nature of the democratic situation.

Both governments and legislators will vary in their degree of accountability and reponsiveness to, and censurability by, the governed. Under direct democracy, legislators will be diminished in power and may be recalled and forced to face re-election, with the possibility of defeat. Under representative democracy, governments and legislators may only be accountable at elections. They may be fairly safe between elections, with either party discipline or electoral procedures (such as fixed-length parliaments) safeguarding them from popular pressures. Those most open to pressures—

members of the American House of Representatives—are dismissable by the voters every other November; subject to locality rules restricting candidatures to local people (thus making them susceptible to local lobbies), and largely without the protection of party whips. When Louis Fisher writes that Congress seems so responsive that it cannot be responsible, he is using 'responsible' in the non-technical sense of behaving in the public interest.[35]

On the other side, however, the American president is not responsible to Congress except that the legislature may very exceptionally impeach him. He is elected for a fixed term of four years, and the nature of his election may not make for very precise mandates. In between elections he struggles with Congress in order to persuade it to endorse his policies. Executives can, however, be responsible to the voters through referendums. Vincent Wright says the referendum in the Fifth French Republic was seen by de Gaulle as a means of re-establishing the link of accountability and political responsibility between the governed and the government.[36] A British prime minister, without a fixed term, can be dismissed by a vote of the legislature and forced to dissolve Parliament in order to seek re-election. British ministers also have to answer parliamentary questions; both censurability and accountability are thus features of British politics.

When we attempt to evaluate how much responsibility should ideally exist in a democracy we are faced with a problem. The amount of upward control will not only depend on institutional arrangements, but on the political maturity of the electorate. Voters who have no desire to use their freedoms effectively will allow governments to wield 'irresponsible power'. If they fear neither accountability nor dismissability, they will not have to be responsive to the voters. It will be necessary only to spell out their policies and defend their actions before the legislature; and with a docile electorate the legislature will also be prone to inactivity. Very few governments indeed do not want to escape from as many pressures as possible.

With periodic elections one might expect that it would be difficult for governments not to be fairly responsible, but election

---

[35] L. Fisher, The Budgetary Process: How Far Have We Progressed? in B. L. R. Smith and J. D. Carroll (eds.), *Improving the Accountability and Performance of Government* (Washington, D. C., 1982), 77.

[36] Wright, France, 144.

results do not always make it clear what voters want the government to do. There are some simple human reasons why elections do not produce very clear guidance about policies and people. In the first place, a considerable proportion of the electorate does not vote. In recent American presidential elections, turn-outs of 55 per cent have been recorded: much less than half the electorate voted for the winning candidate. Again, voters are likely to express judgements with their votes on both past and future policies; but it will never be possible to be sure whether it is performances or prospects which move them most, though there is a good deal of evidence to suggest unpopular past actions, especially if they were shortly before the poll, make more impact than promises about future actions.

Other factors affecting the clarity with which public opinion expresses itself are institutional. For example, if elections are held for executive and legislature simultaneously, as in the United States, it may be difficult to decide what the public wants when, as not infrequently happens, a candidate of one party is elected to the presidency while another party gains a majority in one or both houses of Congress. Again, clear electoral mandates are rare in gubernatorial contests—as Gerald Pomper says, for many reasons, one of them being the American voters' tendency to vote on national issues when choosing their state governor.[37]

At one time it was conventional wisdom that clarity, intelligibility, and precision of intentions sprang from the British situation— only two major parties, one with a majority in the legislature.[38] This resulted in two different programmes at general elections, one of which the voters would choose. Thus they knew what policies to expect, and more than half had to accept responsibility for placing the government in office. The consequence was not only responsive government but also a responsible electorate.

This was contrasted with multi-party situations, with the French Third and Fourth Republics often cited as examples. Many political divisions were emphasized by the electoral system, resulting in legislatures without single-party majorities. Clarity of governmental policy was therefore impossible. As Arend Lijphart writes,

---

[37] G. M. Pomper with S. S. Ledermann, *Elections in America* (New York, 1968) 121.

[38] American Political Science Review, *Towards a More Responsible Two-Party System* (New York, 1950).

'the coalition programme will be a compromise made by political leaders instead of mandated directly by the voters'.[39] Moreover, the parties tended to maintain their policy stances, more concerned not to lose votes than anxious to win them. Hence no clear verdict could emerge from elections, and the electorate therefore had little responsibility for the government. In an extreme case the electorate might move in one direction but the majority coalition government would represent a movement in the opposite direction. This did not encourage politicians to be bold. Brave politicians who, in their efforts to solve their nation's problems, attempted to break up the crystallized multi-party system by seeking for new majorities on new issues tended to accentuate the political chaos. A prominent example was Mendès-France, French prime minister from 1953 to 1954, whose efforts to jolt the Fourth Republic's party system in the course of rationalizing the economy only produced an anti-tax party, the Poujadistes.[40] Here a political leader's clarity invoked a new sectionalism with extremist views.

British adversarial politics, it has been argued, achieved the highest form of representative democracy in the 'doctrine of mandate', which ensured responsibility of both government and electorate. Unfortunately it is seldom so simple, as an examination of British experience demonstrates. In the first place, not everyone in Britain, by any means, accepts the mandate theory. At the opposite end of the spectrum are those who maintain that once a British government is elected it has *carte blanche* to pursue, within the law, any policy it wishes, irrespective of what its leaders may have said at the preceding election. (An example would be the 'doctor's mandate' of 1931: the ailings of the body politic have to be diagnosed, if the metaphor may be extended, before the government can prescribe its medicine.) Yet although the exact status of the mandate theory may be difficult to assess, it is a fact that it is very much a reality in political life. Henry Drucker has pointed out the Labour Party's attachment to 'manifestoism'[41]—the belief that a Labour government must carry out nothing more or less than what the party's manifesto contained at the preceding election. Even the Conservative Party has moved in this direction since World War II. Composing its programme has become much more

[39] A. Lijphart, *Democracies* (New Haven, 1984), 110.
[40] A. Werth, *The Strange History of Pierre Mendès-France* (1957), 87 ff.
[41] H. Drucker, *Doctrine and Ethos in the Labour Party* (1979), 92.

important,[42] and its leaders often draw attention to their fidelity to electoral promises. In general, British governments emphasize their adherence to their mandates, while the Opposition highlights governmental failure to implement declared policies, or governmental perfidy in embarking on measures not previously placed before the electorate.

In fact, though adversarial two-party politics with a first-past-the-post electoral system is likely to produce majority party government (where there is a parliamentary and not a presidential system), and therefore strong, though dismissable, executives it may well not be as responsive to, or representative of, the voters as the multi-party system is. This is because the responses of British parties are often to the pressures of constituency activists, who select parliamentary candidates, rather then to the electorate. The strongly emphasized differentiation between the programmes produces an ideological gap that is unrepresentative of the largely centrist electorate. It is not only that the electoral system merely exaggerates the strength of the winning party in the country, as when Mrs Thatcher in 1983 achieved a thumping majority in the House of Commons with only 43 per cent of support among those voting, it is also that many of the votes for the majority party will be cast *against* its rival rather than for itself. Thus, that its programme receives a majority vote hardly justifies a party claiming a strong mandate.

Conversely, coalition bargaining in a multi-party situation may produce centrist compromises which more accurately reflect the political preferences of most voters. This is argued by Arend Lijphart, who points out that Italy and France have too often been taken as examples of unstable multi-partyism. In some of the small European countries, like The Netherlands with its consociational system,[43] minority parties with stable clienteles and well-differentiated policies are capable of forming enduring coalitions acceptable to the electorate. Here, voters' control is vindicated, perhaps in a rather indirect way, because a succession of coalitions deviating little in their policies and providing conflict-free administration are what the electorate really wants. It is dubious, however, whether electorates feel the same responsibility for governments that result from coalition bargaining after elections. What Maurice Heisler

[42] See J. D. Hoffman, *The Conservative Party in Opposition 1945-51* (1966).
[43] A. Lijphart, *Democracy in Plural Societies* (New Haven, 1977), 23 ff.

calls a European Polity Model has three features: indirect participation by the voters, a decline in the role of legislature,[44] and the effective removal of the mass public from the making of decisions.[45] Hence, though in multi-party systems such as Sweden, Belgium, The Netherlands, and Austria, where executive power is shared between parties, there will be governments more likely in their general policy to express the consensual mood of the voters, there may be less public discussion about policy (even though there may be a very high degree of internal consultation) than in adversarial politics.

So, whatever the type of democratic polity, electoral programmes may be over-emphasized as criteria by which governmental responsibility can be assessed. Responsive governments may choose to desert their mandates when they run contrary to changes in voters' opinions. Should clear indications that public opinion has changed affect the policy formulation of representatives and governments? *How* responsive, in other words, should governments and elected persons consider themselves to be? Once again, it may depend on the force of the declaration of popular feeling. Governor Jerry Brown of California, who was not enamoured of the content of Proposition 13 (limiting localities in assessing property taxes to no more than 1 per cent of the property value), immediately accepted the verdict of the state's voters when in June 1978 they accepted this proposition in a referendum.[46] Whether legislators and governments should constantly undertake their own soundings—e.g. sponsor public opinion polls—in order always to be ready to respond to voters' wishes may depend on their political calculations. If governments believe that commitment to their mandate from the last election will eventually win the next election for them when their programme is completed, they will be prepared to weather the unpopularity of not responding to voters' objections to half-finished business. In such circumstances much will depend on governments' faith in themselves and their policies. Some may be converted by events and desert their declared programmes in order to retain the allegiance of a majority of the voters. Some may follow the voters, others persist in trying to lead them. These are different styles of democratic leadership (as discussed in Chapter 8). It must be said, however, that responsive and responsible government does

[44] M. O. Heisler, *Politics in Europe* (New York, 1974), 38 ff.
[45] Ibid. 70.
[46] Pomper with Ledermann, *Elections in America*, 110.

not necessarily imply only obedience to the voters. It can imply, as Dag Anckar argues,[47] a democratic government that initiates more viable options than citizens can possibly devise. If, retrospectively, voters approve such unmandated initiatives, the criteria of reponsiveness and accountability are both satisfied.

Finally it must be said that there is an element of academic abstraction in much of the discussion about the relationship between democratic governments and their voters. The mandate as an ideal way of judging governmental performance in relation to promises can hardly be realistic when it is difficult to discover what precisely the government is doing. Information is vital if electorates are to know. Thus, in macro-democracy, the media of communication became very important for the proper operation of the democratic system. Mill was aware of this at an early stage when he wrote:

Reading is power: not only because it is knowledge, but still more because it is a means of communication—because, by the aid of it, not only do opinions and feelings spread to the multitude, but every individual who holds them knows that they are held by the multitude, which of itself suffices, if they continue to be held, to ensure their speedy predominance.[48]

And nearly a hundred years later Bryce asserted:

It is the newspaper press that has made democracy possible in large countries . . . Within the last hundred years the development of the press has enabled news to be diffused and public discussions to be conducted over wide areas . . . It is of course impossible for the public to know in any given case what may be the activities that lie behind the action of the newspaper . . . Today the statesman, even if he be a brilliant speaker whose speeches are invariably reported, has a far smaller audience than the newspaper, because it is read steadily from day to day, and he only occasionally . . . The power of the newspaper has two peculiar features. It has no element of compulsion and no element of responsibility.[49]

In the twentieth century the development of broadcasting and, especially, television has added appreciably to the potentialities of the media for disseminating accurate information and instigating vital political discussion. There can be little doubt that for the most

[47] D. Anckar, A Definition of Democracy, in D. Anckar and E. Berndtson, *Essays on Democratic Theory* (Tampere, 1984), 29.

[48] J. S. Mill, De Tocqueville on Democracy in America, *London and Westminster Review* 22 (Oct, 1835) 85–129.

[49] J. Bryce, *Modern Democracies* (1921), 104–19.

part the media have been a failure in this respect and representative democracy has been the poorer for it. In many countries the media, even when focusing on political life, have tended to trivialize debate. Television, in particular, has sought to polarize issues simplistically. The newspapers have often conveyed the biases of their proprietors with little concern for factual accuracy. Moreover, the media's concern for the gladiatorial side of politics has concentrated on top leaders rather than legislative or national debate. For all these reasons the relationship between voters and executives has become the crucial one.

For the ordinary citizen, understanding of political issues now requires unusual effort. Both the lack of information and its distortion have not helped to make political discussion intelligible, and this effect has been exacerbated by two other factors, the increasing technicality of policy and the inability of politicians, or possibly their unwillingness, to explain it. Moreover, where policies are not only complex but also change bewilderingly, both in the life of the same government and from one government to another, the attribution of blame may be difficult. Obviously, responsible government is best served where citizens can not only evaluate responsibility for policies in the short term but also have at least some conception of long-term implications. Where electorates are only worried about immediate outcomes, rational assessment of government performance will be vitiated. The voters will be concerned not about power over policy-making, but only about power over policy-makers. This brings us to the Schumpeterian theory of democracy.

Another Theory of Democracy

Joseph Schumpeter found quite unrealistic the theory of democracy focused around the proposition that 'the people' hold a definite and rational opinion about every individual question and elect representatives to put their views into practice. He countered it with his own definition based on democracy as he perceived its operation in the modern world: 'the democratic method is that constitutional arrangement for arriving at political decisions in which individuals acquire the power to decide by means of a competitive struggle for the people's vote'.[50] This definition is close to the present situation in the democratic world as I have described it immediately above. It

[50] J. Schumpeter, *Capitalism, Socialism and Democracy*, 3rd edn. (1949), 269.

puts a premium on political leadership and electoral competition between élites in political parties. The primary function of the elector's vote is to produce government[51] and not, as the 'classical' doctrine implied, to guarantee that issues be decided and policies framed according to the will of the people.[52]

Schumpeter thus presents a contrast between two theories of democracy: the 'classical', in which individuals, through rational argument, arrive at decisions and elect representatives to carry them out; and his own (the 'Schumpeterian' or 'competitive', as it has come to be called) in which the citizen is not capable of complete rationality, and only chooses between leaders, with organized groups behind them, competing for political power. In so doing the analogy with an oligopolistic market is close. He writes:

Party and machine politicians are simply the response to the fact that the electoral mass is incapable of action other than a stampede, and they constitute an attempt to regulate political competition exactly similar to the corresponding practices of a trade association.[53]

Hence Schumpeterian democracy prescribes a much less important role for the voter, and a much more important role for political leaders, than does classical democracy. In his model, popular power is slight and responsibility of government refers only to dismissability at election time. It is an analysis which the results of the voting studies[54] of the decades following *Capitalism, Socialism and Democracy* supported without much question. The voters were largely apathetic, politically ignorant, and usually averse to much participation in the democratic process. Other writers have since argued that apathy and electoral abstention on the part of the voters may, in some instances, be a reflection of their rationality.[55] What do they have to gain by voting anyway?[56]

---

[51] Ibid. 273.

[52] Ibid. 272. Palle Svensson argues convincingly that the classical theory of democracy is a straw man constructed by Schumpeter to offset his more realistic theory. See his Den klassiske demokratiske teori, *Politica*, Vol. XI, 2 (1978), 5–39. See also C. Pateman, *Participation and Democratic Theory* (Cambridge, 1970) 17 ff.

[53] Ibid. 283.

[54] B. R. Berelson, P. F. Lazarsfeld, and W. N. McPhee, *Voting* (Chicago, 1954); R. S. Milne and H. O. Mackenzie, *Marginal Seat* (1955); E. Burdick and A. J. Brodbeck, *American Voting Behaviour* (Glencoe, 1959).

[55] For example, A. Downs, *An Economic Theory of Democracy* (New York, 1957); also I. McLean, *Dealing in Votes* (Oxford, 1982). 70 ff.

[56] See W. H. Morris-Jones, 'In Defence of Apathy', *Political Studies*, 2 (1954), 25–37.

This question would have angered John Stuart Mill, sometimes considered the philosopher of 'classical' democracy. He saw self-interest as little to do with democracy, writing of the voter:

His vote is not a thing in which he has an option; it has no more to do with his personal wishes than the verdict of a juryman. It is strictly a matter of duty; he is bound to give it according to his best and most conscientious opinion of the public good. Whoever has any other idea of it is unfit to have the suffrage; its effect on him is to pervert not to elevate his mind.[57]

Mill's ideal of democracy consisted of rational people discussing what was the public good and then opting for it. The use of demo-cractic institutions as instruments for personal and collective profit would be detrimental to democracy. Mill feared that only the educated classes possessed the capacity for divining the public good; if universal suffrage were granted, democracy might become 'the exclusive role of the operative classes'.[58] In other words, Mill was dubious about whether classical democracy would work. The problem for Mill was to exclude corrupt, self-seeking interests from power when, with the extension of the voting right, the industrial workers would be in a numerical majority and so capable of enacting legislation in the interests of their own class.[59] On the other hand, he believed that 'nothing less can be ultimately desirable than the admission of all to a share in the sovereign power of the state',[60] and that the electors must possess 'the ultimate power in all its completeness'.[61] Like most Victorian liberals, Mill concluded that if universal suffrage was to be bestowed, all must attempt rationally to seek the common good. This would be accomplished through education, particularly political education, which would come from experience, especially in local politics (see Chapter 4). Quoting the United States as an example, he asserted:

It is only through political discussion that the manual labourer . . . is taught that remote causes . . . have a most sensible effect even on his personal interests; and it is from political discussion, and collective political action that one whose daily occupations concentrate his interests in a small circle . . . learns to feel for and with his fellow-citizens, and becomes consciously a member of a great community.[62]

In the democratic context, therefore, Mill saw complete rationality as the ability to understand causality in the affairs of state. When

[57] J. S. Mill, *Representative Government* (1861), 80.
[58] Ibid. 96.   [59] Ibid. 52.   [60] Ibid. 28.
[61] Ibid. 35.   [62] Ibid. 67.

this quality was widespread, people's view of their self-interest might be identifiable with the interest of the whole community.

Graeme Duncan and Steven Lukes, in a well-known article, agree that the Schumpeterian model is useful as a point of departure in the description of existing democracies, and that it need not be incompatible with traditional notions of democracy.[63] What they take exception to (as I do) is the elevation of a descriptive account into the foundations of a new and realistic ideal, as implied by Berelson, Lazarsfeld, and McPhee, for example, who argue that 'liberal democracy is more than a political system in which individual voters and political institutions operate'. Other necessary features are:

the intensity of conflict must be limited, the rate of change must be restrained, stability in the social and economic structure must be maintained, a pluralistic social organization must exist, and a basic consensus must bind together the contending parties.[64]

As I have argued earlier, this view is inconsistent with the fundamental characteristics of democracy, which encourage dissent and instability. When Schumpeter's model is taken not as a normative theory but as an analysis of the way many contemporary democracies operate, it is a useful point of departure for evaluating what is wrong with present-day democracy. The danger of elevating the Schumpeterian theory to an ideal is that it vastly underestimates the necessity for vigilance in relation to the holders of power, even when they are democratically elected governments, and that it tends to decry the need for citizen participation.

Conversely, Mill tended to intellectualize political decision-making to a degree that even in his day could not have approximated to reality. There is a rationality in self-interest, as Mill conceded, over and above the mere maximization of benefits—in itself a very difficult concept to put into practice in a political context. Even the most untutored individual may know something about his own condition that no one else does. (The wearer knows best where the shoe pinches.) Again, with regard to political education, it is difficult to separate the interest of the individual and public interest. The politically knowledgeable and politically active may benefit themselves as well as the community when they partici-

---

[63] G. Duncan and S. Lukes, The New Democracy, *Political Studies*, 11 (1963), 167–8.   [64] Berelson *et al.*, *Voting*, 313.

pate. Moreover, selflessly working for the common good may be difficult where representative institutions and macro-democracy are in force. Mill identifies some of the problems and not others. For example, he could see the practical difficulty: 'since all cannot, in a community exceeding a small town, participate personally in any but some very minor portions of the public business, it follows that the ideal type of a perfect government must be representative'.[65] Furthermore he was aware of the problems of forming individual opinions in an age when the mass media were beginning to standardize opinion. But he made no allowance for the influence of political parties and pressure groups, and he could not have anticipated how complex shaping an informed opinion would become when governments began to manage economic policy.

Conclusion

Direct and representative democracy are different forms of democracy, though both can be found in almost every polity. In the modern world, direct democracy has often been advocated by those who disapprove of some aspect, or aspects, of representative democracy. They object to the intermediary activities of political parties and pressure groups and feel that matters can be settled by recourse to a simpler and more direct relationship—that between the government and the people. But direct democracy may well not be simplifying when it is introduced at the national level into a highly complex polity with representative democracy. Often it complicates matters even more; and, where recourse to it becomes frequent, it is especially detrimental to the co-ordinative activities of government, especially in the field of finance. On the other hand, at the local level, and nationally for specific issues, its democratic credentials are irreproachable.

In the large contemporary democratic state (macro-democracy as I have called it), representative institutions provide at the national level a practical way of making decisions while trying to maintain democratic procedures and values. But representative institutions, because of their remoteness, their complexities, their delays, and sometimes their factiousness and corruption, may often seem unsatisfactory as instruments of democracy. There can be no escaping the fact that often it is the convenience of governments, rather

---

[65] Mill, *Representative Government*, 28.

than the functions of parliaments as watchdogs for the governed, that has most guided the development of representative institutions in the twentieth century. Because the decline of legislatures and the increasing power of executives may be tacitly sanctioned by the majority of the electorate, it might be argued that democracy is not impaired by such an outcome. As I have argued above, however, it does not follow that the majority always understand the implications for democracy of their attitudes and actions. Put at its simplest, representative institutions provide more opportunities for things to go wrong and therefore demand more vigilance on the part of the democracy-watchers.

Neither direct nor representative democracy, however, offers any intrinsic challenge to inclusiveness, public contestation, or the rule of law. Of course, the spirit in which they are operated is of great importance, and it is not difficult to find instances of usages harmful to democracy. For example, the referendum has sometimes been the instrument of authoritarianism, and fiercely contested elections can lead to breaches of the law. But in themselves they remain part of the machinery of democratic decision-making without any particularly value-laden qualities. The extent to which the ordinary citizen may be involved in either, and so politically educated in the way Mill envisaged, is not necessarily less under direct democracy (as a glance at Switzerland quickly confirms). On the other hand, the organized parties of representative democracy may offer citizens better opportunities for participating in policy-making.

Obviously the relationship between political leaders and the electorate is one of the utmost importance for democracy, though its exact nature is difficult to determine because the interactions between them are subtle and defy analysis. V. O. Key, convinced that voters were not fools, was of the belief that politicians' perceptions of voters' responses must always be a matter of fundamental significance. He warned:

Fed a steady diet of buncombe, the people may come to expect and to respond with the highest predictability to buncombe. And those leaders most skilled in the propagation of buncombe may gain lasting advantage in the recurring struggles for popular favour.[66]

This is an interpretation that emphasizes the importance of political leadership for shaping knowledgeable and responsible attitudes

[66] V. O. Key, *The Responsible Electorate* (New York, 1968), 7.

among the electorate. But while Key saw the voters' positive role in controlling inputs as slight, he was insistent that their negative role in pronouncing on outputs could be decisive. From his study of the 1960 presidential election he inferred:

The odds are that the electorate as a whole is better able to make a retrospective appraisal of the work of governments than it is to make estimates of the future performance of non-incumbent candidates . . . Governments must worry, not about the meaning of past elections, but about their fate at future elections.[67]

Hence governments may be held much more responsible for their performances than their promises.

To what degree responsibility of governments to the governed is a facet of contemporary democracies remains an open question. Clearly, some responsibility is implied by the electoral process: a democratic government must be dismissable. But how much freedom of action a government has between elections is a matter for democratic discussion, and in all democracies it remains open to argument. There are those who strictly adhere to the mandate theory (which in practice, as we have seen, can never actually be implemented), and there are those who maintain that, once elected, governments have autonomous powers. Both sets of disputants are frequently disappointed because political circumstances frustrate realization of these opposed positions. What has more significance for democracy is whether the potentiality for knowing and understanding the government's acts exists. Where citizens are ill-informed about what the executive is doing or proposed to do, public contestation will be sadly impaired. The right to know is clearly an important corollary of the right to vote and the right to oppose. Rationality in decision-making, Anckar says, depends on time to deliberate and on sufficient information.[68] In this sense a government is irresponsible if it does not keep citizens informed of at least the policy options, and allow time to discuss them, before a decision is made.

This question is relevant to the issue of whether Schumpeterian democracy is a condition for concern. The fact that people are not completely rational, and cannot, with imperfect knowledge, ever be so, does not imply that they cannot be *more* rational. That Schumpeterian democracy works, or appears to work, should not satisfy

---

[67] Ibid. 76.
[68] Anckar, Definition of Democracy, 31.

democratic theorists. A system in which rather élite figures packaged by public relations experts claim that they possess more individual competency than their opponents can hardly be one in which responsible leaders and voters emerge. The decline of legislatures is a similar cause for concern. These trends, together with the increasing apathy of the electorate, may be exaggerated in current political science literature, but there is much evidence to support their validity.

One might defend Schumpeterian democracy as an inevitable second best, and also with the argument that in a democractic country the degree of governmental responsibility is, like the choice between direct and representative democracy, a matter ultimately for citizens to decide. Yet even this decision will be difficult where people lack knowledge about constitutional matters and power relationships at the top levels. An electorate educated in democracy is bound to be more likely to hold the government to account.

We must now turn to the apparatus of the democratic state. It has many implications for governmental responsibility and for the relationship between governors and governed.

3

DEMOCRACY AND THE
APPARATUS OF THE STATE

STRUCTURES of administrative power existed long before democracy. In fact, they were a feature of some *anciens régimes*. Theda Skocpol describes how China before 1911 had six hundred years of peace and order, economic expansion, and cultural elaboration under a mandarin class of about 40,000 officials—a centralized, autocratic, semi-bureaucratic administration.[1] States have always had administrative apparatuses though in modern times these have greatly expanded. Richard Eichenberg calculates an average for twelve European states of administrative employment per 1,000 populations. It is 4.9 for 1880, 16.7 for 1920, and 19.0 for 1970.[2] The growth in the numbers of public servants has been a consequence of the increasing scope of the modern state. At the beginning of the twentieth century about one-tenth of gross national products of democracies contributed to public spending: today the equivalent proportion would be about a half,[3] an increase partly the result of the pressures of democratic electorates.

Democracy's impact has varied. In the United States, populistic pressures have resulted in a patronage system with offices tending to rotate with presidents or (at state level) governors. But in most democracies, including Britain, the advent of democratically elected Parliaments ushered in professional, uncorrupt, meritocratic civil services, dedicated to neutrality and impartiality. Indeed, Weber's favourite metaphor of a machine best describes this style of administration. Machines have no life of their own; they can be set in motion by anyone who knows how to work them. They are also composed of several parts, each with distinct function. The more complex their functions, the more difficult they are to operate.

[1] T. Skocpol, *States and Social Revolutions* (Cambridge, 1979) 68.
[2] R. G. Eichenberg, 'Problems in Using Public Employment Data' in C. L. Taylor (ed.), *Why Governments Grow* (1983), 142.
[3] M. Dogan, The Political Power of the Western Mandarins, in M. Dogan (ed.), *The Mandarins of Western Europe* (1975) 5.

A century or more of democracy has seen the administrative
apparatuses of democratic states transformed from this early
'machine'. Perhaps J. D. Aberbach, Robert Putnam, and B. A.
Rockman best characterize the development of the relationship
between politics and administration in four stages.[4] The earliest
form envisages a simple separation. As Frank Goodnow said,
politics expressed the public will and administration executed it.[5] In
an earlier work Putnam described such an administrator as a 'classical bureaucrat',[6] an example of Weber's ideal-type, simply implementing policy. A second form, postulated by H. A. Simon,[7]
conceives the administrator providing objective criteria and information in order to judge policy options, while politicians,
concerned with the pressures of interests, express value judgements
and bring quite different considerations to decision-making. Probably, however, the politicians will eventually choose from those
options bureaucrats declare possible. With the third form the
bureaucrat becomes involved with the interests. As the authors
explain, 'whereas politicians articulate broad diffuse interests of
unorganized individuals, bureaucrats mediate narrow focused
interests of organized clienteles'.[8] In this model, bureaucrats share
both formulation of policy and brokerage of interests with the
politician who is concerned with articulating general policies and
principles. What Putnam calls the 'political bureaucrat' deals with
specialized policies and segmentalized clienteles within a
departmental framework. In the fourth form the distinction
between bureaucrats and politicians disappears, except that the
former still implement policy. Lines of demarcation are blurred,
people move easily from one role to the other, and bureaucrats also
enunciate general policies and principles. This fourth type is more a
tendency than a reality. It is rarely found.

A fifth form not characterized by the above authors might be
where politicians do not enter the decision-making process at all: it
has been depoliticized. The bureaucrats have such a monopoly of
the information, which only they can analyse, that only they
possess the expertise to make a choice between policy options. Such

    [4] J. D. Aberbach, R. D. Putnam, and B. A. Rockman, *Bureaucrats and Politicians
in Western Democracies* (Harvard, 1981) 4 ff.
    [5] F. Goodnow, *Politics and Administration* (1900).
    [6] R. D. Putnam, The Political Attitudes of Senior Civil Servants in Britain,
Germany and Italy, *British Journal of Political Science*, 3 (1973), 87 ff.
    [7] H. A. Simon, *Administrative Behaviour* (New York, 1958).
    [8] Aberbach *et al. Bureaucrats and Politicians,* 9.

administrators, specialized by training, academic discipline, and expertise, may believe political leaders to be unaware of the public interest, which can only be determined by scientific processes. To some extent they may take up the position of classical bureaucrats, but unlike the latter, they are involved in all forms of decision-making. The adoption of various forms of planning has expanded the role of such specialized bureaucrats, or 'technocrats' as it has become common to call them. Technocrats are motivated by professional standards and values. They see the policy-making process as a search for the truth, not the discovery of consensus.

In the real world all these forms are likely to be found in the apparatuses of all democratic states. Classical bureaucracy is not yet dead, but today it is merely one type of role among many. Johan Olsen's categorization of Norwegian civil servants is fairly typical. Of 100 at the top, 27 were engaged in co-ordination, 21 in rule application, 18 in planning, 15 in personnel administration, 10 in preparing laws and rules, and 9 in miscellaneous activities.[9] Olsen argues that the role conceptions of the civil servants reflect a shift from organisational forms based on hierarchical command and professional expertise to forms relying on bargaining and compromise.[10] He finds, however, that the majority of Norwegian civil servants still do not favour engagement in politics.

Administrative control by the state, then, existed before democracy. It is something that democracy has adapted to, and in the process the state apparatus has been modified, sometimes with difficulty. The degree to which different forms are consistent with democratic procedures and values is something we must now consider.

Classical Bureaucracy

Bureaucracy has suffered from almost as many definitions as democracy, but unlike the latter it has often been employed with a pejorative emphasis. Bureaucrats have been disliked by both aristocratic and populistic politicians. Bismarck often asserted that the bureaucracy was the real introducer of the revolution into Prussia, and he described the Prussian civil service as 'the animal with a pen'.[11] Andrew Jackson averred: 'In a country where offices are

---

[9] J. P. Olsen, *Organised Democracy* (Oslo, 1983) 138.
[10] Ibid. 135.
[11] J. W. Headlam-Morely, *Bismarck and the Foundation of the German Empire* (New York, 1899) 61.

created solely for the benefit of the people no man has any more intrinsic right to official station than another.'[12] The public generally tends to see bureaucrats as people behind grilles in post offices or seated at desks in tax offices. Their image is not favourably depicted in the popular press: it is embellished with forms and red tape. Petty functionaires are seen as imbuing their routines with an air of mystery. Unreason seems to lie at the root of their activities.

On the other hand, the conception of bureaucracy formulated by Max Weber envisaged it as the highest form of authority. The underlying values were those of a system of law. The bureaucratic apparatus was neutral and implemented policies and decisions of political leaders in a routinized manner. The bureaucrats were professionally trained, meritocratic, career-oriented, impersonal public servants. They had no goals of their own, for machines do not have goals. All their behaviour was governed by rules, so that essentially the apparatus of the state was controlled by rationality. Victor Thompson calls this type of administrative system, for him largely associated with pre-industrial society, 'desk-class' bureaucracy.[13] Robert Putnam, as we have noted, calls it 'classical' bureaucracy.

In their relationships with the democratic polity and, indeed, with other types of regime, classical bureaucrats preserve a value-free, neutral stance. The administrative apparatus is owned by the political leaders of the country, who may employ it in any way they wish. Hence in a democracy, with successive changes of government, civil servants adapt themselves to changes of style, policy, and personality without a murmur of dissent. In fact, their capacity to do this is one of the important sources of stability in difficult periods when power is being transferred from one party hierarchy to another. The administrators' detachment, impartiality, and anonymity stems from their renunciation of the right to criticize and contest that is so basic to democracy. Hence they have the duty to advise and warn their political masters in private, but once decisions have been made, ultimately by the politicians, the bureaucrats have no role except implementation. Conceivably, they might also behave in this way if, after an armed *coup d'état,* a military

    [12] R. Hofstadter, *The American Political Tradition* (New York, 1955), 51 quoted in C. E. Jacob, *Policy and Bureaucracy* (Princeton, 1966), 16.
    [13] V. A. Thompson, Bureaucracy in a Democratic Society, in R. Martin (ed.), *Public Administration and Democracy* (1965), 221.

dictatorship supplanted democracy. Many German public servants who had been employed by the Empire and the Weimar Republic found no difficulty in working for the Third Reich. Thus the 'neutrality' of a bureaucracy can be exactly what the word indicates: it implies no necessarily significant support for the democratic ideal.

In other ways it is sometimes argued that bureaucracy is contrary to democratic substance and spirit in that bureaucracy imposes secrecy whereas democracy flourishes on open information and publicity. The secrecy of bureaucracy stems from varied causes. Max Weber noted that 'every bureaucracy tends to bolster its position by keeping information secret'.[14] Especially where administrators have high status their mystique can be enhanced by fostering an image of inaccessibility. The filing cabinets may be carefully guarded because information and comments about clients may be confidential—for example, details of a private individual's tax returns. More importantly, policy matters may be deemed secret. This may be a genuine national concern where defence policies are concerned but more often the real reason for secrecy will be a desire to conceal disagreements where a show of political unity is regarded as necessary. In Britain and other countries where the principle of collective Cabinet responsibility is in force it will be particularly damaging to the system if differences of opinion in the ruling party at a high level are revealed. Governments are weaker, it is argued, if their disagreements are known to the public. In such cases civil servants have an obvious duty to preserve the central decision-making from the fragmenting pressures of the pressure groups by concealing the views of the Cabinet members as well as their own views. Collective responsibility is not possible without secrecy about disagreements and so if one conceives collective responsibility as a support for democracy, one may be prepared to accept the amount of secrecy it entails. Conversely, one might argue that the doctrine of Cabinet responsibility is responsible for much of the secrecy in the British civil service (or provides an excuse for it), and that anything that encourages secrecy is detrimental to democracy.

Furthermore, it is maintained that bureaucracy is based on the principle of organizational hierarchy whereas democracy rests on that of equality of citizen rights including the right of participation.

[14] H. H. Gerth and C. W. Mills, *From Max Weber: Readings in Sociology* (1948), 233.

The decision-making of democracy encourages followers to criticize, impede, and reject leaders. Within the bureaucratic framework no such contestation is allowed, and followers are expected to accept leaders and carry out their orders. The hierarchy is usually embodied in a professional career structure of a well-defined and differentiated kind. Bureaucrats' areas of operation are carefully delimited and little discretion is accorded those at lower levels. Policy decisions will be passed down from the political leadership to be executed. The senior bureaucrats, comparatively a small group, will be an administrative élite remote from contact with the pressures of the electorate.

Early bureaucracies, what Weber terms the 'patrimonial'[15] variety, may be further isolated by their recruitment from the nobility. Later versions of a 'pure' type[16] will be characterized by meritocratic standards which may or may not imply closeness to the rest of society. Appointed as a result of their qualifications, largely through the examination process, the administrators of the modern state, it is argued, should ideally be those possessing most merit. What 'merit' means may vary from country to country: for example, in France it may imply possession of cerebral assets only to be found in graduates of the École Normale, while in Britain it might signify certain moral qualities until recently considered more important than mere brains and learning. The normal meaning of the term meritocratic, however, would imply the selection of the best recruits, regardless of class, gender, or creed, in order to run the nation. It thus enshrines the values of equality of opportunity, the French Revolutionary doctrine of *la carrière ouverte aux talents*. The result is a specialised élite with highly educated people at the top. Its claim to power will rest on knowledge, usefulness, and success rather than on the social status accorded by birth to a patrimonial bureaucracy. To the extent that meritocracy is egalitarian, bureaucracy *is* egalitarian; but it does not follow that it is supportive of democracy.

Indeed, it can be argued that any professional form of administration is prejudicial to democracy. Populistic theories of democracy tend to advance this view because they are suspicious of all forms of power, especially appointive, tenured, and centralized power. The experience of the United States illustrates this tendency.

[15] Ibid. 224.
[16] Ibid. 200.

Jeffersonian democracy held that administration involved no more expertise than the ordinary common-sensical man possessed. (It was rather like Lenin's 'administration of things' after the revolution had been achieved.) Consequently no office required special experience or training, and all offices could be filled by election or the appointment of non-professionals. This would prevent the administration from centralizing power: it would remain fragmented, as the Founding Fathers intended. But the price was governmental inefficiency. Boss Plunkitt of Tammany Hall, inveighing against the 'tyranny of the examination system',[17] justified the existence of amateurish, politically biased, and corrupt officials. The Progressive Movement, reacting especially against the local populistic bureaucracies of the boss-ridden cities, was concerned with making local and state government more efficient. As a result it helped to usher in a demand for 'business government' in local and state politics. As Douglas Yates says, 'the model of administrative efficiency bears the strong imprint of the experience of business organization in the United States'.[18] In the United States it is in the field of business activity that balanced budgets, clear goals, rationalized and business-like procedures, and honest administration have been paramount. Pluralist democracy and populist pressures have tended to produce different outcomes in the field of political activity.

Yet pluralist competition tends to represent the ideal of American democracy—the fragmentation and balancing of powers—while bureaucracy, in its political context, is particularly identified with the concentration and centralization of power. Efficiency and bureaucracy are balanced against amateurism and decentralization, and on the whole the latter pair of attributes are traditionally favoured. Bureaucracy is taken to mean 'more government', while Americans want less government and, it is usually argued, this is what their Constitution sets out to ordain.

But there are some unchallenged assumptions in this line of argument. In the first place the connection between bureaucracy and centralization is not absolutely ineluctable. One can conceive quite easily a situation in which more decentralization produces a much larger bureaucratic apparatus and many more rules; and yet

---

[17] W. L. Riordan, *Plunkitt of Tammany Hall* (1963), 16.
[18] D. Yates, *Bureaucratic Democracy: The Search for Democracy and Efficiency in American Government* (1982), 31.

of another situation in which more centralization leads to organizational streamlining and smaller and simpler rule books. Thus the characterization of bureaucracy as a complex and unwieldy administrative machine may be more consistent with a decentralized and deconcentrated political system. Conversely, centralization may imply, at least in some situations, less organizational complexity.

Secondly, the link between bureaucracy and efficiency is not universally accepted. Martin Albrow convincingly demonstrates how some of the early writers saw bureaucracy as the embodiment of officiousness and inefficiency; though Max Weber perceived 'pure bureaucracy' as the most efficient form of administration. It was bound to be so because it represented the highest form of rationality. (We shall deal with this later.) But Weber was concerned, as Albrow argues, to affirm that the specific nature of modern administration and the control of the apparatus of the modern state were conceptually distinct.[19] Weber was not uninterested in the traditional problem of the relation between democracy and bureaucracy but again his organizational model was one which could be used by any type of polity. Similarly, its efficiency will support either an authoritarian or a democratic state. It is *not* that bureaucracy is inevitably anti-democratic, as it is in the American populist tradition, or inevitably pro-democratic. Efficient bureaucracy makes for the continuity of any type of regime.

On the other hand, if bureaucracy is inefficient it will be detrimental to all types. Numerous commentators since Weber have argued that the conclusions of his analysis were unwarranted. Empirical studies such as those of Blau,[20] depicted administrators ignoring rule books and operating their own systems. Others have found organizations without effective strategies because of conflict between sub-groups and/or between individuals and their bureaucracies. Anthony Downs, *par excellence,* has portrayed organizations as incapable of operating rationally and efficiently because of the rational self-interested behaviour of officials seeking to maximize their status, wealth, and power,[21] and he sees increasing bureaucratization as the division of labour in society becomes more

[19] M. Albrow, *Bureaucracy* (1970), 46.
[20] P. Blau, *The Dynamics of Bureaucracy* (1955).
[21] A. Downs, *Inside Bureaucracy* (1966).

complex. But he does believe bureaucracies can innovate, largely as a result of competition between different sections within them.[22] Moreover, he concludes that 'although many citizens in democratic societies claim that bureaucracy as a whole is excessively large in relation to the benefits they derive from it, most would undoubtedly support the existing structure given the option of abolishing it.'[23] Hence Downs perceives great benefits from the operation of bureaucracy. Even though it may be inefficient and irrational at times, it fulfils indispensable functions, he seems to imply. And it can be argued that in spite of the ideological neutrality of bureaucracy, modern democratic states need it more for those allocative and coercive purposes which in totalitarian states are pursued by mobilizing single parties.

Yet it is not bureaucracy's efficiency but its rationality which, I would argue, is its strongest contribution to the democratic polity. 'Rationality' I use here in the sense employed by Weber, incidentally agreeing with Albrow who maintains that central to the Weberian conceptualization of bureaucracy is the rationality of legal authority.[24] Diesing defined legal rationality—one of his five types of rationality—as that of fundamental rules. The tendency of societies to develop rules was the result of a need to attain predictability and formal order.[25] This is consistent with Weber's position: 'The "objective" discharge of business primarily means a discharge of business according to *calculable rules* and "without regard for persons".'[26] It was this lack of arbitrariness, this fairness and objectivity, which most commended bureaucracy to Weber. He saw it best developed where Roman law had flourished. ' "Equality before the law" and the demand for legal guarantees against arbitrariness demand a formal and rational "objectivity" of administration, as opposed to the personally free discretion flowing from the "grace" of the old patrimonial domination.'[27] England, Weber said, with common law, 'retained a less rational and less bureaucratic judicature'.[28] On the Continent Roman law was rationalized into 'a closed system of concepts to be scientifically handled'[29] in the period when bureaucratization was taking place.

---

[22] Ibid. 275.   [23] Ibid. 280.   [24] Albrow, *Bureaucracy*, 63.

[25] P. Diesing, *Reason in Society* (Urbana, 1972), 124. See also R. Hartvig, Rationality and the Problems of Administrative Theory, *Public Administration* 56 (Summer, 1978), 159.   [26] Gerth and Mills, *From Max Weber*, 215.

[27] Ibid. 220.   [28] Ibid. 218.   [29] Ibid. 209.

Thus Weber saw rule-making and rule observance as the rational feature of bureaucracy because the legal and the rational to him, in this context, were synonymous. Bureaucracy was the extension of a 'government of laws and not of men' into administration. Hence it could have nothing to do with popular pressures. He wrote:

> Every sort of popular justice—which usually does not ask for reasons and norms—as well as every sort of intensive influence on the administration by so-called public opinion crosses the rational course of justice and administration—under the conditions of mass democracy, public opinion is communal conduct born of irrational sentiments.[30]

This type of public pressure, even by a majority, Weber saw as a demand for privilege, even though it might be expressed in egalitarian terms. From the populist angle, due process of law (or administrative action, in Weber's legal/rational meaning), might be regarded as anti-democratic, certainly as anti-majoritarian. But fair trials, an incorrupt judiciary, and legal processes open to all, treat everyone equitably and equally before the law, in the same way as rational bureaucracy. Many of the most vociferous protesters against bureaucratic rules are really demanding that they should be treated in a privileged fashion. Equality before the law, like bureaucratic rules operating fairly, impedes the granting of discretion and privilege. Observance of the bureaucratic rule-book is part of the rule of law which, as we have noted, is essential for the maintenance of democracy.

The need to consult rule-books and the structures of hierarchy are causes of another feature of bureaucracy against which popular, or populistic, tendencies fulminate—its delay. Bureaucrats are not noted for producing speedy results. Yet this characteristic may again be another facet of the need to be equitable and detached. Judges and juries may be slow in considering their verdicts. Similarly administrators, in order to be fair, may have to be cautious. Moreover, in democracies they will essentially be responsible to the politicans, who are responsible to the electorate. This is an additional reason for circumspection. Consequently, while some of what is called red tape may be unjustifiable, some can be rightly defended in terms of the preservation of the rule of law and the democratic process.

To sum up: Weberian, 'desk-class', or 'classical' bureaucracy is in

[30] Ibid. 224.

many of its aspects neutral towards democracy. It is likely to be more stable, more efficient, and possibly more centralized than other administrative forms. But it can equally serve authoritarian regimes with these virtues. For this sort of bureaucracy is theoretically an apparatus or machine, a tool for any sort of political authority, best associated with the separation between politics and administration as advocated a century ago by Woodrow Wilson: 'Administration lies outside the sphere of politics. . . . The field of administration is the field of business. It is removed from the hurly-burly and strife of politics.'[31] Bureaucrats did not possess power in their own right; according to this theory, they exercised power for their political masters.

A likely, though not necessary, corollary of neutrality is fairness. Where bureaucracy is positive towards democracy is where it upholds the observance of rules and maintenance of the rule of law. Although, as we have noted in Chapter 1, the rule of law is not a sufficient reason for the existence of democracy, it is a necessary one. A situation in which everyone is equal before the law and is treated in an unarbitrary fashion by administrators is a necessary foundation for the maintenance of democracy. Weberian legality/ rationality may not directly contribute to democratic values but without it democratic regimes can scarcely be viable.

Technocracy

For many reasons the apparatus of the contemporary state no longer closely approximates to Weber's model. The modern bureaucrat, at a senior level anyway, will often be concerned with much more than rule-bound implementation. He will be involved in giving expert advice and exercising highly specialized skills. Here we are dealing with a new phenomenon.

I have already called this technocracy, a term used for the sake of convenience. Like bureaucracy, it is both a concept and a description of a group of people involved in administering the state. (Sometimes the term 'technocrat' has been used to describe a professional politician with certain characteristics but my definition excludes this usage.) A technocrat is a specialized administrator; but the specialization referred to here is not the functional

[31] W. Wilson, The Study of Administration, *Political Science Quarterly*, 2 (June, 1887), 209.

differentiation of the bureaucrat with his clearly defined assignment and hierarchical responsibility. It is the specialization of the qualified expert, the person trained not in administration (or not *only* in administration) but in the sciences or social sciences. The governments of all industrialized countries increasingly consult such people, and they are more and more likely to be appointed to the permanent public service.

Technocracy has inherited many of the traits of bureaucracy. Jack Hayward writes:

Both the bureaucrat and the technocrat claim to exercise power in a rational way; but whereas the bureaucrat is primarily a routine administrator, relying upon conventional wisdom to muddle through by adjusting conflicting interests and enforcing rules in an impersonal manner, the technocrat seeks systematic innovation calculated to increase efficiency, based on assessments of the future rather than loyalty to the past.[32]

The technocrat, like the bureaucrat, tends to operate behind a veil of secrecy: he is anonymous and not usually subject to public criticism. The technocrat also moves within a hierarchy, though in certain kinds of planning there may be an emphasis on teams. Professional and technical qualifications may be more important than position within a hierarchy when plans are being formulated, but for their implementation a chain of command becomes more imperative than ever. The technical apparatus of the technocrat—charts, models, statistical tables, even a language of his own—sets him even more apart than the bureaucrat from the man-in-the-street. Consequently suspicion is likely to be even more prevalent. Moreover, while the populist politician may fulminate against the delay occasioned by the red tape of the bureaucrat, he is more likely to complain about the 'undue haste' of the technocrat.

Thus, though technocracy may have traits in common with bureaucracy, its advent raises new implications about relationships between administrators and democratic political leaders. On the one hand technocrats, like classical bureaucrats, favour a clear division between politics and administration—Putnam[33] found that specialist British civil servants were distinctly of this view—but on the other they do not have classical bureaucrats' likely attitudes towards seeking consensus or responding to political pressures. The

[32] J. Hayward, *The One and Indivisible French Republic* (1973), 100.
[33] Putnam, Political Attitudes, 117.

bureaucrat may hold up the implementation of the democratic majority will but the technocrat attempts hastily to impose his own solution. He is sceptical about democracy because he knows the rational objective answer to the nation's problem, while democratic discussion and democratic politicians will prevent, or at least hinder, its application.

'Technocracy', as a term, appears to have links with both technology and techniques. In fact, these two concepts are technocracy's main components; but whereas technology can be defined as the application of science to industry, technocracy is the application of science to government; and while techniques are skilled methods of achieving purposes, when applied to administration they involve, again, the control of human behaviour. Thus technocracy seems to imply a conjunction of the natural and social sciences. This will commend it to some and condemn it with others.

The growth of science and technology has changed government as it has changed the world. For political leadership it has produced new policy problems at the same time as it has provided new instruments for dealing with them. For example, the increasingly technical nature of war has brought scientists and technologists into government service while the growing complexity of the economy has led to economists also being employed. The recognized importance of research and development for national prosperity, and the awareness that private firms and universities are no longer able to promote it on the scale needed, has led governments to sponsor their own. The American space programme is the outstanding example of this but there are many others of significance. The overall effect is to make science and technology important political considerations, and as only scientists and technologists understand the area properly their power is inevitably strengthened. Some of the earliest technocrats were scientists, and in some countries, especially in Britain with its civil service based on arts graduates, they had difficulty in holding their own against the bureaucrats.

The expansion of the sciences, and more particularly of the social sciences, also makes a scientific attitude towards people, and their attitudes and aspirations, more prevalent. Within the last century what can be described as a 'technology of knowledge' has burgeoned. In the first place, quantification of factual material about the economy and the population provided empirical data, interpretation of which led to the development of statistics—only 'common sense' (it is often asserted), but all too often providing pitfalls for the unwary. The study of the economy was assisted by the identification of measurable variables which could be related to each other. Finally, an enormous technical stimulus to all statistics-based activity was the invention of the computer. Its capacity for storing quantified knowledge and interrelating it changed the quality of policy-making, because insufficient information had long been regarded as an obstacle to completely rational decisions. Now it seemed the latter were within human grasp.

Planning

The scientific approach applied to decision-making is most clearly manifested in planning. Advances in the social sciences, such as systems analysis, cybernetics, and cost–benefit analysis and the production of increasingly sophisticated computers put new life into the idea that with perfect information and the correct application of expert skills all problems could be solved without conflict. Jean Meynaud says that one of the most important components of technocratic thinking is 'the belief that rational analysis and interpretation of facts are liable to bring about unanimity at least among men of good will'.[34] Planning was given a new lease of life by the emergence of a technology of information. The dilemma of planning for the democratic state is that it structures the future and so restricts future political options.

Most policy-making in modern industrialized states contains an ingredient of planning; and there is an obvious connection between planning and technocracy. All planners are technocrats, even if all technocrats are not planners. Indeed, the planner with professional qualifications and, probably, a meritocratic background is the archetypal technocrat. He or she combines the bureaucrat's attachment to order and rationality with the policy-maker's concern for initiative and innovation.

'Planning' as a term has been in use for half a century. It entered into the jargon of social scientists, political commentators, and politicians as a result of the Soviet Five Year Plan.[35] Hence its

---

[34] J. Meynaud, *Technocracy* (1968), 209.

[35] See F. W. Bealey, *Social and Political Thought of the British Labour Party* (1970), 26 where I first made this point, though perhaps with not sufficient clarity at the time. For a misunderstanding, see A. Oldfield, The Labour Party and Planning: 1934 or 1919?, *Bulletin of the Society for the Study of Labour History*, no. 25

earliest associations were with socialism and/or communism; but it was not an essentially socialist idea, owing more to eighteenth-century rationalism than nineteenth-century Marxism. The word as such cannot be found in Marx.

Types of planning can be categorized variously. In the first place it is common to distinguish between physical planning and economic planning, a dichotomy based on what is planned. Physical planning is concerned with the use of land, economic planning with organizing the economy. Of course, the two may well be connected. The people who want to control the allocation of land are often the same as those who wish to control the distribution of resources. Physical and economic planners will have to be associated in industrial location policy, motorway construction, and urban renewal.

Secondly, planning can be categorized according to who does the planning. As Galbraith has so emphatically asserted: 'The modern large corporation and the modern apparatus of socialist planning are variant accommodations to the same need.'[36] There is both private and public planning—indeed, in the 1930s, Hugh Dalton logically perceived five arrangements: 'unplanned Capitalism, Privately Planned Capitalism, Socially Planned Capitalism, Planned Socialism and Unplanned Socialism'.[37] The scale of modern technology makes planning of some kind an absolute essential because consumer needs may have to be anticipated for years ahead. Planning is employed by leaders of both public and private corporations to eliminate as many elements of uncertainty as possible.

Thirdly, planning will vary according to the purposes for which it is intended. Planning for war may involve haste, arbitrariness, and strict discipline. 'War Communism' in the Soviet Union from 1919 to 1921 was characterized by military organization within the economy, including control over labour.[38] Planning in peacetime, for example for industrial expansion, may be much less painful, less arbitrary, and less hurried. Planning for agriculture needs longer cycles and more allowance for the unexpected. Planning for industry can be quantified with more confidence.

(1972), 41. The word 'Planning' cannot be found in *Labour and the New Social Order,* the Party's 1918 policy statement.

[36] J. K. Galbraith, *The New Industrial State* (1967), 51.

[37] H. Dalton, *Practical Socialism for Britain* (1935) 247 n. 1.

[38] B. P. Beckwith, *The Economic Theory of a Socialist Economy* (Stanford, 1948), 170.

Fourthly, planning can be classified according to the sector of the economy with which it deals. Planning on the demand side of the economy will involve interference with consumer sovereignty. Rationing decreases the scope for the individual's exercise of choice and forethought. It may arise in a siege or war economy but it may stem from conscious production planning. Planning on the supply side may involve stabilizing costs, which implies pegging wages and interest rates. What Beckwith calls 'arbitrary planning',[39] the system in the Soviet Union, entails planners fixing both production targets and prices for commodities.

The fifth and most appropriate categorization (for democratic theorists) relates to the scope of planning. It can be seen as a spectrum stretching from planning concerned with highly specific objectives—'operational' or 'blueprint planning'—to comprehensive national planning. The former often relates to local acts of public investment, a bridge or motorway; but it can be a national commitment, as when the Ghanaian government decided to build the Volta dam or President Kennedy promised that America would put a man on the moon. Years of co-operation between science, industry, and the government followed from this latter decision; but though it was national policy it only involved a relatively small section of the nation. Comprehensive planning, however, is likely to affect everyone and to draw all aspects of national life into the national endeavour. As Lindblom says, it implies the 'intellectually guided society'[40] and the 'preceptorial economy',[41] and like Herman van Gunsteren he argues that planning is incompatible with democratic politics.[42] The pursuit of all-embracing societal goals over a decade or two is impossible where periodic competitive elections take place. Democratic electorates are prone to change their minds every four or five years and they are especially suspicious of promises of benefits in the distant future. 'Jam today, not tomorrow' is their customary demand. Hence policies of long-range investment in industry involving great sacrifices in consumption in the present in order to confer prosperity upon future generations need a highly centralized and coercive state, probably backed up by charismatic leadership and ideological indoctrination.

[39] Ibid. 169.
[40] C. E. Lindblom, The Sociology of Planning, in M. Bernstein (ed.), *Economic Planning East and West* (Ballinger, 1975), 101.
[41] C. E. Lindblom, *Politics and Markets* (1977), 161.
[42] H. R. van Gunsteren, *The Quest for Control* (1976), 9.

An approximation to comprehensive planning may be possible temporarily in democracies where national goals are clearly postulated, widely recognized, and compelling. For example, the need to win a war provides a general goal to which all parts of a democratic population are likely to subscribe. The desire for victory, shared by British people of all kinds in World War II, made central direction of the war effort easy. The government undertook planning of the national productive process (though its co-ordinative success has perhaps been exaggerated), in order to ensure a steady flow of military material; it rationed all sorts of resources, both raw materials and consumer goods, because the country was virtually under siege; and for the same reasons it diverted labour into the armed forces and vital industries. The vast mass of the people accepted these constraints because the national end was clear, specific, and readily comprehensible (the enemy could be seen, heard, and felt). At the same time all the necessary democratic criteria, with some few exceptions for reasons of national security, were observed. It was widely realized, however, that once victory was achieved controversy about national goals would again break out. Economic control and direction of labour might become unacceptable. And so it proved.

Comprehensive planning for any length of time is, as Lindblom argues, an intrusion into democratic society. However, this does not prevent other forms of planning being compatible with democratic procedures and values. The best argument against the view that planning and democracy are irreconcilable is to point out that people are planning at all levels of private and public life in every democratic country. Much state planning arises unintentionally. Government intervention is *not* planning, though government planning is always a form of intervention. For reasons elsewhere explained governments intervene in the economy in a piecemeal fashion. Quite frequently as a result of uncoordinated interventions, demands may emerge, perhaps from the bureaucracy, for a tidying-up and rationalization of such activities. Piecemeal intervention will produce an economy which may be 'mixed' in various ways. Often the ingredients in the mixture will have been determined by political pressures, resulting in a situation in which economic rationality is lacking. Rationalization and standardization may then be described as 'planning', even though making for less economic rationality. Indeed, 'rationalizing planning' (in the sense that rationalization means advancing a rationale where rationality is lacking) might well describe a process such as this which does not imply postulating national goals of either a specific or comprehensive kind. It involves co-ordinating government *agents* rather than *policies*.

Alan Budd describes much planning undertaken by democratic governments as resembling the style of planning undertaken by companies in competitive markets. He calls it 'strategic planning'.[43] For example, in the first three decades after World War II many democratic governments were committed to the goal of full employment, quantified by Beveridge as no more than 3 per cent unemployment. It was to maintain this objective that management of economies, widely inspired by Keynesian ideas, became standard democratic practice. Demand was either expanded or contracted through the use of monetary and fiscal policies. Essentially the model was one of a government achieving by manipulation just the right amount of balance between inflation and deflation. The prevailing metaphor conceived the economy as a television set with numerous levers (as with earlier models) and the government, aware of the relationship between the different variables, fine tuning until a perfect image was achieved. This form of planning, if, indeed, it could be called planning (as it often was), put a high premium on economic models and economic expertise, and politicians without any grasp of economics may have found themselves in difficulties. Eventually, however, Keynesian management came to be accepted by politicians of the liberal–centre as well as of the social-democratic left. It was regarded, like bureaucracy, as part of the instrumentation of democratic government.

A much more complex type of management was implied by the attempt to attain other national economic goals. The concept of national growth assumed an expanding economy and involved much more than control of consumer demand. Government efforts to increase the national product could hardly avoid bargaining with employers and unions and bringing them into some tripartite form of consultation. This was based on a general consensus that most people wanted more material prosperity, involving a larger national cake. On the other hand, it did not envisage centralized control. French *planification indicative*, the prototype of this form of planning, consisted of drawing up a probabilistic model which

[43] A. Budd, *The Politics of Economic Planning* (1978), 153.

allowed for freedom of choice for economic actors.[44] Its framework incorporated prophecies, guesses, and estimates about production, and allowed for an expected growth rate. In doing so consultation and collaboration became essential. The pooling of information was particularly important, and this in turn encouraged the search for new information and research based upon it. Goals were clarified and an order of priorities could be established. Even more important, perhaps, was the education of the decision-makers. The rationality of the planners, it was hoped, would be communicated to the other decision-makers—particularly employers and unions —who would be socialized in its values. This form of planning did not anticipate attaining targets but hoped that initial failure would lead to later correction. In the Commission of Modernization, especially, the pedagogy of the French plans became evident. Indicative planning is essentially a learning process during which participants grow into the need to adjust self-interest to national goals. Its imperative is economic growth, its most salient lesson the importance of adaptation.

To sum up: the scale and type of planning affect both the nature of democratic institutions and the operation of democratic processes. With the onset of national economic management, politicians may still formally 'own' the administrative apparatus of the state; but they will not find controlling it so easy. As Guy Peters says, economic and social policy for many nations is being determined by bureaucratic planning bodies.[45] Who formally governs may not be very relevant. Hence

the roles of political institutions are being diminished rather dramatically. They do not have the time and staff to handle most decisions, leaving them with the task of broad policy guidelines on issues where there is always a certain amount of consensus.[46]

Even executives are in decline. Collective executives, finding it less easy to speak with one voice, may be weak in confronting the planners. For example, the Norwegian Cabinet has little say over the draft of the Norwegian Budget, which is drawn up by a group of civil servants and technocrats.[47] And even in Britain the Treasury

---

[44] L. Nizard, Administration et société: Planification et regulations bureaucratiques, *Revue française de science politique* 23/2 (1973), 199.

[45] B. G. Peters, *The Politics of Bureaucracy* (1978), 179.   [46] Ibid. 189.

[47] J. Higley, K. E. Brofoss, and K. Groholt, Top Civil Servants and the National Budget in Norway, in Dogan (ed.), *The Mandarins of Western Europe*, 252–74.

has specialized information about public expenditure which departmental ministers lack. Individual presidential executives are probably better placed to avoid this erosion: the French president, with a seven-year term and a weak legislature, may be best situated of all. De Gaulle especially, enunciating and shaping French goals and controlling his team of experts, was seen to be at the helm of the nation. Extolling the plan as a symbol of a national consensus,[48] he nevertheless provided the best illustration of how to ignore expertise when, against the advice of his economists, he refused to devalue the franc in 1969.[49]

Of course, democratic government should postulate the ends while planners provide only the means; but administrators have both longer time perspectives than politicians and also information of which an incoming government, in particular, may be in short supply. The enunciation of wide economic goals may have perilous consequences, as the experiences of the first Wilson government in Britain illustrates. Highly specific economic goals, like those put forward by Ronald Reagan in his 1980 presidential, quickly crumble when the calculating machines of the technocrats ingest them. The difficulties that many political leaders have in clarifying and co-ordinating national economic policies and evaluating outcomes may lead to unmandated and unpromulgated versions being tacitly adopted by economic planning apparatuses.

Vis-à-vis planners, legislatures are correspondingly weaker than executives. Legislators, because they are more remote from the formulation of budgets, programmes, and plans, find them more difficult to follow. In most cases legislators are much less able to avail themselves of the relevant information. The American Congress, with its powers of investigation (especially the financial powers of the House of Representatives), is an exception. The first three French plans were not even submitted to the French Parliament,[50] though the broad outlines of later plans have been discussed. But even when legislators see the details of plans they may not be much wiser without expertise or research assistance. They may be sceptical about the outlines of plans, but they will have to wait many years to discover whether their criticisms were justified. This is often the case, for example, with educational planning. Attempts

---

[48] Y. Ullmo, France, in J. Hayward and M. Watson (eds.), *Planning, Politics and Public Policy* (Cambridge, 1975), 28.

[49] J. Hayward, *Governing France* (1983), 173.　　　　[50] Ullmo, France, 27.

to modify a plan may be countered by a defence of its necessary integrity. Hence planning weakens all the traditional roles of legislatures except their role of supporting executives. It is hard to resist the conclusion of Coombes and Walkland, that 'much of the economic activity of modern government resembles foreign policy'[51] because of the way it is based on extra-parliamentary negotiation.

This brief discourse about the impact of planning on representative institutions does yield a clue to the effect of planning on democratic procedures and values. For many reasons, the trend toward executive power brought about, as we shall see elsewhere, a form of governmental managerialism. That this is not far-fetched can be supported by the growing tendency in the twentieth century for democratic politicians to appeal to the voter in terms of their superior ability at managing the economy. In Britain, Wilson, especially, saw himself as the manager of an enormous firm. The analogy, however, is both revealing and misleading. Although governments have often borrowed their planning techniques from private industry, there are fundamental differences between the large-scale corporate planning that Galbraith describes[52] and that of a democracy. Weidenbaum argues:

Corporate planning of necessity is based on attempts to persuade the public to purchase the goods and services produced by a given firm. The controls that may accompany the plan are internally oriented. In striking contrast, the government is sovereign. Its planning ultimately invokes coercion. The controls are thus externally oriented, extending their sway over the entire society.[53]

But ultimately, of course, in a democracy, the government can be thrown out by the voters so its coercion may only be temporary. Business planning may be restrained by the rationality of the market, whereas governmental planning is restrained by the rationality of electoral competition. In one case the nature of the risk is loss of wealth: in the other it is loss of power.

It is not entirely inappropriate to see the relationship between modern democratic government and voters as one between a periodically disposable management and critical customers. There

---

[51] D. Coombes and S. Walkland, *Parliaments and Economic Affairs* (1980), 12.
[52] J. K. Galbraith, *The New Industrial State* (1967).
[53] M. L. Weidenbaum, The Second Managerial Revolution, in W. Goldstein (ed.), *Planning, Politics and the Public Interest* (1978), 61.

is evidence to demonstrate that voters want efficient service from their governments and are willing to reward those that give it. Planning would probably be welcomed by voters as an aid to efficiency if they were ever asked about it. The streamlining of decisions, the curtailing of discussion, the reference to specialists—all those factors associated with planning which take little account of democratic values—may be generally accepted by the majority of a democratic public that approves of their use for the execution of successful and popular policies. There is not much evidence of electorates deploring the decline of legislatures.

Different forms of planning, however, have different implications for the democratic process. Centralized comprehensive planning, as we have noted, cannot be found in any democracy except possibly in wartime. 'Blueprint planning' has commonly been used for land-use planning, especially in urban areas. In this field planning has acquired some obloquy when developments such as new motor-ways or bypasses have taken local residents by surprise. The practice of making prior consultation by public enquiry a statutory necessity as in Britain, has grown. In other countries this practice has been extended to other fields. For example, Dorothy Nelkin describes how the governments of Sweden, The Netherlands, and Austria have sought to broaden public participation in decisions involving technological changes.[54] Public participation has been welcomed by some planners as contributing to their information.

Indeed, newer forms of planning such as 'indicative planning' may stress the incorporation of public opinion within the planning process. Andreas Faludi argued that planners should regard pressure groups as a source of creative planning[55] and contended: 'A planner who perceives his role as political is likely to be more successful in this than the planner who sees his role merely as that of a bureaucrat.'[56] Thus French post-war planning, originally conceived as part of a process of depoliticization, has gradually become more consciously political. Yves Ullmo regards 'trans-parency',[57] the application of planning techniques publicly, as important a principle in the execution of French planning as rationality. This has signified, he argues, a movement from *dirigisme* and tutelage towards co-operation with socio-economic

[54] D. Nelkin, *Technological Decisions and Democracy* (1972), 92.
[55] A. Faludi, *Planning Theory* (Oxford, 1973), 122.   [56] Ibid. 81.
[57] Ullmo, France, 24.

groups. Increasingly its aim has been to concert pluralistic activities into a framework for a medium-term economic policy. At the same time the scope of French plans has become more comprehensive. Hence though the change from the Fourth to the Fifth Republic, as Jack Hayward argues, coincided with a 'shift in emphasis within the higher administration from the consensus norms of political rationality to the efficiency norms of economic rationality',[58] the idea that planning was apolitical could not be sustained. In the 1970s it became clear that a great deal of the process of planning was concerned with establishing some sort of consensus between social and economic pressure groups and the planners. French planning, as Ullmo suggests, has an implicit socialization function,[59] though the socializing efforts are not always successful. Whimsically he comments: 'First and foremost, planning, and particularly the preparation of the Plan, acts as a barometer of interest-group pressure, with the government being tempted to break the barometer.'[60] As with much economic policy-making by democratic governments, indicative planning implies a mixture of rationalities.

Political Bureaucracy

The political bureaucrat has likewise a mixture of roles. According to the characterization of Aberbach *et al.* this may involve formulating policy, bargaining with interests, or both.[61] It may comprise the more flexible, more political sort of indicative planning as described immediately above. It may in some countries—for example, France or The Netherlands—portend movement into the political arena. Thus there may be blurring of the lines between civil servant and politician.

The emergence of the political bureaucrat is the inevitable result, as I noted above, of the extension of state intervention and the growth of the public sector. The welfare state and the management of the economy arose in response to democratic pressures. The apparatus of the state has become far too large for its management and detailed guidance to be solely in the hands of representatives of the electorate. As Edward Page writes, 'Given the scale and complexity of modern governments much policy making must in

[58] J. Hayward, *The One and the Indivisible French Republic* (1973), 101.
[59] Ullmo, France, 50.   [60] Ibid. 42.
[61] See Aberbach *et al.*, *Bureaucrats and Politicians*.

fact take place outside the purview of political leaders.'[62] Hence the classical bureaucrat's dichotomy between politics and administration is hard to discover in many areas and at certain levels of national policy-making. The result, as Klaus Schubert argues, is that 'for large areas of modern state administrations the traditional picture of an administrative bureaucracy no longer applies.'[63] Contemporary studies of the attitudes of top civil servants reflect these trends. Olsen reports from Norway:

The role conceptions of the civil servants reflect a shift from organisational forms based on hierarchical command and professional expertise to forms relying on bargaining persuasion. Negotiator/mediator is a role mentioned most often . . . Likewise, most top civil servants find a resemblance more with the role of company manager than with the role of judge.[64]

Putnam found that only 9 per cent of senior British civil servants, and 43 per cent of German, agreed that the interference of politicians 'in affairs which are properly the business of civil servants' was a disturbing feature of contemporary political life.[65] Aberbach *et al.* in their comparative study of bureaucrats and politicians found the former well disposed on the whole to pluralistic pressures. All the indications are that the top bureaucrats in contemporary democracies have adapted themselves to playing what would formerly have been considered political roles.

James Christoph suggests that top British civil servants have five roles.[66] First, implementing policy, which may go far beyond traditional administration because the nature of modern statutes often demands more delegated legislation. Second, advising ministers, where technocrats may have great expertise to offer; though much advice will be information about the background of policy, including the likely reaction of pressure groups. Many top bureaucrats will have sensitive political antennae, partly as a result of long familiarity with the context. (Ministers often will not have this.) Third, advancing the claims of those groups who are regular clients of the department. Spending departments are particularly identified

[62] E. C. Page, *Political Authority and Bureaucratic Power* (Brighton, 1985), 169.

[63] K. Schubert, Politics and Economic Regulation, in F. G. Castles, F. Lehner, and M. G. Schmidt (eds.), *The Political Management of Mixed Economies* (Berlin and New York, 1981), 8.

[64] Olsen, *Organized Democracy*, 135.

[65] Putnam, Political Attitudes, 99.

[66] J. R. Christoph, High Civil Servants and the Politics of Consensualism in Great Britain, in Dogan (ed.), *The Mandarins of Western Europe*, 45 ff.

with certain groups and often negotiate with the Treasury on their behalf. Fourth, attempting to reach a consensus and avoiding conflict in committees. These four roles—implementer, adviser, advocate, and committee-man—will be found in all democratic bureaucracies. The fifth—reciprocating ministerial protection by shielding the minister from media, public, and parliamentary criticism—is only found in British-type government. British civil servants defend the doctrine of ministerial responsibility because it preserves their anonymity and invulnerability from public attack. It explains why British bureaucracy is even more secretive than other bureaucracies.

The fact that political bureaucrats are undertaking numerous forms of political activity does not however in any way imply that they are the same sort of people as politicians. There are numerous differences. Matti Dogan contrasts politicians elected in the limelight with 'mandarins' appointed in secrecy.[67] Politicians can be dismissed by the voters and tend to compete with one another for public esteem, while bureaucrats have an *esprit de corps* and cannot easily be dismissed. They come to dislike sudden political change and try to reconcile a government's values and policies with its predecessor's. Thus top bureaucrats tend to be centrist as Aberbach *et al.'s* data demonstrate.[68] Almost all have had higher education and professional training of some kind so they tend to see decisions in a technical context, even when, as in Britain, many of them may not be technocrats. This distinguishes them from politicians, some of whom, from manual-worker homes, will have no higher education. Politicians are more polarized than bureaucrats and more prone to be ideological. Both groups are sympathetic to democracy but on balance, policiticians are somewhat more committed to liberty than bureaucrats are, and politicians are much more enthusiastic about equality.[69] Aberbach *et al.* also found some support for the view that bureaucrats have a conservative bias in that while 21 per cent of them had less favourable attitudes to both equality ('populism') and liberty ('pluralism'), only 6 per cent of the politicians were in that position. (Most of the bureaucrats in this category were Italians who first entered the public service under Fascism.)

The differences between bureaucrats' and politicians' attitudes are reflected in their varying range of activities and aspirations. As

---

[67] Dogan, Political Power, 4.
[68] Aberbach *et al., Bureaucrats and Politicians,* 115 ff.   [69] Ibid. 236.

Aberbach *et al.* conclude, 'most politicians are better connected to broader social forces, whereas most bureaucrats are enmeshed in networks bounded by the departmental hierarchy, together with the associated interest groups'.[70] All accounts of bureaucrats in democracies reveal that, except for those involved with the national accounting and budgeting system, they operate largely within departmental limits. Consequently, while elected political leaders may relate to voters' reactions, top civil servants will be concerned with segmental pressures. For example, those concerned with welfare benefits may be involved with mothers and old age pensioners. Hence most political bureaucrats will be negotiating and bargaining in well-defined decision-making sectors. Others at the Treasury, however, may be reconciling the outputs of these networks with one another and also trying to steer a course between technocrats and political leaders.

All these intricate bargaining procedures within and between the segmentalized networks produce a type of bureaucrat whose search for consensus is expressed in cautious, incrementalist terms. This applies especially to budgeting policies, where the previous year's proportions will be used as a basis of allocation. Hence a very great deal of bureaucratic policy-making will be at the middle level, and political bureaucrats will normally leave to politicians the resolution of high-level issues. (An exception is in France, where major initiatives 'possibly emerge and certainly are processed on the basis of criteria largely internal to the administrative system'.)[71] In general the picture is not one of top bureaucracy being involved in the formulation of major innovative policies. These still emerge from the political parties and elected politicians.

With classical bureaucracy, the relationship between democracy and the administrative apparatus of the state remained relatively simple. Its undemocratic features are well known. Political bureaucracy may also be secret, remote, hierarchical, and dilatory. Unfortunately these are not its only possible failings. Confidentiality, a natural and proper attitude on the part of public servants, may well be used to conceal policies in the process of formulation, and they may emerge ready for the legislative process without any previous discussion. The more open policy-making of the United States and,

[70] Ibid. 255.
[71] Page, *Political Authority*, 150. In the 1980s the importance of French planning has declined.

to a certain extent, Scandinavia, prevents such circumlocution of public pressures but in many democracies not only is policy formulation hidden from the public but also group discussion and consultation. Where some interests are involved and others not, democracy will not be well served. The remoteness of top bureaucrats has always been a point of criticism, but when they are involved with much more than administration—for example, with bargaining and middle-level policy making—their distance from citizens becomes grievous. It is not so much that in this new situation they develop a corporate identity as that they cultivate departmental and clientelist loyalties. The result is a segmented (and therefore complex) system. An incomprehensible administrative apparatus is much more dangerous when it assumes functions hitherto seen as political.

In these circumstances bureaucracy may be very difficult to control. Downs, as noted above, argued that all organizational forms strongly favour their own survival—indeed, their own expansion. When a higher bureaucracy is much involved with policy-making, and has greater technical expertise and much longer, and more guaranteed, tenure in office than its political superiors, it may well be very powerful. Probably, however, complete bureaucratic control will be unlikely because segmentation of policy making will frustrate co-ordination. Even so, accountability of governments to parliaments and to electorates will be difficult to ensure; the danger that political bureaucracies will abuse their power is very real. Where they have considerable control over information (and most bureaucracies do), then they may easily organize cover-ups to forestall criticism.

The case of political bureaucracy exemplifies the nature of the conflict between efficiency and democracy. Aberbach *et al.* conclude:

The moral dilemma posed by bureaucratic policy making is power without responsibility. The dilemma of policy making by politicians is power without competence. Excessive bureaucratic policy making may lead to a crisis of legitimacy, but excessive political policy making threatens a crisis of effectiveness.[72]

The fact is, however, that the right to make mistakes and to be inefficient is surely one that democratic majorities possess. Just as

[72] Aberbach *et al.*, *Bureaucrats and Politicians*, 255.

Mill argued that free speech included the right to voice untruths, because the enunciation of error assisted the discovery of the truth, so it must be contended that the right to participate in policy-making includes the right of supporting and implementing impracticable policies. Of course, this will at first result in inefficiency in its usual sense; but irrational decisions may educate publics to make better choices at a later stage. Democratic publics cannot learn about policy options where policy options are not presented and explained. It should be possible for political bureaucrats to draw up the technical advantages and disadvantages of options but then to leave the choice of policies to elected people and to electorates.

Conclusion

It is not easy to make an assessment of the degree to which the growth of the apparatus of the contemporary state endangers democracy. There seems to be no evidence of bureaucracy threatening public contestation and inclusiveness. What menace there is rests with the bureaucratic impact upon the rule of law and the accountability of democratic governments.

'Classical', or 'desk-class', or Weberian bureaucracy can be reconciled with democracy without great difficulty. Indeed, I have argued that it is an extension of the rule of law. At its best, classical bureaucracy entails a fair and incorrupt administration treating all citizens alike. Even its delays may be regarded as part of the judiciousness of an impartial system. In its relationships with political authority it remains neutral and impersonal, anxious at all times merely to advise and to carry out orders.

This type of bureaucracy has been attacked by populistic politicians, however, for its hierarchy and its secrecy. Bureaucratic delays are attributed to ill-will and status pettifoggery. The perception that bureaucratic apparatuses tend to extend their size and scope—probably a correct one—lays them open to the charge of inefficiency. And the picture has been drawn, especially in the United States, of an irresponsible administrative élite remote from ordinary citizens. Consequently there is great American resistance to a professional civil service.

The modern European state, on the contrary, as Weber argued, more or less developed with bureaucracy. Although he had misgivings about its extension he did not live to see it becoming the power-seeking octopus it is often portrayed as today. When administrators are only concerned with implementing their political masters' decisions it is not easy for them to arrogate power to themselves. Yet already by the turn of the century, bureaucrats were being given discretion—by decree laws, administrative orders, delegated legislation, etc.—virtually to compose their own laws. In Britain, for example, new social legislation, such as the institution of the National Health Service, gave the minister concerned, often after consultation with the interests involved, discretion to issue more detailed regulations (in practice drawn up by civil servants), within the wider framework of a general Act. Once given these sorts of powers, bureaucrats could not avoid entanglement in political decisions, though at first, perhaps, at a low level. The opposite side of the coin is that politicians are no longer involved in so many 'political' decisions.

With technocracy, the division of responsibility between administrators and politicians will be no longer the former implementing the decisions of the latter. The politicians may no longer have either the skills or the knowledge for policy formulation which may now be left to the technocrats. The politicians indicate their broad aims but the planners refine them in more sophisticated and quantitative terms and indicate how they should be attained. Moreover, the planners may proceed at their own pace and without too much attention to the feelings of the politicians or the public. An extreme view of this case would make democracy redundant because the correct policies to follow would emerge from the technocrats' cogitations over their charts and computer print-outs. In practice, as we have seen, while technocratic planning is likely to diminish the role of representative institutions, it will probably provoke pluralistic and bureaucratic intervention in policy-making and even in implementation,[73] so that what emerges can scarcely be the objectively and rationally most desirable policy.

Planning is the most significant manifestation of technocratic influence in policy-making. Many of its implications can be disturbing for those worried about the maintenance of democratic values. For example, Barbara Wootton speaks of

the temptation to enact unnecessary cultural uniformity . . . amongst those men and women who are personally responsible for making the decisions

[73] A. G. Jordan and J. J. Richardson, *British Politics and the Policy Process* (1987), 233 ff.

which constitute economic planning. It will be strong because it is, generally speaking, easier to plan for uniformity than for diversity. It will be strong because people who arrive at positions of power are, inevitably, people who enjoy the exercise of power.[74]

Although democracy is the political regime providing the best opportunity for diversity of expression it unfortunately does not follow that such an outcome will be inevitable. Standardization may be enjoyed by many people, and they may opt for it instinctively. Again, planning tends to imply centralization, for the latter is seen as the price of efficiency (see Chapter 4). Finally, planning tends to favour continuity and stability, whereas democracy is inherently discontinuous and unstable. The equilibrium of inter-party consensus, and agreement between business and labour, are the circumstances economic planners favour. Democracy does not necessarily reject such situations but in the nature of things it cannot provide them with constant regularity. Moreover, 'unplanning' and 'anti-planning' are at least as likely as planning to emerge as keynotes of democratic debate.

The fact is that in democracies the intellectual tide may sometimes flow towards greater rational guidance of social and economic activity and at other times it may ebb in the opposite direction. Furthermore, the meaning of the term, 'planning' has lost clarity by a process of accretion. In general, in the top circles of democratic decision-making it will usually refer today to the intervention of the state in the processes of forward economic policy-making. In this process, 'political bureaucrats' will be to the fore. As Franz Lehner and Klaus Schubert write, 'Parties and parliaments do not possess to any degree the necessary apparatus for information processing and planning with regard to highly specialized problems, nor do they have a sufficiently professionalized personnel.'[75] Only the American Congress might qualify as a possible exception to this assessment. Since the 1970s it possesses specialized personnel to provide it with information though it does not have the necessary coherence and leadership to plan, and certainly not the autonomy.

'Political bureaucrats', therefore, frequently represent democratic governments in medium- and low-level policy-making that involves

---

[74] B. Wootton, *Freedom under Planning* (1945), 32.

[75] F. Lehner and K. Schubert, Party Government and the Political Control of Public Policy, *European Journal of Political Research,* 12 (1984), 133.

bargaining with organized economic interests. This not only leads to the bypassing of legislatures but also to the declining influence of political parties, which are far too cumbrous either to deal with the resolution of conflict or to steer the economy. Most large governing parties contain within themselves interests which are difficult to reconcile without compromising general economic objectives. The capacity of parties to formulate policy guidelines and programmes, Lehner and Schubert argue, is often rather low.[76] Andrew Gamble and Stuart Walkland draw attention to the dysfunctionality of British adversarial politics for economic management.[77] Party conflict, and in particular two-party alternation in government, may result in very erratic steering of the economy. Parties may have difficulty in adjusting their manifestos to changes in economic conditions and in circumstances where U-turns are required, political bureaucrats may take over the tiller by default.

As noted in Chapter 2, the reaction between party government and the electorate creates problems of accountability. The transfer of policy power to bureaucracies, however, aggravates the difficulties of responsibility and responsiveness. As Lehner and Schubert, among others, explain, the Weberian concept of rational bureaucracy cannot be reconciled with political bureaucracy's creation of law.[78] This may lead to role confusion and affect its legitimacy. Although politicians may respond badly to changed economic circumstances, they are more sensitive to changed public opinion than bureaucrats and technocrats who (depending on economic stability and technical expertise for economic steering), may find it hard to respond to either. Political bureaucrats, as we have seen, are not usually insensitive to political considerations but their loyalties are to segmentalized 'policy communities', and their solutions are frequently of an incremental kind. In all contemporary democratic regimes they still leave the articulation of major issues to political parties. Policies implemented in response to highly politicized issues, however, may sometimes make less electoral impact than medium- and low-level policies, emanating from bureaucracies.

Dennis Thompson has written perceptively of the problems of maintaining democratic accountability where elected representatives play increasingly diminishing roles in the formulation of

[76] Ibid. 134.
[77] A. M. Gamble, and S. A. Walkland, *The British Party System and Economic Policy 1945–1983* (Oxford, 1984), 152.
[78] Lehner and Schubert, *Party Government*, 135.

policy.[79] What he characterizes as the 'hierarchical model', *par excellence* the British system with its supposedly well defined jurisdictions, has become a series of issue networks in which the civil servants may initiate policy and bargain with pressure groups. Ministerial involvement in policy-making has been vitiated by the rapidity with which British ministers are reshuffled. They are not long enough in a department to master it and consequently can bring little influence to bear on decisions. The greatest objection to the hierarchical model, however, is that it leads to people criticizing the procedures rather than the policies. The bureaucrats who make the policies escape scrutiny, while the ministers, for the most part not responsible for policy, take responsibility ritualistically, meaning that they escape punishment because everyone knows they cannot fairly be held to blame. Thus in the British system specific policy-makers are unaccountable (in public anyway) and virtually undismissable. They remain largely unknown and invisible. Only the government as a whole can be punished.

With what Thompson calls the 'professionalist model', it is argued that no institutional provision for accountability is necessary. Bureaucrats are aware of the public interest and their dedication to it is selfless and detached. Yet even so they may become insulated from public criticism, especially where decisions are technical. The unquantifiable values of the assumptions underlying cost–benefit analysis may remain unexposed, while the sums themselves, even if published, may be incomprehensible to most of the electorate. The idea of 'peer review', members of a profession criticizing and ranking one another, may break down when such a unifying matter as a wage claim for everyone arises. Here their sense of vocation may be subverted by their collegial and corporate concern for their colleagues. The isolation and superior aloofness of this type of bureaucracy, best exemplified by the French civil service, can scarcely assist accountability, though it may in the short term encourage efficiency.

Democracy, of course, has nothing to do with efficiency in the strictly economic sense. Even if the majority of a democratic electorate want the maximization of material benefits in an intuitive way they may not know how to use their votes to express this desire. There is a mass of evidence, however, to support the view that

---

[79] D. F. Thompson, Bureaucracy and Democracy in G. Duncan (ed.), *Democratic Theory and Practice* (Cambridge, 1983), 236 ff.

voters' demands are by no means entirely materialistic all the time: for example, foreign-policy issues arouse patriotic emotions and also may be expressed in moralistic sentiments. In fact, democratic decision-making can only be reconciled with efficiency in terms which economists would find unfamiliar. These would imply that inefficient decisions made by democratic majorities were beneficial in the long run, maximizing satisfaction because people derive great benefit by learning from their mistakes but learn little while enjoying the less flawed policies of bureaucrats. 'Good government is no substitute for self-government' does not only apply to colonial territories. Citizens may profit from the democratic right to choose inefficiency.

Clearly, certain democratic values may be challenged by the growth of both bureaucracy and technocracy. They increase the distance between leaders and led, already brought about by representative institutions. This remoteness is hardly a situation in which trust can grow; in fact, suspicions of what governments are doing has increased as policies have become more complex and less intelligible. The speed with which technocrats may operate may threaten accountability: the decline of legislatures is an indication of this trend. Where policy emerges half from a planning commissariat and half from group bargaining, responsibility for policy may be hard to establish, though the voters may well still hold the political leaders responsible. Thus one arrives at what, in the late twentieth century, has become not an unfamiliar feature of democracy—politicians taking the blame for adopting policies they do not properly understand.

The position is only bearable because the voters are not, in general, concerned to reach complete understanding. They judge politicians and parties in terms of outputs, not inputs. Successful economic policies are rewarded and unsuccessful penalized. On the other hand, especially in local situations, there may be sudden citizen revulsions classically expressed in the reaction 'the first we knew about it was when the bulldozers turned up'. It is rare for national decisions to evoke this response, but U-turns in economic policy may often leave voters puzzled and uncomprehending. Lack of understanding and the seeming remoteness of both elected and unelected authority may lead ultimately to suspicion and the decline of trust.

The relationship between the apparatus of the state and the

politicians and voters is of the greatest importance for democracy, yet democrats have never entirely come to terms with it. It is, for example, difficult to envisage how British voters would respond to the question 'Are you in favour of abolishing the civil service or do you think we should retain it?' Their probable bemusement could spring from an inability to perceive modern society without bureaucratic administration. After all, bureaucracy, like the state itself, dates from three or four centuries before democracy. Without the organized framework of the state, much of it served and maintained by bureaucracy, the decision-making process we know as 'democracy' could scarcely exist, and while democrats may be heavily critical of bureaucracy they would quickly find it impossible to operate the modern industrial state without it. The problem, therefore, is a dual one: democrats not only need to ensure that bureaucracy and technocracy do not endanger democracy; in order to be successful in such an undertaking they need to understand the implications of the interrelationship between democracy and the state apparatus.

4

DECENTRALIZATION AND CENTRALIZATION
The Democratic Dimension

How power should be diffused is a problem for all states. The most common diffusion is territorial. Variations can be represented along a scale between hightly centralized states where central governments have great powers, at one end, and highly decentralized states at the other. 'Centralization', however, is a term that can be used to describe other types of strong central control. For instance, where there is a briskness and clarity of decision-making and implementation—the chain of command is taut, and orders are clear and smartly obeyed—then a state may be described as centralized. This might not coincide with territorial centralization. Where power is aggregated and concentrated in a few hands—again, not necessarily at a geographic locus—one may also speak of centralization. Finally, state intervention in order to control more and more functions is sometimes described as a centralizing process. Actually, an omnicompetent and powerful state is not inevitably one centralized in territorial terms, because decentralization can sometimes be a more effective framework for state control. All these meanings of centralization can be conceptually separate, though they are often linked in reality.

In this chapter, however, I am first concerned with centralization and decentralization as territorial phenomena, and how they are related to democracy. It would simplify to suggest that how a democratic state chooses to divide power between the centre and the localities is ultimately a matter for its citizens through the decision-making process. Frequently such a structure dates from the beginning of the polity and is bound up with the circumstances in which compromises were effected between different social and political forces. For example, Switzerland and the United States are federal states because both began as confederations or alliances between sovereign entities. Such states could only be inaugurated because the sub-units were accorded considerable autonomy. Federalism was the result.

All states, except micro-states, have territorial divisions for decision-making; but the way this decentralization is structured differs markedly from one state to another. In the first place the geographical pattern varies greatly. Some states have only two tiers of local government: others three or more. Where there are fewer tiers there are likely to be larger and fewer local government units which are more likely to be organized politically by parties. This will provide electoral organization and, possibly, a clearer articulation of issues, though the parties will probably articulate national issues. Other things being equal, therefore, simplicity of territorial division may not make for more accountability of local government.

Whether simplicity or complexity of local government structure is the more conducive to democracy cannot be easily pronounced upon. That a simple structure allows central government to predominate might be regarded as a vindication of the democratic process when national majorities favoured such an outcome. (The difficulty is that they seldom, if ever, explicitly come down on one side or the other.) Complexity of structure, on the one hand, may be regarded as an instrument of democracy, leading to repeated checking and revising of decisions; while on the other it might be perceived as an obstruction to the popular will. Accountability in either case may be enhanced or diminished: it depends on to whom one sees a democratically elected body properly accountable.

More commonly, decentralization relates to the division of functions. It is difficult to separate the pattern of local government from what it does. Some democratic central governments may choose to devolve numerous functions to local government: others may retain many for themselves. Quite frequently in the twentieth century there has been a good deal of movement of functions, backwards and forwards from one tier to another, except in federal states where written constitutions will define the division of functions between the central government and the states, provinces, and cantons. The latter, of course, may then devolve functions to their local governments.

In most democratic countries the decisions about what functions should be local and what should be central have not featured in public debate, unlike those about what should be privately, and what publicly, owned. Communications and transport are usually centralized. There is some variety, however, as between different democracies. For example, French policing and education are largely centralized services, while in Britain both are within the scope of local government. On the whole, however, the recent tendency has been for central governments to deprive local governments of their functions. Especially has this been so with public utilities. At the beginning of the twentieth century most British municipalities ran their own gas and electricity works and hospitals, but by mid-century these had been removed from their control and grouped in much larger units. Brian Smith, writing of the National Health Service in Britain, with 'syndicalist representation' on 'toothless community health councils', lamented: 'Studies indicate that these particular ad hoc bodies serve to protect the interests of the medical professions, rather than the wider public or community interests.[1] The growth of the welfare state has led in most countries to greater bureaucratization and centralization. Here both equality and efficiency have been favoured at the expense of local democracy.

A democracy that has considerable decentralization of structure and function with the lowest levels of government active in operating numerous services may still be highly centralized in many senses. If law and custom allow the central government rigorous controlling powers it may restrict the operations of local government very much. Here it becomes apparent that in few unitary democracies does local government have great financial autonomy. In the first place central governments tend to control potential sources of revenue for local government and provide a large part of it. For example, in Belgium, Denmark, Ireland, Luxembourg, The Netherlands, Portugal, and Britain, more than half of local government revenue in the late 1970s came from central government grants.[2] Fred Riggs has written: '. . . in the developed countries, local self-government, to the extent that it is effective, rests on the ability and willingness of local communities to tax themselves for a substantial part of the service they want'.[3] On this criterion, much of local government in the democratic world might appear ineffective. But Riggs does not specify how much he would regard as a substantial part.

---

[1] B. C. Smith, *Decentralisation* (1985), 131.
[2] Ibid. 101.
[3] F. W. Riggs, Bureaucrats and Political Development, in J. La Palombara (ed.), *Bureaucracy and Political Development* (Princeton, 1963), 137.

Of course, the high proportion of central government funding does affect the autonomy of local government, though not necessarily directly. If it is commonly known by voters that their local authorities are in receipt of a vast amount of centrally raised money they are likely to assume that its independence, and therefore its importance, is greatly reduced. But evidence shows that it is the type of control over grants rather than the dimension of the hand-outs which is more significant. For example, block grants from central government, allowing freedom of distribution, are much less centralizing than 'specific' or 'categorical' grants which specify exactly the services on which the money is to be spent. There are many other ways, however, in which central governments can control local government spending. When central government lays down standards, which it frequently does, local government freedom is restricted. Or central government, while not precisely allocating amounts, may set ceilings on specific expenditures. Finally, when local governments borrow from central government, often for capital expenditure, they will inevitably incur various controls. Certainly in Britain in recent years of recession, while the proportion of central government grant to local authorities has decreased, the strictness of central control has increased. There is no necessary association between the degree of independence and the amount of funding from central government.

What is more important is the control central government exerts over the revenue-raising of local governments and the type of taxation it allows. Where local governments depend upon property taxes for most of their non-central revenue they may run into difficulties, for property taxes are inelastic and, in times of inflation, real revenues may be difficult to sustain. Property-tax rises are also electorally damaging as they are very visible and often demanded in lump sums. On the other hand, where, as in Scandinavia or Switzerland, local governments can raise their revenue from local income tax, they have been less financially embarrassed, less worried by inflation, and less open to central government intervention.[4] Where central governments have monopolized income tax for themselves, local governments have been less financially buoyant and more under central control. Hence, while during the inflationary period local government expenditure in all democratic industrialized countries tended to increase more rapidly than central government

---

[4] Smith, *Decentralisation*, 101.

expenditure, the fiscal crisis was worst where local tax systems were inelastic, as in Britain.[5]

Whether more local autonomy will be any more popular with the voters is a different matter. Local income tax increases might lead to less central control and make local government more independent but they are as likely to be as visible, and therefore as electorally damaging, as rises in property taxes. The fact is that central governments find it much easier than local governments to increase their revenues annually without too much turbulence. When public expenditure was greatly expanding local governments everywhere would have been not unwilling to allow central government to shoulder an unequal share of the burden. In actual fact, in many cases they found themselves in a position of financial embarrassment as a result of statutory obligations to carry out centralized services. No matter what taxation system appertains locally, it seems, local authorities in modern industrial democracies are bound to be in receipt of a high proportion of their revenue from the centre. Local income tax will make them more independent and so more locally accountable, but the greater measure of autonomy may not make local councils any more popular. It might lead to demands from voters for centralization.

The evolution of the financial relationship between centre and localities seems to have led to local governments being entrusted with increasing responsibilities for central governments' social policies, and therefore with more funding. The vast growth of public expenditure in the twentieth century, and especially since World War II, reflecting egalitarian values, has been almost invariably centralizing because standards laid down at the centre allow little local discretion. Since recession arrived in the late 1970s, the proportion of national expenditure devoted to centrally administered services has somewhat increased (largely because unemployment benefits belong to this latter category in most countries) but it has not altered the relationship appreciably. Indeed, with the advent of cuts in public expenditure and a drive for efficiency, even at the expense of equality, an even stricter control by central governments has ensued.

This brief account cannot do justice to the more formal aspects of central–local relations, but it does reveal the extreme complexity of

---

[5] K. Newton and T. J. Karran, *The Politics of Local Expenditure* (1985) is a good account of the recent British experience.

the problem and the difficulty of stating outright whether a particular democracy is centralized or decentralized. Sub-system government may receive more functions from the centre and be allocated more funding, and yet, as a result, be more controlled by central government. Even federalism may co-exist with increasing concentration, if not centralization, of power.[6] This is because the informal elements in the situation are often so important. These may belie the conventional wisdom about local democracy.

Democracy and Sub-system Government

Much of the conventional wisdom, however, is complicated by the conflating of the ideas of decentralization and democracy. In point of fact, decentralization could be applied in an authoritarian state. Not infrequently, even in democracies, the reasons for decentralizing functions are pragmatic and bureaucratic. The results may be rather harmful to democracy. In general, decentralization is taken to be 'good' and centralization is presumed to be 'bad'. Local autonomy, it is argued, should not be sacrificed to the demands of the centralizing national state: it is a basic democratic value and any encroachment on it is undemocratic.[7] With the autonomy of sub-system government is associated its diversity. Thus, 'diversity' becomes a democratic value while standardization, even worse, uniformity, must be undemocratic. Hence the argument appears to be: local autonomy, diversity, decentralization, and 'the good' against local dependence on central government, uniformity, centralization, and 'the bad'.

To a large extent this dichotomy is historical. James Fesler sees the hankering for decentralization as part of a nostalgic romanticization of small-town and rural society.[8] In many countries the autonomy of local government was much more of a reality in the past. In Britain, for example, the corporations of the boroughs before reform had an autonomy so entrenched that they were free to indulge in all sorts of corruption. The Municipal Reform Act

[6] Smith, *Decentralisation*, 120.

[7] It has been argued that the principle of subsidiarity, allocating functions to the smallest possible group, is fundamental. See M. Frenkel, The Distribution of Legal Powers in Pluricentral Systems, in R. Morgan (ed.) *Regionalism in European Politics* (1986), 74. See also *The Federalist*, Essay xvii, and E. B. F. Midgley, *The Natural Law Tradition and the Theory of International Relations* (1975), 202 ff.

[8] J. W. Fesler, Approaches to the Understanding of Decentralization, *Journal of Politics*, 27 (1965), 536. See also his *Area and Administration* (Birmingham, Al., 1949).

1835, introducing elected councils, made Treasury sanction necessary for raising loans.[9] Parliament was soon imposing central
control and, to some extent, laying down standards of behaviour to
which local government had to conform. Thus the British golden
age of local government autonomy was before democracy raised its
ugly head.

Those who romanticized local autonomy perceived centralization as a soulless juggernaut mowing down ancient particularities.
They associated it with mass society, relating it to a cultural process
of standardization; or, alternatively, the imposition by the
metropolis of its values upon the provinces. Furthermore, centralization was regarded as part of a policy of integration by means of
which an enveloping state would absorb local cultures, perhaps
assimilating linguistic and ethnic minorities into the majority
culture.

In actual fact it is difficult to sustain these equations, and to argue
that a system of local government is essentially democratic. On the
contrary, it could be that public contestation, inclusiveness,
accountability, and the values of democracy, such as tolerance,
trust, and constitutionalism, are better nurtured by a completely
centralized regime. This may seem an unexpected assertion, but it
can be supported in various ways.

For example, it can be affirmed that the only majority which
counts is the majority of the whole nation. Any other majority is an
impediment to the realization of the popular will and obscures its
clarification. The logical conclusion of this is a completely
centralized state in which all local decisions are made at the centre.
In practice, of course, local demands have to be dealt with and local
services administered, and therefore, in this type of state, local
administration would be carried out by field agents of central
government. France used to approximate to this model; the possibility is not a mere arid abstraction.

It would seem, however, that inclusiveness might suffer where
participation in political life could take place either at the centre or
in pressure groups and political parties whose main impacts must
be at the centre. This objection would lay stress on local politics as
an arena in which the enfranchised citizenry participate. There is no
compelling mass of evidence, however, that citizen participation is

[9] J. Redlich and F. W. Hirst, *The History of Local Government in England*, rev.
edn. (1958), 130.

always higher in local politics. On the contrary, the empirical data points to the opposite conclusion: in Britain roughly twice the proportion of people turn out at general elections as at local elections.[10] In France the discrepancy is not so marked.[11] Corresponding figures in the United States show higher turnouts in presidential elections and congressional elections than in many local elections, though some of the latter may have a very low abstention rate.[12] In general, the politics of national government encourage a higher participation than the politics of local government. Electoral participation in local politics is so low in many democratic countries that voters can hardly regard it as an important citizen right or duty.

Similarly, it is difficult to contend that public contestation—democratic rights of organized opposition to authority—is enhanced by any form of sub-system government. Are central governments likely to be more repressive of freedoms of expression and the right to oppose than local governments? In general, the answer must be that democratic freedoms are likely to be infringed more in local situations. Parochial opinion may often be narrow-minded opinion, and local pressures may bear heavily on the local eccentric and dissident. The view that social harmony is the ultimate good, so common in small towns, may produce a smothering consensus that is not good for democracy.[13] In contrast, at the national level, unpopular minority groups may publicize their discontents without personalizing them. It is the damage, and feared damage, to personal relationships which makes for avoidance of conflict in small communities, in addition to the dead weight of cultural tradition. For many reasons innovation is more likely to stem from the centre.

[10] J. Gyford, *Local Politics in Britain* (1976) 125, quotes local election turnout in England and Wales at contested elections varying from 37.6 per cent to 48.0 per cent in the 1950s and 1960s.

[11] D. E. Ashford, *British Dogmatism and French Pragmatism* (1982), 77. Sixty-six per cent of voters turn out at local elections in communes of over 30,000 population 82 per cent in those under 30,000. 85 per cent vote in presidential elections and 80 per cent in legislative elections.

[12] Statistics on American local elections are difficult to acquire. S. R. Lyons, Who Votes and Why (Robert A. Taft Institute of Government, New York, 1981) says local elections do not attract voters to the same degree that state and national elections do (p. 39). I should like to acknowledge the help Jack Fenton gave me with this data.

[13] See F. Bealey, Small Group Politics, in V. Bogdanor, *The Dictionary of Political Institutions* (Oxford, 1987), 567–8.

Local representative institutions are better defended as a counter-weight to central power. All central governments, including those that are democratic, have a tendency to act in an arbitrary way. Along with other institutions and associations, local governments may act as a check on such behaviour. They will often have a political composition different from the party or parties in power at the centre, providing compensation for those parties not in the central government, and enhancing the political diversity of the country. It is also argued that local people can make decisions about local matters of which central government is ignorant. In this way local representatives are more representative of, and responsive to, local feelings and local movements of opinion. There are some choices which can only be made properly by those on the spot who have day-to-day contact with local people and local circumstances. By this criterion, the important option is not that between either centralizing or decentralizing functions: it is the choice of what functions should be centralized and what decentralized. For example, as Jim Sharpe argues, where the quality of a service is unmeasurable, but personal and visible only locally, as with health and hospital care, accountability to a near, locally elected body is more appropriate.[14] Central government is not well placed to defend consumer interests.

Another common argument in favour of local democracy, espoused by John Stuart Mill, is that it is a school in which democratic theory and practice can be learned by citizens because, unlike national politics, it is an area where the issues are near and intelligible. Evidence on this is mixed. In Britain, as we have seen, participation rates are a good deal lower in local than at national elections. It is hard to substantiate the view of George Jones and John Stewart that British local electorates have cast their votes increasingly about local issues.[15] Complaints about services, which one would think are more easily made to local councillors, are frequently expressed to local MPs.[16] The movement generally in Western Europe towards larger and fewer local government units[17] can hardly have made local representatives less remote. Certainly in

[14] L. J. Sharpe, Functional Allocation in the Welfare State, *Local Government Studies*, 10 1 (1984), 35.

[15] G. W. Jones and J. D. Stewart, Policy Making in Central and Local Government Compared, *Local Government Studies*, 9 (1983), 74.

[16] Gyford, *Local Politics in Britain*, 135.

[17] L. J. Sharpe, *Decentralist Trends in Western Democracies* (1979), 9 ff.

pre-1975 three-tier English local government, county government—
—the most distant tier for most citizens—appeared to be least
known to them.[18] After 1975, with local government reorganization, national parties became more prominent in local politics, as
the result of the latter increasingly being perceived in terms of
national issues and the fortunes of the national parties at Westminster. The outcome of this may well be less accountability of local
government, with local elections being the occasion for verdicts on
national events. On the other hand, large second-tier units—such
as the provinces in Spain, where considerable powers have been
devolved from the centre in response to ethnic and cultural
pressures—may give local elections greater meaning and produce
electoral turn-outs as high as in national elections.[19] Here large
units provide a focus for identifiable autonomy, but it is not that of
the self-governing locality.

Efficiency, Effectiveness, and Local Government

Much rhetoric in favour of 'good' local government, however,
relates to its efficiency and its effectiveness: efficiency referring to
administration and effectiveness to success of local political action.
How one measures success will depend on one's angle of approach.
Thus, local people might see success in terms of satisfying local
demands, a democratic perspective. National politicians and
bureaucrats, on the other hand, will see effectiveness of local
government in terms of its assistance to central government.
Democratic local government has developed an instrumentality for

[18] Frank Bealey, J. Blondel, and W. P. McCann, *Constituency Politics*
(1965), 246.
[19] J. M. Bochel and D. T. Denver, *The Scottish District Elections 1977* (Dundee,
1977), 84, and 93, reveals that 36.2 per cent of the candidates and 20.3 per cent of
the winners among them were Independents. The same authors, in *The Scottish
District Elections 1984* (Dundee, 1984), 84, 93, give respective figures of 27.7 per
cent and 14.2 per cent. John Bochel helped me greatly here. D. S. Bell (ed.),
Democratic Politics in Spain (1983), app. 198, gives a 79.6 per cent turnout at the
Spanish 1982 general election. In the 1986 regional election in the Basque country
there was a 71 per cent turnout. *(The Times,* 2 Dec. 1986). Keith Medhurst
confirmed this. I am grateful to Eugenia Salvador for providing me with much data
on recent Spanish elections. In her Las Elecciones en Espana: Homogeneizacion o
territorializacion del voto? (Paper given to the Italian Society of Electoral Studies at
Padua, Oct. 1985) she notes that parties on national lines are predominating in
regional elections except in Catalonia and the Basque country.

national government which may threaten to subvert its democratic nature.

At the same time, elected local representatives have tended to undergo the same derogation of status that has afflicted national legislators—they have been overtaken by bureaucracy (see Chapter 3). The 'new managerialism'[20] has either given local representatives roles they were not intended to play or led to local administrators exercising leadership in policy-making. Technocracy has also appeared at the local administrative level. Planning, both physical and economic, has had a great deal to do with this. In Britain, as Jack Brand demonstrates, the demand for planning at the local level had both local and national origins.[21] Locally, suburban sprawl in the large cities raised the issue of control of land use. Nationally, the need to channel industry into distressed areas was recognized in the Town and Country Planning Act 1947 which gave the Board of Trade powers to do so. Then, in considering the needs of different parts of the country, the government, almost by necessity, was forced to think in regional terms. Regionalism (see below) might be necessary to provide the proper framework for correcting economic imbalance, and this was recognized in the Distribution of Industry (Industrial Finance) Act 1958, encouraging development in areas of persistent unemployment. The creation of larger local government units in the local government reform of the 1970s was a reflection of central government concern with economic management.

British reorganization was overwhelmingly supported by the professional groups, who sought a new and more rewarding career structure as well as what they perceived as a more efficient system. Among these the most pushing were the planners, whose professional association had expanded from 1,645 members in 1948 to 4,165 in 1969.[22] Their duties were not as clearly defined as civil engineers or sanitary experts, nor were there the same central government standards to which they were obliged to adhere. As Sharpe perceptively writes of the services provided to local authorities by professional groups:

where there is a high degree of discretion involved and professional autonomy is essential, a potential threat to effective democratic government

---

[20] For a discussion of corporate management, see J. D. Stewart, *The Responsive Local Authority* (1974).

[21] J. Brand, *Local Reform in England* (1974), 26 ff.   [22] Ibid. 68.

is posed. The service gradually comes to serve objectives set by the professional group or groups running the service rather than those of its recipients or society at large. Some form of control external to the professional group is therefore necessary.[23]

And he concludes that the local authorities themselves offer the best focus for the loyalties of professional officers, thus counteracting 'incipient syndicalism'.

Samuel Beer has pointed out how professional groups at all levels tend to 'speak the same language'—to have the same training, attitudes, and values. There is likely to be close contact between professional groups within all levels of government, and agreement between them is very probable. This technocratic nexus, remote from ordinary citizens, is a centralizing factor in all modern industrialized democracies. Ranged against them in the United States is the complex bargaining structure of inter-governmental relations. Beer described a 'topocratic' lobby—the National Governors Conference, the Council of State Governments, the US Conference of Mayors, and the National League of Cities—whose pressure on federal government vastly increased in response to technocratic activity aroused by the federal programmes of the 1960s. Beer saw the topocrats as a decentralizing factor because the general effect of their pressure, while reducing the federal government's 98 per cent categorical grants in 1966 to 75 per cent in 1975, was to provide more block grants and general revenue sharing.[24] The impact of these two latter devices was towards more autonomy (at the same time as a movement towards less equality). Yet the procedural requirements attached to all forms of federal aid in the United States, and constraints in respect of areas such as the environment, equal rights, and personnel, have led gradually to more control over all types of federal assistance.[25] Centralization in recent years has been by the states. American local government, as G. Ross Stephens has argued, has lost much of its independence.[26]

---

[23] Sharpe, Theories and Values of Local Government, 174.

[24] S. Beer, Federalism, Nationalism and Democracy in America, *American Political Science Review* 72 1 (1978), 18 ff. D. C. Nice, *Federalism: the Politics of Intergovernmental Relations* (New York, 1987) 56. notes, however that revenue sharing was only 7 per cent of the national grant system.

[25] Advisory Commission on Intergovernmental Relations, *Intergovernmental Grant System,* 14 (1978), Epilogue, 67.

[26] G. R. Stephens, State Centralisation and the Erosion of Local Autonomy, *Journal of Politics,* 36 1 (1974), 45 ff.

To sum up: whatever the abstract democratic credentials of local government, one must face the fact that the industrialized modern state cannot do without it. Its *raison d'être* may be practical rather than rooted in democratic theory. Governments cannot do everything at the centre. They need agencies in the localities to administer the numerous services—for example, transport and telecommunications—that are demanded by the exigencies of national survival as well as by the pressures of democratic electorates. Some services can be administered through local agents of central government; but in democracies demands that would be better carried out by locally elected bodies are bound to arise.[27] Local representative democracy can hardly be avoided.

Once the practical arguments are accepted for local democracy, the vexed question of what form it should take remains on the agenda. The prolonged, subdued, and somewhat confused debate in every democracy has ranged around four concepts: accountability, autonomy (the assertion of the identity of the local community), efficiency (the best use of resources), and fairness (the most equitable way for distributing them). The different aspects of the choice between more or less centralization can be considered in terms of these complex ideas. Sometimes they can be partly reconciled, though never wholly. The difficulties of analysis lie in the way the contenders in the debate have used them to support their own cases. It is an argument in which motives are often rather obscure. 'Democracy', as so often, may be employed as a weapon by those who are much more in favour of more autonomy, or greater efficiency, or less equality, than they are of more accountability.

Inter-governmental Relations

A further dimension of the relationship between national and local representative democracy complicates the analysis. There are not only institutional relationships between different tiers of local government, but also bargaining relationships. Moreover, there is bargaining between local politicians and technocrats and national

---

[27] Though it might take the form, as in 19th cent. Britain, of separate local elected bodies for specific services. See R. A. Dahl, *Who Governs?* (New Haven, 1961), 200 ff., for a description of this pattern in New Haven. See also K. Newton, Community Decision Makers and Community Decision Making in England and the United States, in T. N. Clark (ed.), *Comparative Community Politics* (New York, 1974), 62 ff.

politicians and technocrats at the centre and in the localities. The
negotiations and bargaining relationships transect the jurisdic-
tional. This produces a certain dualism.

Some neo-Marxists have described central government as
concerned with production and local government as involved with
consumption. Cynthia Cockburn argues that local government is 'a
key part of the state in capitalist society' because the services it
provides 'help to reproduce the labour force although the inception
of the welfare state was a shift in the balance of power in favour of
the working class'.[28] This theory interprets the recent re-structuring
of British local government, with bigger units and more technocratic management, as reflecting the power of capital. Paul Corrigan
writes: 'monopoly capital has attempted to move as much
democratic power away from the locality because it is in the sphere
of locality that the working class as a class has some possibility of
mass politics.'[29] Working-class control of city councils might
provide a springboard to socialism, as in Bologna; but the advent of
much larger units in British local government, he argued, would
impede such an outcome. Manuel Castells perceived opportunities
in local politics for working-class direct action which might be as
useful as the ballot box.[30] Local government might become a real
centre of working-class power.

One does not have to be a Marxist to accept that entrepreneurial
and managerial leadership has long since deserted local politics and
redeployed its major efforts at the centre,[31] but Labour and socialist
parties have taken a similar course. Their egalitarian programmes
of redistribution, planning, and public ownership probably make
centralization inevitable. On the other hand, such parties often give
pre-eminence to local political action in their early history.
Consequently, when such action is advocated locally after several
decades of fair success at the national level it is likely to be a sign of
decline—indeed, of desperation. Farce rather than high revolutionary drama may be the outcome, as the events of 1984–6 in
Liverpool demonstrate. A bifurcation on class lines of the two
arenas of operation does not have general validity.

[28] C. Cockburn, *The Local State* (1977), 41, 62.

[29] P. Corrigan, The Local State: The Struggle for Democracy, *Marxism Today*
(July 1979), 209.

[30] M. Castells, *La Question urbaine* (Paris, 1972). See also C. C. Pickvance (ed.),
Urban Sociology: Critical Essays (1976).

[31] See F. Bealey, Business Leaders in Local Politics in Britain and the USA. Paper
given to ECPR, Lancaster workshop, March 1981.

Peter Saunders suggests, more convincingly, a duality based on issues. He explains: 'While social provisions have been fought over and ultimately determined through political mobilization in the competitive sector of the polity, economic questions have been settled through a process of bargaining and compromise in the corporate sector.'[32]. This model, discussed at some length in Chapters 6 and 7, seems less apposite when transformed into a central–local dichotomy with the argument that the 'competitive sector' largely appertains to the local level and the 'corporate sector' to the central. Countervailing forces to capital operate at both levels through political parties and pressure groups. It would seem (to me anyway), that while what Saunders describes as social consumption may perhaps once have been local, it was forced to become highly centralized in its decision-making in order to be effective. Jim Sharpe is surely correct in pointing out that 'the local level in most countries no longer . . . monopolises social consumption, if it ever did'.[33] Perhaps the models of the Marxists and Saunders overestimate the power of democratic local government.

It is not always easy to assess how much power remains in the hands of local leaders. Undoubtedly this will vary with changing political circumstances and with the functions concerned. Much bargaining at the local level will relate to private and public investment and state support for it. At the grass roots, local political leaders may act as brokers between the locality and the central authorities. Normally secrecy has attended these bargainings. Francois Dupuy writes of France: 'The system also operates secretly. Business is conducted between the initiated, and all transactions are made offstage . . . It is allergic to public debate. Universal suffrage is a formidable sanction and one to hide from.'[34] Frequently in Britain local leaders such as mayors have, through constituency MPs, approached both firms and government bodies. Normally secrecy has attended these bargainings. For example, in Peterhead in the 1970s, with the discovery of oil, the provost undertook lengthy negotiations with the oil companies without the matter even being discussed by the Burgh Council.[35] In Sweden

---

[32] P. Saunders, Why Study Central–Local Relations? *Local Government Studies* 8 (Mar.–Apr. 1982), 60. It is easier to agree with him that investment has precedence over consumption in the ultimate stage of national policy-making. This applies not only to capitalist democracies.   [33] Sharpe, Functional Allocation, 41.

[34] F. Dupuy, The Politico-Administrative System of the Department in France, in Y. Meny and V. Wright, *Centre–Periphery Relations in Western Europe* (1985), 98.

[35] Frank Bealey and John Sewel, The Politics of Independence (1981), 119.

open decision making characterizes such negotiations, which are much more institutionalized than in Britain: County Employment Boards and Regional Development Funds nearly always support local investment applications for the maximum loan available.[36] The main bargaining is at the centre, where there is a clash between the local desire for stimulating employment and the government's wish to eliminate risks. In almost all countries local governments need central support. National governments will not be able to proceed without local knowledge. Economic investment, especially the location of new industrial plant, will produce situations where local politicians can provide assistance, while people at the centre will, as it were, be presenting a prize of a new steel mill or power station to the highest bidder. Jeanne Becquart-Leclerq describes how French mayors and central administrators are involved in a network of informal trading of favours in order to circumvent the rigidly bureaucratic structure. The relationship must be covert because communes compete for amenities and so the system is not far removed from clientelism. What the author calls 'collective mystification' precludes democratic accountability.[37] In France there *is* local power, largely related to the mayor's skill and connections with both bureaucracy and elected authority.[38] Douglas Ashford argues convincingly that French local authorities not only wield more power at the centre than British, but also that the whole system of intergovernmental relations in France is more pragmatic.[39] The *cumul des mandats* is the main factor: many French mayors are also deputies. Sidney Tarrow contrasts the French situation with the Italian.[40] In both countries local leaders are brokers between local authorities and the centre, but the processes are very different. In France, technocrats may provide the expertise to acquire planning permission for programmes of capital investment. In Italy, where administration is weaker, the system is

[36] R. Henning, Regional Policy Implementation Through Bargaining, Paper given to ECPR, Freiburg workshop, March 1983.

[37] J. Becquart-Leclercq, Relative Power and Center–Periphery Linkages in French local Politics, Sociology and Social Research 62 (1977), 37. See also her *Paradoxes du pouvoir local* (Paris, 1976).

[38] J. E. Milch, Influence as Power: French Local Government Reconsidered *British Journal of Political Science*, 4 (1974), 139–62.

[39] Ashford, *British Dogmatism and French Pragmatism*, 361. Even the strong presidential executive of the Fifth Republic has been forced to recognize local political leadership.

[40] S. Tarrow, *Between Centre and Periphery* (1977), 7 ff.

clientelistic. Luigi Graziano describes how a local political boss in Southern Italy gained votes for his party by finding jobs in public works projects and a state-run tobacco firm.[41]

In the case of Britain, Patrick Dunleavy has commented upon the 'constellation of the national–local government system', the network of relationships between local authorities and departments, ministers, MPs, and political parties, determining the parameters within which local authorities operate.[42] Similarly Rod Rhodes and his two collaborators write: 'Local government's future would seem to be bleak, encompassing both a loss of functions and an increase in direct control . . . those rules of the game derived from an acceptance of local self-government are challenged by the extension of bureaucratic rationalisation in a corporatist system'.[43] They refer to the history of the Consultative Council on Local Government Finance (CCLGF), set up by the Treasury in 1975 after local government reorganization in order to determine the level of Rate Support Grant in England and Wales. Before (since 1967) the two parties to this annual negotiation had been the relevant government departments (largely the Department of the Environment) and the local government associations—the local authorities' pressure groups. The CCLFG, ostensibly a continuation of the earlier bargaining process, was in effect an even greater restriction on local government autonomy. The change of economic climate accentuated the Treasury's determination to be sole manager of the economy and to control public expenditure. The local government associations, earlier incorporated into central government processes and hence unable to obtain anything but marginal concessions—were from 1975 onwards nearly as much under the direction of the Treasury as were government departments; though when in May 1981, Jack Smart, chairman of the association of Municipal Authorities, said 'We are almost at the end of local government as we have known it in this country,'[44] it was probably less a comment on the strictness of Treasury control than on the attitude of the Government to local government sensibilities. In centralized Britain, however, in spite of all the

---

[41] L. Graziano, Patron–Client Relationships in Southern Italy, *European Journal of Political Research*, 1 (1973), 22 ff.

[42] P. Dunleavy, *Urban Political Analysis* (1980), 105.

[43] R. A. W. Rhodes, B. Hardy, and K. Pudsey, Corporate Bias in Central–Local Relations, SSRC Discussion Paper No. 1, March 1982, 16.

[44] Ibid. 75 ff.

complexities of central–local interrelationships, there is a relatively more uniform and simple formula than in federal and decentralized United States where 'layer cake' federalism has given way to 'marble cake' federalism, though the marbles (lumps of federal government power) have decreased in size under the deregulating policies of presidents Carter and Reagan.

Although there are many varieties of centre–local relations in democracies it is unlikely that they have anywhere a rational pattern. Good brokerage and inside knowledge are likely to be at a premium, though less so in Sweden where freedom of information reigns. Methods of stimulating local investment may easily deteriorate into patronage systems. They will become inegalitarian and inequitable. Moreover, it will be difficult to reconcile them with democratic principles such as the 'public interest', governmental mandates, and accountability. Bargaining, by its very nature (as we shall see in Chapter 5), is suspect as a democratic activity. The extension of government economic intervention into the locality has resulted in the mixture of political and economic decision-making which is so much a feature of the contemporary democratic state. The different responses to it reflect differences of political culture and structure.

Yet essentially the implications for all governments in the democracies are similar. The growing acceptance of the obligations of governments to manage economies since the inter-war depression (much accentuated by the inflation of the 1970s), set against the needs of the burgeoning welfare state, has produced a situation of tension in which governmental policies have to be more clearly defined and closely controlled. Public expenditure is still the focus of clash between central and local governments, as in inflationary times; but governments are becoming much more anxious to 'check credentials', regularize activities, and formalize bargaining. Much closer inspection of claims and declared goals, much keener evaluation of performances, and much sharper examination of competing priorities can only result in greater centralization in nearly all senses of the term. Although mutual interdependency remains, local government may become more dependent on the centre, and so in many senses less independent. To what degree this is an effect of economic recession since 1973 and to what degree it is the result of longer centralizing trends is not easy to assess.

Decentralizing Movements

The centralizing tendencies of the twentieth century have often been recounted—the accelerated advance of technology, the increasing division of labour, the concentration of industry, the development of national and international communications, and the growth of the state. In spite of these trends it would be unrealistic to overlook the increasing demand for decentralization emerging in many democracies. Sometimes this has been a reaction to various centralizing currents—political, economic, and cultural—although at other times it has arisen for reasons of practicality and efficiency. On occasions both responses have been combined. Hence the implications of decentralization for democracy are somewhat mixed. Some will claim that it makes for more autonomy and efficiency, others less of both, and yet others will prefer either a preponderance of autonomy over efficiency, or vice versa. It is a matter of judgement and taste.

The cultural reaction against centralization takes two forms. One is a partly aesthetic and partly intellectual response to the impersonality of the big city, the other is a sub-national response from the periphery to the centre of the nation state. Both rest on the concept of 'community'. But perhaps the equation of democracy with *gemeinschaft* is best seen in the institution of the community council which seeks to represent the interests of a few people at the lowest level of identification of all—the urban neighbourhood or rural village. The idea that Fraternity (held by Robert Wood to be inimical to Liberty and Equality),[45] is the unique characteristic of the small community, and therefore that small communities are the most democratic, dies hard even though it does not receive much support from academic research. Frederick Bailey,[46] suggesting a yearning for harmony as its basis, quotes Srinivas's remark that Indian villagers are not face-to-face but 'back-to-back'. In Bologna, where community councils were adopted in 1963,[47] the scheme may have been endorsed by all the political parties only because it

[45] R. H. Wood, *Suburbia* (Boston, 1958), 274 ff.

[46] F. G. Bailey, Decisions by Consensus in Council and Committees: With Especial Reference to Village and Local Government in India, in M. Barton (ed.), *Political Systems and the Distribution of Power* (1965), 6.

[47] F. Kjellberg, A Comparative View of Municipal Decentralisation: Neighbourhood Democracy in Oslo and Bologna, in Sharpe (ed.), *Decentralist Trends in Western Democracies*, 85.

enabled each of them to dominate a different neighbourhood. Daniel Moynihan[48] describes how in New York the Community Action Programmes mobilized racial conflict. As conflictual situations are natural to democracy, this outcome is not necessarily an objection. The trouble in small communities is that once open conflict is initiated it often proves irresolvable.

Another argument for community democracy—that it increases participation—is sometimes confirmed. Francesco Kjellberg reported that 82 Italian cities had neighbourhood councils by the early 1970s, and that they appeared to have had some success in stimulating citizen interest in public affairs. On the other hand, the success of such councils in Sweden was short-lived, and only 40 per cent of them remained after a few years of operation.[49] In the United States, Moynihan reports that elections held among the poor to choose representatives for Community Action Programmes governing boards resulted in turn-outs of, for example, 2.7 per cent in Philadelphia and 0.7 per cent in Los Angeles,[50] while a study by Douglas Yates showed that middle-class leaders dominated neighbourhood government.[51] In Britain, although community councils were recommended in a Labour Government White Paper in 1970, they have been allowed only in Scotland, where they have not been enthusiastically received. Voting for them is lower than for any representative institution. In general, then community councils have not increased participation and it does not seem likely that they have fulfilled their other suggested role, that of 'attracting a new and different type of representative into local government'.[52] This potential was realized in the United States, where Moynihan comments that the one positive result of the Community Action Programme was the training it afforded to a generation of new urban political leaders.[53] Unhappily for them, they were unable to compete with the older institutions of city hall. Thus the Community Action Programme became an odd amalgam of mass protest and a much wider mass apathy.

[48] D. P. Moynihan, *Maximum Feasible Misunderstanding* (1969), 114.
[49] Kjellberg, Comparative View of Municipal Decentralisation, 86.
[50] Moynihan, *Maximum Feasible Misunderstanding*, 137.
[51] D. Yates, *Neighbourhood Democracy* (Lexington, 1973), 112.
[52] Redcliffe Maud, chap. 5, p. 18, quoted in Warren Magnusson, The New Neighbourhood Democracy: Anglo-American Experiences in Historical Perspective, in Sharpe, *Decentralist Trends,* 138.
[53] Moynihan, *Maximum Feasible Misunderstanding,* 130.

Views about neighbourhood democracy differ widely. Brian Smith says it may become 'a form of repressive tolerance',[54] meaning that it re-creates the ideology of small-town consensus that suppresses dissent. From the opposite pole Daniel Moynihan writes: 'we may discover to our sorrow that participatory democracy can mean the end of both participation and democracy.'[55] There seems no good reason why there should not be neighbourhood democracy that is neither oligarchic nor anarchic. Community Councils may usefully fulfil the role of local pressure groups, bringing to the notice of local government the discontents of their neighbourhoods. Local councillors may not wish to raise such grievances where they belong to the majority party and the objection runs contrary to council policy. One may well question, however, whether neighbourhood councils could be entrusted with important executive functions, and without these their concern with policies can only relate to bringing pressure on local administrations.

The sub-national reaction against centralization has usually inspired demands for autonomy for areas inhabited by cultural and linguistic sub-groups aspiring to some form of semi-separation. Such areas are frequently called 'regions'. Pressure for regional solutions has come disproportionately from such groups who maintain that their own areas have different characteristics from the nation as a whole and therefore need more self-government than a unitary state can allow. Other arguments for regionalism have been technocratic and based on the view that a region is the optimum size of territorial unit for economic planning. Whereas democracy features strongly in the arguments of the nationalists, calls for 'efficiency' have characterized the rhetoric of the planners who have often been concerned to restrict decision-making to a few people. Of course, although the two trends are diverse, they have sometimes been combined. Democracy and efficiency are not *necessarily* contrary values.

Arguments in democratic terms for regionalism are based on the familiar view that more intelligible decisions will be made in provincial cities than in metropolises: there will be more participation and governments will be more accountable. Where regions are culturally and/or linguistically distinct this will be especially so.

[54] Smith, *Decentralisation*, 184.
[55] Moynihan, *Maximum Feasible Misunderstanding*, 164.

With the first flush of self-determination there will be an emancipation of enthusiasm for democracy. Hence supra-national democracy will also be improved, with the realization of more democratic forms at the sub-national level leading to more legitimacy and stability for the democratic state. On the other hand, it can be argued that devolution to regions might lead to fragmentation and eventual disintegration of the state. Democracy would collapse in the social and political chaos. Which way a process of regional devolution and decentralization will go is bound to be problematic. There seems no prospect of the Italian regions or German *laender* seceding from their respective national territories. The Spanish regions can be mentioned with less confidence. In Canada the granting of wider autonomous powers for Quebec, where a separatist movement had a majority in the provincial legislature, has not ended in a independent Quebec and the fragmentation of the Dominion. Even if a democratic state were to splinter, the outcome might not be unsatisfactory for democracy if the fragments all adopted democratic regimes. On this count the Balkanization of the globe might improve the chances of democracy surviving in the world.

Arrested before fragmentation, the process of decentralization may lead to the half-way house of federalism. Yet federalism has seldom resulted from such a sequence: it is likely to be born where like-minded territories with confederal aspirations adhere together, as in the instances of Switzerland and the United States. It is a nation-building exercise which could be described as centralization, though 'integration' would probably be a more apt word. The outcome is a decentralized state in which 'states' rights', or provincial/cantonal autonomy, may be regarded as an essential component of the national version of democracy. *Local government autonomy*, however, may be no more assured in federations than in unitary states: it will be dependent, as we have noted, on how much power the states, cantons, or provinces accord to their local authorities. Questions of efficiency and equality will be complicated by three tiers, and federal governments commonly find redistributive policies even more difficult to handle than do unitary governments. State governments may compete with city governments for federal funds and the right to allocate them, and complex intergovernmental problems of co-ordination, as in the United States, may be even more troublesome than in unitary states. Another version of federalism, however, is the West German model with its horizontal division of powers between a law-making centre and implementing *laender*. This was not the result of intergration but of conscious decentralization. Although Rod Rhodes surmises that the stage has probably been reached at which federalism has no distinct meaning,[56] it would seem that all versions of it are characterized by territorial divisions of the state into large units with considerable powers. The second tier is thus provided with an alternative focus of identity that can never be possessed by small units of local government.

Opponents of decentralization, devolution, and federalism would normally be found among either centralizing egalitarians or centralizing technocrats. The egalitarians argue that the democratic state must carry out the wishes of the democratic majority, and if that majority wants a redistribution of national resources (as it commonly does, in spite of a recent inegalitarian surge), then this must be done uniformly and in relation to economic and socio-demographic categories (the poor, widows, children etc.), not geographic areas of the country. Thus any attempts to devolve powers of economic intervention would be inegalitarian. Hence the conviction that 'we would be better making our own decisions' is often based on the view that the improvement will be in material conditions, though other gains may be cultural realization and a more identifiable 'sub-national' character. Often equality and efficiency are associated as sub-national groups tend to be geographically peripheral. Arguments for equality between regions, however, hardly strengthen the case for centralized democracy as democracy is a priori neutral between equality and inequality (see Chapter 5). The degree of equality within a democratic polity is a matter for it to determine by democratic process. Where a polity has decided by the normal procedures that benefits shall be universal to certain categories of people, considerations of territorial equality cannot be entertained without distorting the democratic decisions. If, for example, it were decided to award social benefits to each region on a per capita basis irrespective of economic and socio-demographic variations between the regions, the result would inevitably be inegalitarian; and if the regions were allowed to set up their own scales of old-age pensions or family allowances there

---

[56] R. A. W. Rhodes, *Control and Power in Central–Local Government Relations* (1981), 77.

would be inequality between similar categories in different regions. In either instance many would argue that the outcomes were either unjust or inefficient or both.

The technocratic objections to decentralization relate to considerations of efficiency. Planning is normally a centralized, and centralizing, process because it requires control over political subunits. Control from the centre, however, as we have noted, does not necessarily rule out some administrative decentralization, and for some purposes this may be deemed more efficient—especially if it is not involved with local representative institutions. National economic policies such as demand management may have an inequitable impact as between regions. Regional economic policies may set out to compensate regional inequalities by state action. Thus 'regionalism' has become a technocratic concept, involving the creation of intermediate bodies between central government and local government purely for purposes of economic planning. Vincent Wright describes how the French planners under the Fifth Republic, realizing that the 90 *départements* were inadequate even for consultative purposes in 1958, grouped them in 22 *circonscriptions d'action regionale* with a co-ordinating prefect in each to co-operate with a local regional expansion committee. Each had a small think-tank, a *commission de developpement économique regional* (CODER). He says of the latter that they were 'quickly colonised by traditional elites and economic decision-making was not rationalised but anchored in the time-honoured system of inter-departmental bartering.'[57] Later, in 1972, the regions were clearly designated public, and not local, authorities, though the CODERS were replaced by regional councils and economic and social committees. Thus triumphed the opponents of radical regional reform. These were local traditional élites who dominated regional decision-making and ensured that incrementalism based on bargaining between the *départements* prevailed over a rational distribution of resources based on regional needs; technocrats belonging to Paris-based technical corps whose appointments preceded the advent of regionalism; and the prefects whose power had been progressively eroded by the rise of both technocracy and regionalism.[58] Its supporters were the new economic élites created

[57] V. Wright, Regionalisation under the French Fifth Republic: the Triumph of the Functional Approach, in Sharpe (ed.), *Decentralist Trends in Western Democracies*, 198 ff.   [58] Ibid. 209.

by rapid industrialization in the 1950s who wanted government support for investment and public works. They secured the support of the Planning Commissariat in Paris, which argued for greater rationality through economies of scale derived from larger units.

The main point about all these innovations is that though they modified the decision-making structure they were little to do with democracy. The communists and socialists, with their Jacobin tradition of centralization, were initially opposed. But the new Socialist Party, reformed in 1971, changed tack and became committed to the election of regional councillors. Yet both parties, Wright comments, continue to perceive regional democracy within a centralized model. He believes that political decentralization alone can legitimize local planning decisions, but neither the old notables nor the new functionalist entrepreneurs are willing to support it: 'Functional regionalism has triumphed and regionalism based on effective political decentralization has failed.'[59] It is too early yet to assess whether the Mitterrand reforms of 1981–3 have resulted in either effective decentralization or more efficient local planning.[60]

It does not follow, however, that decentralized economic planning is inconsistent with democracy. Franz Lehner suggests that 'in federalist countries with a high degree of inter-governmental co-operation and bargaining, the load of organised demands on government can be reduced'. Certainly in the Swiss case a rather high growth rate was not vitiated by complex consociational and direct democracy.[61] Efficiency and regional democracy can coincide. Again, West Germany seems to have discovered such a formula, owing to uniformity of law and policy-making at the centre, with a diffusion of responsibility for detailed economic policy-making in the *laender*. Nevil Johnson[62] explains this success of decentralization by local government's commitment to efficient provision of services, consistent with the German tradition of municipal autonomy and initiative. As a result participation is high.

[59] Ibid. 224.

[60] See Y. Meny, Decentralisation in Socialist France, *West European Politics*, 7 (1984), 65 ff., and M. Kesselman, The End of Jacobinism? The Socialist Regime and Decentralisation, *Journal of Regional Policy*, 2 (1985), 179.

[61] F. Lehner, Pressure Politics and Economic Growth: Olson's Theory and the Swiss Experience, in D. C. Mueller (ed.), *The Political Economy of Growth* (1983), 213.

[62] N. Johnson, Some Effects of Decentralisation in the Federal Republic of Germany, in Sharpe, *Decentralist Trends in Western Democracies*, 244.

Politicians often start their careers in local government, making their names in *laender* politics before going on to federal politics.

Regional development policy may be relatively successful when the localities are concerned with the detailed decisions. Similar success seems to have attended the evolution of Norwegian municipalities,[63] which had no significant part in national plans for regional development until the late 1970s. Change occurred when the central government began financing local development officers and fishing and agriculture advisers to co-operate with local mayors and councils. They provided what Tarrow calls a 'technocracy of the base'[64] with an expertise to exploit organizational programmes and the confidence to be firm with 'technocracy at the centre'. Thus the political entrepreneurship of the mayors, linked with the expertise of the local technocrats, produced a successful decentralized local economic investment policy.

To sum up: the urge for decentralization is for the most part a reaction to the centralizing tendencies of the contemporary world. Whether it is a democratic reaction or not will depend on the circumstances. Decentralizers are not necessarily democrats even when they press for regional self-determination: decentralization may be a device of planners for more effective economic management of regional investment policies. Such a development may not be democratic and may not even be efficient. Yet there is evidence that both more efficiency and a healthier democracy may sometimes result from some forms of decentralization.

Conclusion

This chapter has been concerned with two questions: the nature of central–local relations in contemporary industrialized democracies, and the implications of it for the democratic process. Without some understanding of the former, approaches to the latter are hardly likely to be profitable.

The difficulties of assessing the extent of centralization are many. The term, as I indicated at the beginning, has at least three components. Moreover, trends clearly vary as between one democracy

[63] H. O. Larsen, Local Development Activity in Norway: A Policy from Below. Paper given to the 12th International Political Science Association conference, 1982.
[64] S. Tarrow, P. J. Katzenstein and L. Graziano, (eds.), *Territorial Politics in Industrial Nations* (New York, 1978), 16.

and another. Furthermore, one's comparative perspective will be affected by the time-scale one adopts.

In terms of administration there can be little doubt that there is a trend in all democracies towards greater centralization. This can be confirmed by asking questions related to six dimensions of central–local relations. If we ask who pays, the answer must be that more and more local services are paid by central government. If we enquire who delivers the services, then the answers vary greatly from country to country. There has been a tendency, however, for either central government or centralized quasi-governmental bodies to deliver more services, though the *volume* of services administered by local governments may well have increased. This may explain why the answer to whether it is central or local government that has proportionately increased its numbers of public servants is generally that it is local government. A larger proportion of local government servants are currently employed delivering national services through the channels of local government (e.g. education). Fourthly, if we ask how much central governments prescribe standards and lay down conditions, we find that almost everywhere they do so increasingly. Even in the federal United States, in all these instances the emphasis has been towards centralization.

The fifth and sixth questions are more fundamental: who has final jurisdiction over local authorities' fields of action and who makes the policies created by local government? Taking these two questions together reveals the problems of making an assessment: final jurisdiction and legal and constitutional position may not always be very enlightening indicators of the ultimate sources of power. Clearly central government must exert final sanctions over local government, except under federalism where the states, provinces, or cantons have entrenched powers subject to some overall legal authority such as a Supreme Court. So it is difficult to estimate to what degree local governments have retained scope either for initiating their own local policies or modifying central government's policies.

Here another dimension of centralization enters into the reckoning. The growth of the welfare state, which as we shall see was brought about partly by democratic pressures (Chapter 5), has given central government many more functions and led to a proliferation of public services and their bureaucracies. In many democracies local government has been called upon to assist in running these services at the local level, in the process becoming an instrument of central government. Henry Schmandt and John Goldbach saw American local government moving from the 'political city' through the 'administrative city' to the 'dependent city'.[65] Local government's chief function has become one of relieving the strain on overloaded central government. It also provides a useful coordinating function at the local level for services which are, in their origins, national. It is practicality and efficiency, rather than democracy, that tends to be the rationale of local government systems.

From a historical perspective this is scarcely surprising because, as I have observed before, modern nation-states did not begin as democracies. Local administration, as national, preceded the advent of democracy, after which representative institutions at the central level became the salient feature of the political scene. Indeed, in some democracies there was no popular clamour for representative local democracy, which tended to be advocated on abstract, intellectual grounds. Prominent exceptions to this can be found where the idea of local democracy had an earlier legitimacy and a more popular basis as in the United States though, as I have noted, local government even there has been subjected to centralizing pressures from the states.

Hence there lies at the heart of the subject a permanent ambiguity, as Sharpe has so cogently argued: 'local government is subordinate to central or senior government, but at the same time has the potential for independent power because it is elected, derives part of its revenue from its own tax, and employs its own staff'.[66] Local councils have many of the attributes of democratic legislatures and they are responsible to local voters, but at the same time they are accountable to central government. Smith does not greatly exaggerate the position in many countries when he writes: 'Local democracy can offer the appearance of self-determination without its substance.'[67] Local democratic institutions are no guarantee of local autonomy.

In fact, national public opinion, as we have observed, has often been indifferent to local autonomy. The pressure from nation-wide

[65] H. J. Schmandt and J. C. Goldbach, The Urban Paradox, in H. J. Schmandt and W. Bloomberg, Jun. (ed.), *The Quality of Urban Life* (Beverley Hills, 1969), 493.

[66] L. J. Sharpe, Is There a Fiscal Crisis in Western European Local Government?, *International Political Science Review*, 1 2 (1980), 203.

[67] Smith, *Decentralisation*, 195.

majorities for both efficiency and equality has often led to the erosion of local independence. Bureaucratic criteria often lead to greater centralization: the assumption that efficiency and largeness of scale are related seems ineradicably prevalent. Again, the pursuit of egalitarian and standardizing measures has frequently resulted in local government losing functions and powers. National majorities, it is difficult to refute, should normally outweigh local majorities. Moreover, the former will decide when exceptions to the rule can be permitted.

Indeed, if efficiency and equality militate against local autonomy, it is pertinent to enquire whether local autonomy or 'localism' is a necessary democratic value, or merely a romantic notion as Fesler maintains? Is democracy weakened where local identification with local politics is weak? Would democracy be endangered where, after long and informed discussion, a majority of citizens voted to abolish local governments? Does sub-system government bolster what I have indicated are the necessary components of democracy—public contestation, inclusiveness, the rule of law, and governmental responsibility?

There is no way in which these questions can be answered authoritatively, and clearly the position will vary in time and place. Not infrequently local values may run contrary to democratic values; indeed, demands for more local autonomy may stem from undemocratic impulses. Populist separatism may be intolerant and disorderly. Public contestation may be more difficult in such circumstances in the local, rather than the national, contest. On the other hand, it is difficult not to accept that possibilities of participating in political discussion and decision-making are much greater at the local level. The issues may be more familiar, and there are more opportunities for many amateur politicians—retired people and women in particular—to give some time to the community. It can be a training ground for younger politicians, who quite frequently begin their careers on local councils where they learn many of the skills and roles they will need later in national legislatures. In Britain, local government increasingly has become a springboard from which aspiring politicians launch themselves into national politics.[68] In such ways, local representative democracy provides supports for national representative democracy.

[68] J. Gyford and M. James, *Political Parties and Central–Local Relations: Initial Impressions*. Paper given to Political Science Association conference, 1980, p. 8.

Yet John Stuart Mill's hope for British local democracy has scarcely been realized.[69] It has not educated local citizens and enriched local life in the way nineteenth-century liberals anticipated it would. Its main task has become that of co-ordinating at a local level numerous programmes devised by central government, which as Sharpe points out, in Britain is not by nature or tradition an operational authority.[70] The upward accountability of local government (except in federations to province, canton, or state), is to central government, downward accountability being democratically to the electorate. British local government in particular must be regarded as an example of considerable responsibility yoked to limited power.

This may explain why many British local councillors are not unduly worried about relinquishing functions to the centre. Especially in lower-tier units, elected representatives have been only too pleased to rid themselves of responsibilities which have become too awkward.[71] Moreover, local electorates, in spite of their protestations of local patriotism, may know very little about who runs what. There is much evidence to suggest that what British voters care about is the amount and efficiency of services; and that they have difficulty in distinguishing the outputs of central government disbursed by local field agencies from those of local government administered by a locally elected council.[72] All the outputs may be perceived by the voters as emanating from an indeterminate and remote 'them', an impression enhanced by the similarity of the two bureaucracies inhabiting similar blocks of offices and dispensing attentions with like impersonality.

Consequently, the responsibility of local governments to local electorates may sometimes be a farce. Where the voters cannot distinguish the impacts of local government actions from those of central government, they will not be able to reward or penalize their local representatives appropriately. If they are provoked to

[69] J. S. Mill, *Representative Government* (people's edn. 1886), 112 ff.

[70] L. J. Sharpe, Theories and Values of Local Government, *Political Studies,* 18 2 (1970), 167.

[71] For example, there was little or no organised opposition from local councillors to the abolition of the Scottish small burghs. See Bealey and Sewel, *The Politics of Independence,* 255 and Michael Dyer, The Politics of Kincardineshire, Ph.D. thesis (Aberdeen, 1973), 1135.

[72] M. Horton, *The Local Government Elector* (1966). Enquiry carried out by Government Social Survey for the Committee on Management in Local Government (Maud Committee).

vote, and many are not, they may not do so very meaningfully. On the other hand, even if the voters are well informed about the provenance of polices, they may still vote to punish or reward local governments according to their view of the record of the central government. Thus the true protestations of a local council majority that the central government is to blame for a rise in municipal rents may fall on deaf ears, and the voters may then demonstrate their displeasure with the central government by voting against the incumbent council. It is difficult to discern anything even approximating to a mandate emerging from many local elections.

No democratic theorists would be likely to quarrel with Saunders's assertion that the present state of central–local relations in democracies has generated a new tension between the principles of rational planning and democratic accountability.[73] This tension, noted in Chapter 3, exists because the majority of citizens will not always be motivated by a desire for rationality and efficiency. As Sharpe warns 'we cannot assume that enhancing system capacity is preferred by the majority of citizens to the accessibility of government, the accountability of that government, the sense of community within the given polity'.[74] When the rationalizers produce polices that are not rational, however, the assumption becomes even more suspect. Sharpe demonstrates how British local government reorganization had two functional emphases—the city–hinterland thesis and economies of scale—both of which have since proved to be dysfunctional. He concludes: 'At the heart of the matter it is that it is just as important for local government to be democratic as it is to be functionally efficient.'[75] Whether it is 'just as important' or 'even more important' is clearly a value judgement.

Local government cannot be properly democratic unless it is accountable to some degree. This further depends on its capacity to tax its citizens and on their willingness to prefer taxing themselves to losing their local representative institutions. Thus in the last resort it is the value judgements of citizens and their support for local autonomy which determine the character of the local democratic process. Demands for local autonomy, moreover, may either spring from a sense of regional or local cultural identity or be raised

[73] Saunders, Why Study Central–Local Relations? *Local Government Studies* (1982), 60. See also his *Urban Politics* (1979).
[74] L. J. Sharpe, The Failure of Local Government Modernization in Britain: A Critique of Functionalism, *Canadian Public Administration*, 24 1 (1981), 106.
[75] Ibid. 114.

by certain individuals, such as local businessmen, who feel it is to their economic advantage. Whatever the case, local autonomy is a value independent of local democracy, though where the two have long been associated they may be perceived as fused together. In this latter case the stronger the sense of local identity, the more likely people are to want to retain their local democracy.

The cry of local autonomy may often be raised when democratic governments impose uniform standards. Democracy encourages, indeed guarantees, diversity of expression, but not diversity of action. Ed Page illustrates how, because local government autonomy in Britain is seen as a 'good thing', British oppositions are always using it as a stick to beat centralizing governments.[76] But British governments of all ideological complexions have worried little about depriving local government of its powers. Moreover, local autonomy may not be perceived as important by either local politicians or voters. Indeed, Page suggests, in Britain it is held in cultural disdain.[77] Majorities in many democratic electorates may prefer standardization and feel little regret over the ironing out of local idiosyncracies. Rationalization and efficiency imposed by central authority may sometimes be the voters' preference. So much will depend on how they view the balance of advantage and disadvantage.

In one sense there can be no dispute that centralization has greatly increased in all democracies. The scope of governmental activity has been extended to wider and wider areas of national life. Technocratic and bureaucratic needs as well as egalitarian pressures have been at the roots of this development, as we have observed. The results have often, though not always, been what the majority has usually desired—larger outputs of services and more equity in distribution of benefits. As against this the extension of government intervention has vastly proliferated the complexities of government and led to decentralization in another sense—the tautness of control from the centre has suffered. Slackness and elaboration of governmental structures have provided many opportunities for the exercise of local power through consultation, bargaining, and political pressure. These trends have been evident since the nineteenth century though subject to periodic fluctuation.

[76] E. Page, The Value of Local Autonomy, *Local Government Studies*, 8 (1982), 23 ff.
[77] Ibid. 37.

Decentralist forces have had some success in times of prosperity when the national cake was expanding and there was a scramble for slices, with the government as slicer having problems of controlling allocation. When recession looms, as from 1973 onwards, with a contracting cake, the slicer has much more power. But there is no general rule determining the degree of efficiency of central control. A well-known organizational theorist says that the solution to the question of how much centralization there should be is a matter of finding the optimum degree of centralization/decentralization.[78] Each case should be decided on its merits.

What are the implications of these tendencies for democracy? It has been argued that local democracy might not be needed.[79] It is not necessary, within any democracy, for all associational forms to be democratic. The degree of oligarchy or democracy is fundamentally a matter for them to decide. Would it necessarily be detrimental for a large democratic state to abolish its local representative institutions and operate through local field agencies? Might this not be a solution for Britain, where local government has roused little enthusiasm among the voters? The local government system has never been an issue at any general election and has remained a matter on which British governments have made decisions on grounds of political expediency, conventional technocratic wisdom, and administrative convenience.

The answer must surely be that there are several reasons why it would be damaging for a democratic state to abolish local democracy. One, already mentioned, is its function as a training ground for national politics.[80] This is important though hardly compelling in itself. A second is the impact such a decision would make upon the functioning of national representative institutions. It could hardly fail to evoke a feeling that *all* the nation's democratic procedures were threatened. A disjuncture between a national democracy and a local autocracy could ultimately be demoralizing. Thirdly, local democratic politics should contribute to the vitality of the participatory process throughout the nation. Unfortunately this is

---

[78] M. Z. Brooke, *Centralization and Autonomy* (1984), 166.

[79] G. Langrod, Local Government and Democracy, *Public Administration*, 1 (1953), 25.

[80] Bealey *et al.*, *Constituency Politics*, 407; M. Parkinson, Central–Local Relations in British Parties: A Local View, *Political Studies* 19 (1971), 440; C. Mellors, Local Government in Parliament: Twenty Years Later, *Public Administration*, 52 (1974), 223.

not always evident. Elsewhere I have written of participatory local democracy in Britain being a failure,[81] but there are countries where turn-out at local elections exceeds turn-out at national elections.

A final judgement might be that local government of some kind, even if it is not local democracy, is an essential part of any large state. It is not practical for the modern democratic state to do without local government, and difficult for it not to imbue local government with the paraphernalia of representative democracy. Whether a local government system, once inaugurated, should have a more centralized or a more decentralized, structure is likely to depend much more on administrative considerations than on democratic principles. Where popular pressures result in more decentralization, perhaps regional autonomy, local participatory democracy seems more likely to flourish. In many democracies, however, locally elected councils do not have the jurisdiction to undertake important local decisions, which often result from secret bargaining with central government. This is merely another factor weakening the accountability of local government to local voters. But most of them may not strongly desire more accountability. They may prefer more local autonomy, or more equality, or more efficiency and central control, at the price of less accountability. The option in these terms has, of course, never been put to any of them.

[81] Bealey and Sewel, *The Politics of Independence*, 252.

5

EQUALITY, DEMOCRACY, AND THE DISTRIBUTIVE PROCESS

AT first sight, equality seems to be one of the simplest concepts—much simpler than democracy. It has a quantitative connotation. Equal means equal. As Sartori says, the notion of equality is much more intelligible than that of liberty.[1]

To some, equality and democracy are almost synonymous. It is assumed that countries with democratic institutions will either be egalitarian or striving towards less inequality. In such contexts, 'democratic' is used as an adjective to describe situations where differences of hierarchy and status are not emphasized. It is especially prone to be used in this way in the United States. In another sense, 'democracy' goes back to Aristotle who used it to describe a polity in which the ordinary people were in power (and did not govern for the common good). Aristotle regarded social and economic egalitarianism rather disapprovingly, but he did acknowledge a clear connection between the rule of the demos and equality.

Democracy as I have defined it, however, except in one important respect, is not *necessarily* more predisposed to equality than to inequality. The exception is civic and legal equality. Universal suffrage guarantees a right of participation in decision-making at the minimal level. The rule of law, freedom of the person, and freedom of expression should ensure that citizenship rights are possessed by all. Although these civic liberties may be dismissed by some egalitarians as screens behind which all kind of inequalities are preserved, it needs to be stressed that they are not equalities found in every time and place. On the contrary, even in democratic countries they represent hard-won gains, the outcome of struggles in some cases for centuries. In 1647, during the Putney Debates within the Cromwellian Army, the Leveller leader, Colonel Rainboro, demanding manhood suffrage, said: 'the poorest he that is in England hath a life to live as the richest he'.[2] This

---

[1] G. Sartori, *Democratic Theory* (1962), 328.
[2] Quoted in A. D. Lindsay, *The Essentials of Democracy* (1929), 12.

counter-claim against unequal civil rights was later promoted by the Chartists in the nineteenth century, but not acknowledged fully until the twentieth. In fact, equal rights of citizenship are too recent an acquisition for their success or failure as instruments for the furtherance of other equalities to be assessed with great precision.

Naturally, democracy has been sought after, where it did not exist, by those who hoped that it could be used for egalitarian purposes. As the poor, more underprivileged people always outnumbered greatly the rich and privileged, this was not a foolish expectation. Certainly the well-off minority anticipated the extension of the suffrage with apprehension, the most fearful of them expecting arbitrary confiscation. This did not happen; and although it may seem a fair inference that democracy has led to a less unequal distribution of resources, the proposition is not universally accepted. While Gerhard Lenski saw the advent of democracy as the most important factor making for greater social and economic equality,[3] Robert Jackman, consciously refuting him, argued that both democracy and the decline of great inequality are the results of economic development.[4] Christopher Hewitt's findings suggested tentatively that the more democracy a country experienced, the less inequality it would condone.[5] Whatever the case, and it is not a matter for argument here, there seems to be no necessary association between democracy and equality.

Indeed, democratic countries could theoretically be concerned with promoting greater inequality, while authoritarian states might be ruled by autocrats determined to make everyone exactly equal. And this is not far-fetched. It can certainly be argued that there is greater economic equality in the Soviet Union than in the United States; and we have numerous contemporary examples of democratic countries where the majority of the electorate seem to have opted for greater inequality, or less equality. I say 'seem' because most of the majority apparently choosing greater inequality might want 'more equality' with the few rich though 'less equality' with the

---

[3] G. Lenski, *Power and Privilege* (1966), 428 ff.

[4] R. W. Jackman, *Politics and Social Equality* (1975), 74 ff.

[5] C. Hewitt, The Effect of Political Democracy and Social Democracy on Equality in Industrial Societies: A Cross-National Comparison, *American Sociological Review*, 42 (1977), 450. Franz Kraus, in The Historical Development of Income Inequality in P. Flora and A. J. Heidenheimer, *The Development of Welfare States in Europe and America* (1981) also supports this, arguing that Jackman used an unreliable inequality indicator.

more numerous poor. Equality with whom? is often an appropriate query.

Thus equality is not at all the simple concept which it might at first sight appear to be. When we say 'all men are equal', we are not implying, Benn and Peters argue, that they possess some attribute or attributes in the same degree, but that they ought to be treated alike.[6] How are we to understand the expression 'more equality', enquires Sartori?[7] There are numerous kinds of equality, and he suggests greater equality may be attained by balancing inequalities against each other. Hence people with more wealth may be accorded less power. Equality of what? is another pertinent question.[8]

Democracy and 'Fair Shares'

Yet even if equality is an obscure and scarcely obtainable objective, there can be little doubt that egalitarianism in some form is a feature of all democratic societies. The belief that a democratic society can, or should, be more equal remains a fairly salient feature of many citizens' thinking. Equity may be commonly accepted as a principle even if equality is regarded as unattainable and impractical. 'Fair shares' may be a virtually meaningless slogan; nevertheless it is often a powerful feature of the rhetoric of democratic politicians. Arguments about the unequal division of wealth, status, and power are the stock-in-trade of most democratic political parties, as well as a subject of vigorous debate among social scientists. Let us first examine the distribution of wealth in its relations to the democratic process.

Suppose national material resources are represented by the proverbial cake and the citizenry by nine people—a family of five and a family of four. How effectively would democratic processes resolve the problem of dividing up the cake? We must rule out four of Brian Barry's social decision procedures. Combat, contest, lottery, and authoritative determination all would lead to renunciation of the democratic process. This leaves bargaining, discussion, and some method of voting.[9]

[6] S. I. Benn and R. S. Peters, *Social Principles and the Democratic State* (1959), 108.   [7] Sartori, *Democratic Theory*, 342.

[8] For a treatment of the principles of allocation and equality see F. Oppenheim, *Political Concepts* (Chicago, 1981), 96 ff.

[9] B. Barry, *Political Argument* (1965), 85 ff.

John Rawls in his *Theory of Justice*[10] writes that the obvious solution is for the one who divides the cake to have the last slice, the others having chosen before him. But this assumes that the fair division is an equal one, and that there is an agreement about who should do the slicing. Rawls is concerned with a just, rather than a democratic, society. In most democratic societies the majority of people will not be imbued with Rawlsian ethics, and their ideas of equity and fairness are likely to be influenced by their own claims to limited resources and their ideas about the validity of others' claims. They will tend to perceive everyone else as motivated by rather selfish motives, whether or not they recognize their own selfishness. They will not think their vision is obscured by a 'veil of ignorance'.

Hence when the subject is the distribution of a material resource, a discussion on the merits of the case is hardly likely to result in unanimous acclaim of the morally right, or fairest solution. There would need to be a decision about criteria to be regarded as merits. The hungriest, or most hard-working, or oldest, or youngest, it might be argued, deserve larger shares. After this there might be another stage in which it was discussed whether there should be equal shares in the favoured category. Whether these arguments were accepted or not might depend on the relationships between the people involved and how well they were able to assess the validity of the claims. It would also depend on how altruistic or selfish they were. It would be a matter both of values and information.

Perhaps the eventual course would depend on how much family ties were dominant. If no other consideration weighed and if they were rational egoists, the family of five would quickly want to resort to majority voting so that they could outvote the family of four and obtain all the cake for themselves. (After which similar difficulties of sharing might arise within the family.) The family of four, if they anticipated this might happen, would argue against any sort of voting unless it were one in which one individual–one vote did not appertain. Perhaps they might argue that each family should have a block vote of one, thus resulting in a stalemate.

If family ties were weaker, however, the argument might continue for a long time. The family of four, thinking they were about to be outvoted by the five, might buy off one of the five

[10] J. Rawls, *A Theory of Justice* (Harvard, 1971), 85.

by offering the defector a bigger slice of the cake. This sort of coalition-building might go on for some time. For example, if the family of five had previously agreed to 20 per cent each, the family of four might offer a 24 per cent share of cake to the one of the five with the weakest family feeling and take 19 per cent each themselves. While the potential defector is considering the offer his own family will offer him a 25 per cent share to retain his support, reconciling themselves to an 18.75 per cent share each. Such a process might go on almost indefinitely, producing the cycles of bargaining without outcome described by David Mueller.[11] Faced with the prospect of endless haggling about what is only a very small material resource, the costs of time and nervous energy might persuade the participators that some simple settlement, such as equal slices, was a sensible compromise. On the other hand it might not, and decision-making by combat might ensue. It would depend most of all on the interrelationships of the parties concerned: how much they trusted each other; how much they had learnt from their bargainings; and how much imagination they could bring to solving the problem.

The example of the cake may seem simple and like a laboratory situation in that it postulates no outside factors. But it can, in fact, be applied to the position of a whole society. For instance, if a macro-democracy were really dividing up a cake, whatever the proportions decided everyone would receive only an invisible crumb, so no one would worry about the principles employed or the outcomes. With benefits and costs negligible, what James Q. Wilson calls 'majoritarian politics' would ensue.[12] Again, where a society has many groups constantly engaged with arguing about benefits for large numbers of people so that the process becomes institutionalized, the outcomes may well be incremental changes for everyone, though the procedure will be facilitated if the aggregate of resources becomes slightly larger all the time. (This implies some economic growth.) But where one large indivisible public good is to be allocated, for example an airport, aluminium smelter, or nuclear power station, we are faced with a zero-sum game. At least a cake can be sliced, but here we have 'winner takes all'.

In such cases the decision is likely to be political, but it is unlikely that most democratic governments would entrust it to a majority

[11] D. C. Mueller, *Public Choice* (Cambridge, 1979), 38 ff.
[12] J. Q. Wilson, *The Politics of Regulation* (New York, 1986), 367.

vote. Authoritative allocation based partly on geographic and economic factors—for instance, an aluminium smelter is best sited on a deep water inlet—would be applied. Argument behind the scenes might be intense, and political factors would be bound to loom large. It is said that when the Beeching cuts on British Rail were first mooted, a perceptive civil servant noted that some of them affected marginal constituencies held by the government.[13] These railway lines were reprieved. Again, the fear of offending voters in certain areas may lead to uneconomic sharing of public goods between one part of the country and another. This is merely another illustration of how little democracy has to do with efficiency. An often-quoted example is that of the Labour government in 1969 which was so concerned to win a by-election at Hull that it offered the bribe of the Humber Bridge.[14] Though the bridge has since proved to be very costly, the by-election was won. But equity may have little part in such decisions either. Where decisions are made in order to win marginal constituencies by allocating large public investment to them, the outcomes will seem unfair to supporters of the government in other constituencies possessing majorities so strong that they do not need to be placated.

To sum up: there are some fundamental facts about democratic redistribution derivable from the parable of the cake. Firstly, where there are two different groups whose corporate interests are entirely in conflict, democratic dialogue cannot properly begin. If democratic decision-making is imposed upon a society so divided, the majority group will constantly outvote the minority group on every issue. In these circumstances democracy cannot develop. The situation mirrors that in countries where ethnic, cultural, and religious divisions cause great distrust. Unfair sharing of public goods is a likely concomitant of such dichotomy exemplified in polities like Northern Ireland, Zimbabwe, and Sri Lanka.[15] Public disorder and civil war are not unlikely outcomes of such situations if federal or consociational solutions cannot be adopted.

Secondly, it demonstrates that where a body of individuals, whether in alliances or not, are given the task of sharing resources among themselves, and where there is no clear majority, they are

---

[13] R. Crossman, *The Diaries of a Cabinet Minister,* iii (1975), 603.
[14] Ibid. 449.
[15] This phenomenon is best dealt with in A. Rabushka and K. A. Shepsle, *Politics in Plural Societies: A Theory of Democratic Instability* (Columbus, 1972). In my opinion this is a grossly neglected book.

likely to be plunged into time-consuming haggling. Discussion on the merits of the case is likely to be transformed into manœuvrings about the criteria, each party concerned either with producing criteria to suit its own case or with manipulating the terms of the given criteria to its own advantage. Consequently the assumption that satisfactory outcomes are likely to emerge from democratic discussion about allocation where rules and principles are laid down may lead to even more frustration. (This was the experience of wage-bargaining in the British civil service's Whitley Councils in the 1950s.)[16] Bargaining implies uncertainty, with neither side knowing the strategy and expectations of the other. If one side is informed about the other in this way it will be at a great advantage. If it is misinformed it will be at a great disadvantage. Bargaining thus puts a premium on espionage, bluffs, and threats: whether one is contending for a slice of cake or for a piece of legislation, these same features prevail. Ed Lindblom, however, sees it as one form of 'partisan mutual adjustment', the process by which people in disagreement resolve their differences. He writes that 'coping with value conflicts is built into the very model of the process. In the face of conflicts over the proper weights to be given value, the various devices of partisan mutual adjustment bring participants to decisions or resultant policies.'[17] Most bargaining will end in a decision embodying rough-and-ready justice.

Thirdly, although macro-democracy is concerned with large collectivities—electorates, legislatures, political parties, etc.—some decisions will be taken by a few people at the top. Maurice Duverger sees of the two levels of political analysis: the macro-political, dealing with group relationships, and the micro-political, dealing with relations on the individual plane. At the micro-political level—in ministerial committees, in administrative committees, in the executive committees of political parties[18]—the type of manœuvring we have noted affecting the slicing of the cake may well apply. Let us turn then from abstraction to distribution in the real world of large-scale democracy.

Distribution by the Market

The most common method of acquiring wealth in democratic

---

[16] An example of this can be found in Frank Bealey, *The Post Office Engineering Union* (1976), 310 ff.

[17] C. E. Lindblom, *The Intelligence of Democracy* (New York, 1965), 240.

[18] M. Duverger, *The Idea of Politics* (1966), p. x.

societies is through the sale of one's labour. Market allocation existed long before the advent of democracy and wage levels have been political issues in all types of regime, but under competitive capitalism wages should be fixed by individual contract between employer and worker and, therefore, external intervention should not enter into it. The higgling of the labour market then reflects competition among workers for jobs and among employers for workers. Ideally, perfect information is a condition of perfect competition. In fact, with numerous small employers all bidding for labour and others wanting to enter the market at the first opportunity, it will be very difficult to know what is going on. Luck and access to information may be the basis of success. But uncertainty is regarded as the price one pays for an economic system supposed to produce the largest aggregate wealth. Wage-earners who believe that inequality is inevitable under every system may accept capitalism because it provides a larger cake with potentially bigger slices for everyone, including the prospect of disproportionately larger slices for themselves. The people with the smallest slices may feel their undeservedly low rewards are part of the unfathomable operation of the market. It is all a lottery like life itself, and nothing can be done about it. Conversely, other people may blame their own deficiencies for their low material rewards and not the system.

Competitive capitalism, however, as far as it ever existed (for perfect competition is really an economist's ideal model), essentially pre-dated democracy, going back to the period when there was a political economy where the masters held political power and the workers had none. Adam Smith was aware of this when writing in the eighteenth century, of workers' predicaments in a strike when all the magistrates were employers.[19] Political leadership, at that time, could escape blame for economic conditions because it was not held responsible for them. Once an extended franchise arrived, workers began to combine for both economic and political action. Poltical leaders, forced to bid for workers' support, could not easily escape commitments to improve industrial conditions. Thus state intervention in the market, including the labour market, became part of a new political economy associated with democracy.

Of course, payment for labour is only part of any economic system. Competitive capitalism provided wider markets for goods and services. Consumer sovereignty ensured that sellers had to

[19] A. Smith, *The Wealth of Nations* (1776), 74.

respond to buyers' preferences: thus there is a certain parallel between a totally competitive market and democracy. In practice, however, consumer pressures have never had anything like the force of producer pressures. Markets are far too differentiated and consumers' tastes too variegated for consumers to have become organized forces. Occasionally democratic governments have introduced price control; but in general it is on the production side of the economy that governments have intervened and affected people's shares.

In contemporary democracies many goods and services are still allocated by the price mechanism, though it is not as flexible as it was. The capitalist system has changed. With corporate capitalism (as I shall call it), concentrations of capital dominate some markets. Large oligopolistic corporations fix prices and compete in terms of product quality. They often plan years ahead so that great emphasis is placed on research and development. Hence corporate capitalism is organizational, rather than individualistic. The consumer may still exercise considerable sovereignty: exactly how much is a matter of some dispute. (There is a good deal of evidence to suggest that it is impossible to persuade consumers to buy a product they dislike.) On the other hand, among brands which differ only slightly the consumer may be guided by advertising. Unlike competitive capitalism, where information is hard to come by, though complete information is essential to the perfect market of the model, corporate capitalism provides a vast mass of information about a smaller number of choices for the consumer. Unfortunately some of it is misinformation.

The great corporations with large bureaucracies often operate on an international basis, and the scope of their activities is such that they can affect national and even international economic life. The general ethos they provide is one of stability, though of less opportunity. It has become more difficult for any individual entrepreneur to enter any market dominated by the corporations. The obverse of this is that there are fewer risks, though sudden price hikes may, as in the 1970s, result in consumers having less goods unless they increase their incomes. The policy changes caused by large corporations' activities force governments to advise and to consult them. Reciprocally, such corporations must be concerned about changes in governments' economic policies.

The distribution of wages under corporate capitalism usually operates through collective bargaining between organizations of employers and trade unions. One of the primary features of the bargaining situation is that the outcome is unpredictable. Large-scale collective bargaining is especially so. The employer's disposition to reward each worker according to his view of the worker's merit has to give way to collective determination in which numbers, organizing skills, and the threat to withdraw labour are all factors. Standardization of wage rates may threaten the weakest employers and at the same time subsidize the laziest or least efficient workers. The results of collective bargaining are the outcomes of conflicting oligarchic hierarchies within a mixed economy. The uncertainties of the process inject unpredictability into the political power pattern as well as into the economy. Where the democratic state is the employer, as in the public services, the process is inevitably partly political.

Perhaps one might still exaggerate the number of wage settlements arrived at as a result of collective bargaining. It varies in proportion to the degree of trade-union organization of the labour force: in the United States it is 19 per cent and in Sweden 84 per cent. Yet for the most part it is the largest, most modern, industries which settle wages in this way, and it is extremely likely that collective bargaining will become the most common method of awarding wages in contemporary democracies. Indeed, in one non-democratic state with a centrally directed economy and a one-party system, Poland, it recently nearly acquired the same importance. In Britain, national collective bargaining in two large industries, coal and cotton, dates from the late nineteenth century. In Scandinavia wage bargaining has become highly institutionalized and centralized, though in France it has only relatively recently become established on a large scale.

The outcomes of collective bargaining, however, despite occasional trade-union rhetoric to the contrary, seldom have much to do with equality. Indeed, negotiated wage settlements are as likely to make for inequality. Gains made at the bargaining table at the expense of employers are also made at the expense of workers in other industries, because a wage rise pushes up prices in one's own industry—corporations especially being quick to safeguard profits. And it is not the trade unions in the weakest, most poorly paying industries who are best at obtaining wage rises. The reverse is more likely to be true. Consequently many collective bargaining successes such as may occur in times of inflation have the effect of sectionalizing the labour force. Workers and trade-union leaders in one industry become conscious of competing against workers and trade-union leaders in others. Inequality increases. Prime Minister James Callaghan, addressing the 1977 Conference of the Trades Union Congress, was referring to this when he condemned 'the double talk' about free collective bargaining, claiming that it would not bring 'more socialism in our time'.[20]

The operations of corporate capitalism, in fact, reveal how far the actuality of contemporary life in democratic countries is from abstract ideas such as fairness, justice, and equality. As an allocative process it produces results which often appear (and often are), unfair, unjust, and inegalitarian. Whether or not corporate capitalism holds the support of the majority of democratic electorates is not easy to say as it is not usually a specific issue at elections. (Nor would it be an easy question for sample surveys.) Where it does feature, in those democracies where large Communist parties contest elections (in Italy for example), electorates have not so far chosen an alternative system.

Explanations for this vary. One common set of explanations attributes it to capitalist distortion of people's ability to assess their self-interest, effected by capitalist control of the media of information. If one assumes, however, as I do, that while the electorate may not always be aware of their own interests they are frequently better at assessing them than either politicians or intellectuals, one is led to the conclusion that after decades of democracy people have come to prefer capitalism to its alternatives. Again, if this is so, several factors may be at the roots of this position. A dislike of change is a fairly common human predisposition; the feeling that a system with which one is familiar, in spite of its inequalities, is better than a new system promising fairer shares is in keeping with the cautious conservatism of ordinary people. More quantitatively, the size of the average share may outweigh inequalities between shares. Hence a belief that inegalitarian capitalism bakes a bigger cake and provides larger slices than egalitarian socialism may outweigh considerations about differentials. The widespread belief that in the United States and Japan, for example, the average manual worker has considerably higher living standards than in Socialist Eastern Europe powerfully offsets assertions that in the

[20] T.U.C. *Conference, Report* (1977), 433.

Soviet Union wage differentials between management and labour, and between different sections of the working class, are less great than in capitalist countries. The average democratic voter appears to use his franchise largely, though not entirely always, for pragmatic, self-interested purposes.

Corporate capitalism within a democratic regime results in many complexities of distribution, and often, to the ordinary citizen, it may seem little different from the lottery of competitive capitalism. The process may seem just as arbitrary, if not more so; the information just as incomplete, and possibly as misleading; and participation by the individual may be just as ineffective. But a collectivistic rather than an individualistic society implies different structures and orientations of power. Consequently, ordinary citizens are more likely to see their troubles caused not by their lack of enterprise or bad luck, but by the backstairs influence of sectionalisms other than their own. The 'invisible hand' has become a sleight of hand. We shall see later in Chapter 6 how sectional pressures complicate democratic decision-making.

Distribution by the Government

Complexity is further increased by another form of distribution common in all contemporary modern states—direct allocation or re-allocation by government decision. Two processes are at work: governments provide public goods and services, or sometimes cash payments; and to pay for this they impose direct and indirect taxes. Hence the procedure is mainly redistributive. In most contemporary democracies as much as two-fifths, in some cases even half, of gross national product is redistributed. The system, familiarly called the 'welfare state', is often regarded as an inevitable feature of modern democracy.

The basis of the welfare state lies, however, not only in democracy but also in nationalism. Weber describes[21] how the need of dynastic monarchs for revenue for defence led to the nationalization of taxation and thus the foundation of bureaucracy. The need for a healthy factory workforce and fit recruits for the army, as well as the tactic of forestalling the demands of the newly enfranchised working class, explains Bismarck's pioneering of social benefits in

[21] M. Weber, *The Theory of Social and Economic Organisation* (1947 edn.), 377 ff.

Germany in 1881. Thus a healthy, contented citizenry can be regarded as a national asset by non-democratic regimes. Many public goods can contribute towards this desired situation. Obviously public health is one such, and national public education is another. Hence most education in the modern state is not allocated through the market but provided by the state. Again, calculations of national security arise here because well-schooled armed forces are necessary for modern defence. National ownership of public utilities, especially railways and telecommunications, has often been influenced by the same factor. Indeed, the pressure of labour and socialist parties for the welfare state and the public ownership of industry has usually been complemented by that of rationalizing, pragmatic, conservative nationalists.

Among ordinary democratic citizens, pressures for the welfare state and public ownership were confusingly mixed. Self-interest, altruism, and ideology all contributed to the mix, which varies from one country to another. Pressures for public ownership were stronger in depressed industries and in manufacturing and least in service industries or where there was new technology. Some trade-unionists expected larger pay packets from nationalization; other people thought that competitive markets were wasteful, and that amalgamation of modern firms under one corporation would be more efficient; others again saw private ownership and the profit motive as immoral and hoped socialism would usher in a co-operative commonwealth in which the state would allocate fair shares and people would work for the common good rather than their own enrichment. Yet public ownership never had the electoral appeal of the welfare state, demands for which sprang from two basic values—security and equality. The former concept embodies insurance against sickness, unemployment, and old age. It also includes the payment of benefits for children. It provides support, therefore, 'from cradle to grave', a safety net to protect the less affluent members of society, what the Webbs called the 'national minimum', a standard of living below which no one should be allowed to sink. Once these benefits began to be perceived as 'social rights', a concept developed by Thomas Marshall[22] that earlier received official status in the Weimar Constitution of 1919,[23] the principle of 'universality' began to creep in. Clearly, old age,

---

[22] T. H. Marshall, *Citizenship and Social Class* (Cambridge, 1950).
[23] Flora and Heidenheimer, *Development of Welfare States*, 19.

ill-heath and children are afflictions visited on almost everyone, irrespective of income or social position. The perception of public education as part of the welfare state, a quite logical progression, entangles it with the principle of 'meritocracy'. Thus what was envisaged originally as a state-instituted ambulance for the worse-off becomes a pantechnicon full of goodies for everyone. The popularity of the welfare state with the middle classes, and hence with a very wide spectrum of the democratic public, provides the democratic process with a considerable problem.

Indeed, the 'distributive state' is a source of numerous difficulties. Controversy, for example, arises over the provision of public goods and over the allocation of priorities among them. Should we have a new set of multi-headed nuclear missiles or a new cluster of technological universities? Do we need more or fewer power stations, and do they take precedence over new developments in the health service? How the investment portion of the cake is divided will be a troublesome item on the political agenda of all democracies, because here one is not only allocating for the present but also for the future. Welfare benefits will not involve the same uncertainty because they are divisible, precise, of immediate impact, and with values easily comparable with those of the market. The welfare section of the cake is one of which the slices are well known and well defined.

In the end these different processes are, to a greater or lesser degree, associated in policies and in people's minds. People will be affected by taxation, welfare benefits, collective bargaining, and in the long run by the allocation of public investment. Both gains and losses will be experienced by most: a veritable complex of swings and roundabouts. This will lead to resentment as between categories which are likely to become organized sectional forces. The groups concerned, as Peter Flora and Arnold Heidenheimer relate, 'after several generations of welfare state development . . . have developed more sophisticated expectations, more alternative strategies and fewer notions of ignoring or opting out of the system'.[24] Furthermore, the competition of the political parties, especially where they are fairly evenly balanced in a two-party system, will produce a pattern of raids across the party divide for groups of voters—there will be attempts to attract old age pensioners or marginal tax-payers, for example, by offering adjustments to

[24] Ibid. 32.

payments. As Jurgen Kohl explains, 'the logic of competitive politics holds that governments faced with the alternative of losing public support will tend to meet new demands without imposing new burdens'.[25] But this will be impossible in the end without increasing the gross national product. Thus the general economic policies of democratic government will need to be modified in order to take account of all these considerations.

The Distributive Impact of Economic Policy

The commitment to full employment adopted to a greater or lesser degree by all industrialized democracies after World War II was a policy with strong distributive implications, inevitably strengthening trade-union bargaining pressures and increasing inflation. One way of looking at the policy, as Fred Hirsch reminds us,[26] is as a method of avoiding distributional conflict. Yet it did have a certain redistributory effect because inflation tends to penalize the rentier class and people on fixed incomes. At the same time, Keynesian theories had general support, especially from the left. A communitarian, more fraternal, approach to social and economic problems had been engendered, especially in Britain, by the experiences of World War II. The idea that one could spend one's way to prosperity was naturally welcome. Politicians of all parties came to accept that when one had to choose between more unemployment and more inflation, the latter was to be preferred. The electorate, with its memories of inter-war depression, was too much in support of the proposition for the politicians to reject it. Similarly in the 1960s the policy of accelerated growth in the economy was intended to conciliate distributive pressures and was received with general approval by many voters and political leaders alike.

The collapse of this consensus in the 1970s with the onset of the recession brought in its train a more inegalitarian society. With the abandonment of the full employment policy we have, in all the advanced industrial democracies, a much larger group of unemployed people at one end of the social spectrum, while lower progressive taxation (partly in response to electoral pressures) has

---

[25] J. Kohl, Trends and Problems in Postwar Expenditure Development in Western Europe and North America, in Flora and Heidenheimer, *Development of Welfare States*, 308.

[26] F. Hirsch, The Ideological Underlay of Inflation, in F. Hirsch and J. H. Goldthorpe (eds.), *The Political Economy of Inflation* (1978), 270 ff.

allowed the rich to retain more of their earnings. To what degree this increase in inequality threatens democracy is a matter of some controversy. Raymond Plant, writing of the contemporary problems of the liberal capitalist welfare state, warns:

The lack of an agreed moral basis for distribution means that the state will lack legitimacy and create tensions when it cannot resolve if it remains in the arena of seeking distributive justice. The only solution is to uncouple the state from distributive processes, and confine its role to securing the general legal and procedural rules for capitalist enterprise.[27]

John Hall argues, surely correctly, that inflation put the mixed economy under strain some time before growth declined. He continues with respect to 1973: 'The ending of economic growth in or about that year has meant that the inherently unstable combination . . . has finally become unstuck.[28] He concludes that zero growth would result in 'a war of all against all'. Thus the arrival in power in 1979 of a British government with monetarist, anti-Keynesian principles should have resulted in great social disorder. Andrew Gamble says that the importance of Keynesianism for Hirsch was that in the circumstances of mass democracy and universal political participation it provided the missing legitimacy for a predominantly capitalist system.[29] Hence with the collapse of Keynesianism, the capitalist system would lose its legitimacy and social peace could no longer be maintained. Distributive injustices would lead to disorder and so democracy would be under threat.

It would be foolish to contend that the retreat from Keynes, the economic recession, and recent voters' revolts against the scope of taxation and the size of public expenditure have not resulted in greater inequality and social tensions. Very probably the riots in some British inner-cities in 1981 were to some degree a reaction against the new policies. On the other hand, although public disorder of this kind constitutes some threat to the rule of law, it must be put in perspective. The question that needs to be answered is, why has disorder not been so much worse in a period in which public expenditure has been curtailed and unemployment has been higher than in the 1930s? The answers to this are many. Firstly,

[27] R. Plant, Hirsch, Hayek and Habermas: Dilemmas of Distribution, in A. Ellis and K. Kumar (eds.), *Dilemmas of Liberal Democracies* (1983), 53.
[28] J. Hall, The Conscious Relegitimation of Liberal Capitalism: Problems of Transition, in Ellis and Kumar (eds.), *Dilemmas of Liberal Democracies*, 71.
[29] A. Gamble, Economic Growth and Political Dilemmas: Post-war policies in Britain, in Ellis and Kumar (eds.), *Dilemmas of Liberal Democracies*, 93.

public expenditure has not been as severely cut as some imagine.[30] Secondly, the unemployed are better provided for than in the 1930s (when they rarely rioted anyway). Thirdly, people appear to blame the international economic situation as much as the government. Fourthly, people's economic expectations were probably nothing like so high as some academic commentators imagined. The voters were much less likely to expect politicians to keep their promises than had been feared. Finally, the new political economy had been legitimized through the ballot box. It may not have been legitimate to the unemployed, people in the inner cities, and Keynesian intellectuals; but its implications were not unacceptable to the majority of the electorate. Thus increased inequality was sanctioned by democratic processes.

Specific economic policies may sometimes arouse sudden resentments. People may be aware of the rewards accruing (or seeming to accrue) to relations, friends, and neighbours, and they may react much more strongly against what they see as the very unfair relative net gain of some groups close to themselves, perhaps in some straightforward matter such as an increase in old age pensions. They may not be so aware of much larger relative net gains of groups socially distanced from them. Or, again, a sudden new tax policy may produce highly charged and organized protests, like the Poujadist reaction to Mendes-France's sales tax. But taxes may be most painful when they are visible. Harold Wilensky[31] notes that the anti-tax movements in both California and Denmark sprang more from an objection to visible taxation rather than from the size of the tax. In fact, California, did not even have high tax rates. In between these extremes of comprehension the system may appear far too complex for ordinary voters to understand. They may well view it, as after all they always have, as something unfathomable. As they do not expect it to be very 'fair' they will feel alienated only by its grosser aberrations.

The Allocation of Position

When we turn to the allocation of position we move away from abstract models about cakes and material products towards the

---

[30] A. G. Jordan and J. J. Richardson, *British Politics and the Policy Process* (1987), 223 ff. show how the Conservative Governments post-1979 have failed to cut public expenditure in the way they intended.

[31] H. L. Wilensky, Leftism, Catholicism and Democratic Corporatism, in Flora and Heidenheimer, *Development of Welfare States*, 346.

world of power and prestige. By 'position' I refer to leadership roles in society, the economy, and the polity. The capacity to command, lead, and guide others takes a variety of forms in different times and places. The young adventurous entrepreneur, of the type described by Schumpeter,[32] emerged in a society in which leadership had been feudal, based on land, inheritance, and prescribed status. Position under competitive capitalism could theoretically be obtained through application, hard work, self-help, enterprise, and resourcefulness. American millionaires, so the legend ran,[33] had begun by saving their nickels earned in newspaper rounds. The political replica of this was the progression from log cabin to White House. In a highly flexible society brought about by the rise of capitalism, everyone, it was argued, had the opportunity to lead. It was an assertion of the rewards of merit earned by the exceptional few. In America, where this view was especially firmly held, there was, indeed, quite early in the nineteenth century, as De Tocqueville witnessed,[34] a society more egalitarian than any the world had ever experienced. This may be explained, however, by the absence of feudalism rather than the presence of capitalism.

Whatever the case, one of the developing features was the specialization of leadership. Under feudalism all forms of leadership—social, economic, and political—had tended to remain undifferentiated in the hands of the aristocracy. Some early capitalists enjoyed political activity, particularly at the local level; but most found running their business enough. Enriching oneself was more easily expedited through the economy than through the political system. Consequently, with the rise of capitalism, leadership tended to be more specialized and differentiated. More social and economic mobility, however, evoked an ethos of egalitarianism, even though it was still very difficult for ordinary people to reach the top of the ladder in any walk of life. Specialized leadership, moreover, implied a very different method of allocating positions. Both in capitalist and socialist countries, the need for organization and management, in industry and in other fields such as public service, has produced a demand for people trained in various super-

[32] J. A. Schumpeter, *Theory of Economic Development* (New York, 1934), 89 ff.

[33] Frances W. Gregory and Irene D. Neu, The American Industrial Elite in the 1880s, and W. Miller, American Historians and the Business Elite, in W. Miller (ed.), *Men in Business* (New York, 1962 edn.), 194 ff. and 321 ff.

[34] A. De Tocqueville, *Democracy in America* (New York 1954 edn.), 229 ff.

visory skills, and this demand is met by a supply of recruits from the educational system. Education is today another method of competing, far more prevalent than entrepreneurial competition; but even in industry and commerce high-fliers in the twentieth century have more often begun by excelling in a series of examinations than by cutting a dash at buying and selling for profit.[35] Not that higher education does not allow for the needs of the market, but it does this by training corporation executives, research scientists, technologists, bureaucrats, and technocrats.

Thus it is not easy at first sight to characterize modern education as egalitarian. Although there is universal access, the results seem positively inegalitarian. This is so because equal right of access is not the same as equality of opportunity. Indeed, they could only be the same if everyone was identical when they began their education, instead of which children not only have congenital differences (unless one believes we are all 'equal in the womb'), but also widely varying family backgrounds. John Charvet points out that an extreme condition of complete equality of opportunity would be that parents should not rear their children.[36] Absolute equality of opportunity implies a period of training during which everyone would be treated equally.

In fact, a race or series of races is a useful analogy. In order to compensate for inherited differences and socialization in the family, 'handicapping' would be allowed after every race in order to prevent inequality emerging. Once the final race began, however, there would no be handicapping: competition would be the rule. Here we have a recognizable system with a certain amount of equality tempered by meritocratic values. Ultimately, 'equality of opportunity' implies that 'opportunity' will be more important than 'equality'. A system of free, compulsory, standardized education with egalitarian rhetoric, as in France, for example, can still have élitist values and produce a highly specialized, self-consciously intellectual meritocracy. Meanwhile, access to higher education remains limited everywhere.

[35] For example, W. L. Warner and J. C. Abegglen, *Occupational Mobility in American Business and Industry* (Minneapolis, 1955), 176, demonstrate how after 1892 factors involved in achieved status influenced occupational succession into the business elite.

[36] J. Charvet, The Idea of Equality as a Substantive Principle of Society, *Political Studies*, 17 (1969), 1–13.

The allocation of hierarchy under corporate, or advanced, capitalism results in a competition for position rather than a competition for markets. The swiftest in the race secure the glittering prizes. Most people of average pace secure skilled manual or clerical jobs, and the slowest have to be content with the poorest-paid manual jobs. Mobility is always possible, though winning the pools, sport, or the pop scene are seen as more likely avenues for advancement than entrepreneurial success. Otherwise promotion is not easy for those in routine clerical and manual jobs with little of a career structure outside the public service and the corporations. Hence competition for position will not trouble the majority of the population of industrialized countries; but among the professional and managerial minority it will be a salient concern for most of their working days.

A society of this kind inculcates very different values from those of competitive capitalism. The archetypal leader is not the adventurous entrepreneur but the cautious manager; not the individual responsible to himself but the 'organization man' responsible to committees and boards; not the founder of business dynasties but the meritocratic 'spiralist' moving from firm to firm as he seeks promotion; and not the profit seeker in the market but the corporation politician often advancing himself by whom he knows rather than what he knows. Adaptability and conformity are all prized qualities in this type of society. As William Miller writes, 'Learning the ropes in most organisations is chiefly learning the who's who, what's what, why's why of its informal society.'[37] To some, the system by which the individual gains advancement in this organizational complex may seem to resemble uncomfortably the *nomenklatura* of the CPSU.

Whether capitalism as it has developed in the late twentieth century strengthens or weakens democracy is a question that can only be answered in the most qualified terms. In many people's minds the two processes are conflated in a structure unconsciously or consciously labelled 'the system'. Certainly it is not always easy to separate the causal connections between democracy and corporate capitalism. It is clear, however, that the distributive system which has emerged, although more egalitarian than in the past, is still quite inegalitarian. Wealth is still distributed quite unequally in

[37] W. Miller, The Business Elite in Business Bureaucracies in Miller, *Men in Business*, 304.

spite of efforts at redistribution. Leadership, which by its nature cannot be redistributed to any great extent and must always be with us as long as we have organized society, has become more accessible with a measure of increased social mobility. On the other hand, with the march of meritocracy and many more people receiving higher education and specialized training, the competition for position and status has become fiercer.

Many of the problems facing democratic countries arise from the basic incongruity of the economic and political systems. At the lowest level within the polity there is complete political equality: the franchise is allocated equally, irrespective of status or wealth. On the other hand, status and wealth are distributed in very unequal portions. Democracy provides the opportunity for these inequalities to be mitigated by groups gaining control of the sharing process and in some countries they have had limited success. On the whole, however, business has adapted itself to democracy without being too incommoded. Hence wealth in democracies tends to be allocated through a modified, corporate form of capitalism within a negotiated framework of regulation and restriction. Mixed economies—partly competitive, partly commanded by the state, and partly determined by collectivistic bargaining—present a rather confused pattern of activity. In this situation, Who gets what, when, how? may be difficult to ascertain. As the process is controversial and open to public argument there is much dissembling.

The allocation of position has tended increasingly to be by the prinicple of equality of opportunity. Certainly with the growth of organization and the advance of industrialization, as well as with extended education, the professional and managerial classes have expanded greatly and access to them has become easier. But it would be a mistake to interpret this as a move towards a very egalitarian society. These classes with greater skills and more knowledge ('they not only know the ropes, they pull them', as a friend put it), tend to play the educational machine to the advantage of their children. Indeed, Christopher Hewitt discovered no association between democracy and access to higher education.[38] Consequently, in societies where the historical rhetoric is as dedicated to equality as in the United States, or to meritocracy as in France, a good deal of inequality of opportunity still exists. Thus

[38] Hewitt, The Effect of Political Democracy, 459.

the pursuit of meritocracy remains a feature of modern democracies. Whether if it is ever completely attained it will make democracy any stronger must remain an open question.

The Public and the Distributive Process

It is not easy to assess how much these outcomes represent the failure of the democratic process. To what degree are demands for a change in distributive principles, and in the size of shares, frustrated by hiatuses in democratic decision-making? Are people interested in distributive methods, or only in the outputs from the system?

Robert Dahl lists numerous options[39] for distributing income, including the classic Marxist principle, 'from each according to ability, to each according to needs'; and he enquires whether failure to be consistent about any such prescribed options arises from incompatibility with the workings of the economy, or because of 'civic orientations', the values citizens hold towards their political arrangements and institutions. He comes to the conclusion that no particular distributive principle should be 'accepted without question as a principle of distribution that the demos in a democratic socialist country either would or should adopt'.[40] In practice, however, it seems unlikely that any democratic country adopts its distributive criteria in a very conscious way. Occasionally they become something of an issue at elections when politicians of left and right may bandy words such as 'public ownership' against others such as 'private enterprise'. In Britain the 1945 general election is often cited as the one in which this form of ideological dispute became most salient.

Even when such principles are at issue, the real interest may be in the outcomes. There is little doubt that many British voters who supported public ownership in 1945 saw it as likely to be more efficient and productive of larger material rewards. (There were public servants who warned them this might not be so.)[41] It seems highly probable that, especially as the twentieth century has proceeded, most democratic voters' prime concern has been economic self-interest. The questions to which they address themselves are of a calculative kind. 'If I vote for X will the

---

[39] R. A. Dahl, *Dilemmas of Pluralist Democracy* (1982), 135.　　　[40] Ibid. 137.
[41] For example Bryn Roberts, secretary of the Public Employees. See *TUC Conference Report* (1944), 87 ff.

increased family allowances his party offers be more than the increased income-tax I shall have to pay?' 'If I vote for Y will the freer collective bargaining his party will allow offset the rise of prices which will follow?' Unfortunately, with the mixed economy it may be very difficult for the voters to discern the answers. It is not only that the politicians blur their policies, it is also that they often do not really know the likely results. They may not understand the operation of the economy and its impacts on the policy process; but even if they do, they cannot reliably predict the economic climate when they hope to hold office, dependent as it is on external factors.

Mixed economies are composed of so many roundabouts and swings that calculations may be difficult at the best of times. Much of the trouble will arise from changing differentials as between social benefits and levels of wages. It may be that certain politicians may be regarded as responsible for these. On the other hand, benefits or losses that occur may be attributed to outside circumstances. There is both the rationale of national economic policy and the give and take of the free market to consider. It is thus difficult to define the allocative criteria. They may result from neither a form of 'public interest' nor a 'hidden hand' but the clash of group interests.

Where distributive policies can be attributed neither to luck nor to people who are visibly responsible they will give rise to suspicion and feelings of injustice. As I have already argued, individuals may feel they do not get their deserts with the market, but what they get may be accepted as the luck of the draw. In a command economy they may disagree with the criteria, but at least the criteria are likely to be known. Under a mixed economy they may vary from one part of the economy to another. For example, there may be a wage policy in the public sector but free collective bargaining in the private sector. Dependent on which sector fares better, it is only natural that the people in the other sector should demand the more rewarding form of allocation. Usually groups from the least prosperous industries, or from non-productive services in the public sector, may find their best strategy is that of reference-group bargaining, i.e. to aim at linking their rewards to those of similar groups in prosperous industries. But groups of employees in the latter will be in a better position to argue their claims in terms of the state of the industry. Neither luck nor well-defined criteria, in this situation, seem to determine awards. Perhaps some of both is involved; but political factors will also be important. And political factors will change with political leaders.

Where the economy is in a serious inflationary situation, as in Britain or Italy in the 1970s, all these considerations become more acute. Differentials between various types of awards may become very much out of normal alignment, either because of the operation of the market or because of government policy. People will feel threatened by rising prices and everyone, in the first place, may suffer some deprivation of income which they feel is undeserved and for which they may be unable to attribute responsibility. Ultimately they will blame both the government for not doing anything to alleviate the situation and other groups whom they will see, rightly, as having pushed up prices in winning new wage awards. As a result of such experiences they will develop strategies and attitudes based on their knowledge of the impact of inflation.

The overall strategy will be never to fall behind and if possible to keep well in front of everyone else. Moreover, this aggressive policy will be assisted by submitting a larger wage claim than it is guessed other group-bargainers will advance and by presenting it more quickly than usual—jumping one's place in the queue, as it were. Thus a union which operates in this way may be making a pre-emptive strike. The knowledge that after a wage scramble all prices will rise and that the country will be no wealthier does not deter this strategy—rather it encourages it, for in such a situation it is completely rational to desire the advantages of enjoying a wage rise for as long as possible before prices increase as a result of members of other unions following suit.[42] But after some experience of the inflationary cycle even trade-union members will realize there is something almost confiscatory about a large trade union advancing a claim for a 30 per cent wage increase. It will be threatening to deprive members of other unions of part of their livelihood, especially if it sets in motion an avalanche of further claims.

It is a situation in which each group attempts to gain as large a share of the distributive function as possible. Especially where the state is actively involved in allocation (to a greater or lesser extent the position in all modern societies), it thus represents a challenge to the authority of the state. As C. S. Maier writes, 'Rapid inflation

[42] Trade-union strategy in inflation is discussed in M. Laver, The Great British Wage Game, *New Society*, 9 Mar. 1980.

involves the search for constant income shares and thus the attempted coinage of each group's respective scarce goods. Coinage, however, has been a traditional prerogative of sovereignty. Inflation tends to erode sovereignty'.[43] Samuel Brittan argued that in Britain this dilemma was one of the internal contradictions of democracy, a form of government which he considered likely to pass away within the lifetime[44] of contemporary adults. Politicians find it difficult to abandon inflationary policies because of the coercive pressures of group self-interest in the market place, and because of their electoral practice of outbidding their opponents with unfulfillable economic promises. On the other hand, Brittan continued, the voters did not interest themselves in economic policies; only in their outcomes. They did not understand that on a national level the same principle held as in their private lives—more of one thing means less of something else. Consequently electorates tended to expect too much from government action at too little cost and to praise and blame governments for things which were largely outside their control.[45] This latter defect, the inability to apportion responsibility, is bound to have serious implications for the working of democracy.

Assessment of Brittan's argument must rest largely on one's interpretation of what he means by 'coercion'.[46] If by coercive groups he means those which break the law, then clearly by my definition their activities are undemocratic. On the other hand, if he means they exert power, though not in an illegal fashion, then whether they endanger democracy or not is bound to be a matter for controversy. They may thwart the goals of democratically elected governments attempting to manage the economy, but unless such goals are embodied in law it is not easy to characterize their actions as undemocratic. Of course, obstruction of all kinds, such as strikes and boycotts, may be nuisances which some people may feel *ought* to be illegal; but as long as such activity is legal it is not undemocratic. Therefore a critic's only redress is to campaign for the passage of legislation to make what was legal illegal. Otherwise, in cases where the legality of trade-union behaviour is in some doubt as in some instances of 'withdrawing an essential service

[43] C. S. Maier, The Politics of Inflation in the Twentieth Century, in Hirsch and Goldthorpe (eds.), *Political Economy of Inflation*, 41.

[44] S. Brittan, The Economic Contradictions of Democracy, *British Journal of Political Science*, 5 (1975), 129.

[45] Ibid. 139.   [46] Ibid. 130.

from the market place and using coercion to keep out substitute supplies,'[47] one can only have recourse to the courts. Brittan may regard this as a very unsatisfactory solution, but democracy is not concerned with giving satisfaction to individuals or protecting them from exercises of legal power they do not like. It *is* concerned with deciding whether any exercise of power should, or should not be, legal. Unfortunately, in the case of British trade unions, their legal status is frequently redefined by the democratic process so that the status quo seldom has the stability which makes for legitimacy. This should not imply, however, that the law with regard to trade unions can be overlooked, and even flouted: on the contrary, for democrats it should mean that its observance is a matter for greater delicacy of treatment and commitment on the part of those involved. (The problem of trade-union power is certainly not to be dismissed lightly, and I shall deal with it at greater length in Chapter 7.)

It is not that the generation of excessive expectations, as Brittan puts it, is not a problem for democracy. The objection to his analysis is that he lays the blame unequally on the irrationality of the voters rather than on the irrationality and irresponsibility of the politicians. Moreover, he looks only at Britain, whereas his argument seems much weaker if one contemplates Scandinavia, or Holland or West Germany. Even in Britain, however, people may be more economically educable than Brittan maintains. His example of people irrationally preferring a rise of £4 a week in common with everyone else, rather than £5 if everyone else were awarded £6, may not be an instance of the 'money illusion' so much as an appreciation of real wages. If people expected inflation to increase more in the second case, so that they were worse off in real terms with £105 a week than with £104 as in the first case, it would be more rational to accept the £4 a week rise.[48] The recession since his article was published has ensured more recently that British political leaders have *not* been indulging in political auctions. They have not needed to because the voters have very quickly adapted to the new economic situation and greatly lowered their expectations. In fact it may well be that ordinary citizens are nearer to everyday economic reality and so adjust more quickly to changes in it than do their political leaders.

Inflation and deflation both present problems for democracy. In

[47] Ibid. 137.   [48] Ibid. 158.

the inflationary situation an atmosphere of unreality is engendered. This is particularly the case if the money illusion is not quickly understood; but even where it is, as I argued, it may be quite rational in the short term to pursue escalating wage claims. In circumstances where demands are also made with increasing frequency, many people, especially those with weak bargaining positions and on fixed incomes, may come to feel that the distributive process is becoming less and less fair. All sorts of rumours may arise about the high and undeserved pay of other groups. Consequently feelings of injustice and distrust may hold sway, and a call for undemocratic action may be aroused. Inadequacies of the government and political leadership in dealing with such a situation may accentuate the difficulty, especially if the politicians have been responsible for disappointing the expectations of either specific groups or the general public. It has been argued that the electoral consequences of counter-inflationary action will deter democratic politicians from undertaking it, but this is merely a counsel of despair, for it should not be impossible to convince a democratic electorate of the need for deflationary policies in inflationary circumstances. Of course, if it becomes impossible then chaos may ensue, in which case democratic government may break down. In the end, democratic solutions will depend on the responsibility and intelligence of both politicians and citizens.

Deflation is not taken to be such a problem. It requires a sober rather than a heady response. Wages may rise little, or remain stable, and distributive injustice will arise from many people losing their jobs. Feelings of insecurity among those still employed will also develop, especially if the unemployment rate persistently rises. It may well happen, however, that those who remain employed will maintain, or even improve, their living standards because of the stability of prices. They may feel sympathy for the unemployed but have few practical suggestions for helping them. In such situations trade unions are notoriously ineffective: indeed, their insistence on maintaining wage rates may keep unemployment higher than it would otherwise be. Even so, there may be little protest, in a country where trade unionism is strong, at such refusal to lower wage rates. Social protest may be palliated by high rates of unemployment relief and, possible, by work-sharing. Unemployment becomes a social and, ultimately, a political problem when people have been unemployed a long time and the expression of discontent may become serious where a particular group of people have a much higher rate of unemployment. Hence young school-leavers, or blacks in the inner cities or immigrant guest workers, who may especially suffer, may react violently. But these outbreaks are likely to be sporadic and they will hardly encourage other employed workers to revolt. Indeed, periods of long-term unemployment may be periods of relative tranquillity. People's expectations will be greatly diminished and politicians will not need to outbid each other as during inflationary times. It is much more difficult, anyway, to make exaggerated promises about more jobs than it is to make them about higher living standards, and where governments adopt monetarist policies they may feel absolved from taking responsibility for the economy. Consequently recessions, which almost certainly lead to a more unequal distribution of wealth, seldom seem to provoke social unrest or political disturbance. The 'relatively deprived' in this situation are the poorest, least skilled, most politically underprivileged section of the population.

Conclusion

Democracy cannot escape the difficulties of distributive policy even though some may wish there was no such involvement. Classical liberal theory envisaged the economy and the polity as separate entities with the latter only acting as a referee in the economy, making sure the rules were observed. This conception, never realized in practice at any time, for people have used political power in every era to interfere with market forces, was doomed to certain death under democracy. The vast masses of underprivileged people, once they entered the decision-making process, were bound to demand all sorts of constraints upon competition. Hence today's mixed economy is a natural result of democracy.

This outcome, however, with its complex distributional system, has not proceeded far towards an egalitarian society. Whether such a society is a necessary concomitant of democracy or not is anyway open to argument; but in its beginnings democracy and equality were often seen in association. Since then forms of redistributive justice have been frequently presented as programmes to be adopted by democratic states. Hence an egalitarian presence pervades much debate about social and economic issues in democratic countries, producing a tension between democracy's promise of equality and its disappointing performance in practice.

Equality, as I have argued, it not the easiest of concepts to define. Human beings are not equal because they are not identical (fortunately) even at a biological level. Equity, or 'fairness', may be a rather more meaningful concept; but it is not easy to envisage how democratic procedures will help to reach a solution generally accepted as fair. Equal voting rights, applied to the problem of trying to reach a fair distribution of resources, may result in the breakdown of democracy and a reversion to physical combat or authoritative allocation. Any invocation of the merits of the case or attempts to lay down criteria for dividing a material resource may lead to frustration and cynicism. There is bitter disagreement about what is fair and/or deserving of reward. Thus at its most elementary level, simple distributive justice may not be compatible with democracy. Indeed, with micro-democracy, the personalization of the allocation may be detrimental to trust and respect for rules.

With macro-democracy this latter difficulty may not arise but other problems are magnified many times over. The complex procedures brought to bear upon vast resources have led to further complications. This was perhaps inevitable given that the enfranchisement of the many was largely the enfranchisement of the underprivileged. Modern democratic states with their mixed economies, however, in spite of disappointing many egalitarians, have not collapsed in a welter of cynical frustration, although the distribution of wealth and income has been a foremost issue in them all, with the possible exception of the United States.[49]

Putting aside non-democratic forces espousing 'more equality', the main advocates of considerable redistribution have been the social democrats who have seen the democratic state as an instrument for allocating resources more fairly. Only a few social democrats have advocated absolute equality. Equality of opportunity, allowing scope for the profit motive and for ambitious climbers, has been the equality most favoured. (When Hugh Gaitskell, the leader of the Labour Party, said 'socialism was about equality', he certainly meant equality of opportunity.) The result of decades of debate and, in some case, much time spent in government, has been to concoct an amalgam of both forms of equality. Social democratic parties espouse a 'national minimum', a certain standard of material comfort and service below which redistributive efforts

[49] A. Lijphart, *Democracies* (1984), 130, considers the USA, Canada, and Ireland as the only democratic countries in which the socio-economic dimension does not have high salience.

should prevent people sinking. In addition, their expansion of opportunity, mainly through family policies and education, prepares people to *compete*.

On the whole, such parties have increasingly been reluctant to press the redistribution of capital through public ownership of the means of production, distribution, and exchange. Indeed, they have been more concerned in expanding the national cake rather than slicing it up more equally. Thus the 'white-hot scientific revolution', the drive for increased technology by the Labour government in Britain from 1964 to 1970,[50] was a simultaneous attempt to increase investment and productivity and to extend social benefits. The implication was that if people had bigger shares they would be less inclined to ask for equal shares. Generally speaking, this rationale has found acceptance from the main supporters of democratic socialist parties, the industrial workers, who also assert their claims through trade unions. Both the workings of democracy and the economy—both the political and economic markets, one might say—have propelled social democratic politicians towards policies of expanding wealth, in the private and public sectors, as well as those designed to distribute it more fairly.

Both socialist political parties and trade unions are responses to the distribution of wealth. But the former are not as accommodative to inequality as unions invariably are. Frank Parkin says: 'Collective bargaining does not call into question the values underlying the existing reward structure, nor does it pose any threat to the institutions which support this structure'.[51] But he does not perceive trade unions' and voters' influence as the cause of what he calls the de-radicalization of socialist parties. Rather does he explain this in terms of socialist political leaders being affected by their position and their contacts with the values of what he calls the 'dominant' class. Consequently the fact that much inequality exists, Parkin argues, is a demonstration that it is much more commonly the case that members of the underclass take their political cues from their party leaders than the reverse.[52] He couples this with the assertion that working-class support for social democratic parties has not fallen. This is difficult to maintain if Northern Europe, including Britain, is the area to which he refers. Surely sections of

[50] See F. Bealey, *The Social and Political Thought of the British Labour Party* (1970), 224 ff.
[51] F. Parkin, *Class, Inequality and Political Order* (1971), 91.   [52] Ibid. 129.

the British working class became attached to collective bargaining in the 1970s because they saw it as a much better way of advancing their demands than through the Labour Party whose policies had less appeal? The majority accept the reward structure as the one in practice most likely to produce the highest benefits. Parkin, like Brittan, underrates the rationality of working-class people when making decisions about their own material needs.

It is easier, therefore, to justify the distributive system in present-day democracies in pragmatic rather than in egalitarian terms. Bargaining groups often deploy quite unequal resources and operate within a context which gives one more power than another. The outcomes may be inegalitarian but are accepted as part of a familiar process which produces not too inequitable results; and there is a sense in which public opinion may have a role. Collective bargaining may occur in 'smoke-filled rooms', but frequently its participants operate within a blaze of publicity. Thus, if the outcomes are regarded as very unfair—perhaps wage differentials have been badly flouted—government may face pressures to control wage bargaining, and sometimes respond to them. (It depends on how much electoral damage governments perceive may be done by acceding or not acceding.) Governments may, as we have seen in Chapter 3, be themselves involved in bargaining with the groups concerned. (I shall discuss this further in Chapters 6 and 7.)

The bargaining process, it might be objected, is a long way from approximating to the classical theory of participatory democracy. It puts a premium on strategy and tactics and on the structure of argumentation. Samuel Bacharach and Edward Lawler portray bargaining as a game of managing impressions or manipulating information,[53] which emphasizes misleading one's opponents about the situation, including one's own resources. They maintain: 'The relative amount of information parties have about each other is a critical determinant of a party's tendency to bluff.'[54] But bargainers may even bluff about the amount of information. In all these subterfuges, moreover, they may confuse their own followers and the public all of whom may wish they could participate. Hence the secrecy and somewhat arcane manœuvres characterizing much bargaining, as well as the uncertainty of assessing its outcome,

[53] S. B. Bacharach and E. J. Lawler, *Bargaining* (1981), 42.
[54] Ibid. 172.

infringe the democratic criteria of inclusiveness and accountability to a considerable degree. Especially where governments become involved, the complexity may defy any attempt to discover the 'truth' and so to enforce responsibility to the electorate.

On the other hand, Lindblom's analysis of 'partisan mutual adjustment' perceived bargaining as often enhancing democracy. This is largely because he envisages it operating within the framework of the American political system, where decision-making is unusually open, public surveillance at its greatest, and the legislature the point of access for most interest groups.[55] So accountability may be often realized. Moreover it must be remembered, as I argued in Chapter 2, that where there are competing party leaderships, as in Britain, they may consistently misinform in order to secure electoral advantage, their arguments uncomfortably resembling Pareto's 'derivations'.[56] Unhappily, conventional respresentative democracy (or 'numerical democracy' as we shall later call it), like bargaining, can lead to untruth, irrationality, and unaccountable policy-making. It is bound to produce results that many will regard as unfair.

In practice what a group means by fair is consistent with what it perceives as its deserts. It is a subjective concept which can be rationalized by reference to certain criteria and the rewards of other proximate groups. The effect is to produce a trend towards sectionalism in which the communitarian attitudes usually associated with social democracy find it hard to flourish. Inflation, in particular, has been very detrimental to social democracy. The anti-welfare movements in the United States, Britain, and Denmark (to name only a few), demonstrate how the clock of the welfare state might be put back. Taxation has become unpopular with the more prosperous manual workers, who have become less willing to contribute to the provision of social benefits. Inflation has helped to drain the reservoir of working-class solidarity.

A society in which there is persistent and vigilant concern about other people's rewards, as Britain today, is not one of harmonious consensus. It is characterized by a certain envy, often the product of exaggerated rumours. (In fact, officially promulgating everyone's earnings might be a wise policy.) Groups may feel threatened, both by the collective bargainings and the industrial behaviour of other groups. Conversely, government intervention in the bargaining

---

[55] Lindblom, *The Intelligence of Democracy*, 311 ff.
[56] S. E. Finer (ed.), *Vilfredo Pareto: Sociological Writings* (1966), 237 ff.

process may also constitute a threat. In Britain such a situation has produced a set of tough, sectionalized groups determined to safeguard their own privileges and differentials; and it is thus not easy to identify a willingness to accept economic policies reflecting a consensus view. To a great degree, however, the blame for this position of distributive instability is not laid by citizens on democratic processes.

As for the distribution of position, the main effect of democratic and economic pressures (it is not easy here to evaluate their respective significances) has been to enlarge the professional and managerial classes, what Milosz calls the 'intelligentsia',[57] and to stimulate a more mobile society. Old-time democrats would have thought this development helpful for democracy and there is much evidence to suggest that better educated people are more comprehending and more supportive of it. But the process has also produced the vestiges of a discontented intellectual proletariat, for there must be a limit to the leadership positions which any society can support. A stratum of professional people and managers *manqués* could conceivably provide some threat to democracy as the nucleus of an extremist movement allied to other relatively deprived groups. In an economic recession this might especially be the case.

Whether citizens are satisfied with their slice of the cake or their position in the hierarchy may depend on two factors: whether they feel relatively deprived or rewarded, and whether their expectations are fulfilled or disappointed. When a policy they expect will result in relative deprivation does so, they are not as likely to be aggrieved as they are with unexpected relative deprivation. Unexpected relative reward may delight some, but it often produces grievous, unexpected relative deprivation for others. And unexpected deprivation, especially if it is a substantial rather than an incremental redistribution of wealth and hierarchy, may result in social upheaval. As Gary Runciman writes, 'The upsetting of expectations provokes the sense of relative deprivation which may in turn provide the impetus for drastic change.'[58] But revolutions and *coups d'état* are not necessarily associated with general economic decline: like Runciman, many commentators believe prosperity encourages a revolution of rising expectations. Political institutions may be

[57] C. Milosz, *The Captive Mind* (1980), 143 ff. He distinguishes the intelligentsia from the intellectuals.
[58] W. G. Runciman, *Relative Deprivation and Social Justice* (1966), 22.

endangered by groups whose high expectations have been unfulfilled.[59]

It is a far cry, however, from sketching this model of the relationship between political stability and economic and social change to arguing that economic crises such as depression and inflation are both necessary preludes to the collapse of democracy. War, education transforming intellectual values, and cultural conflicts may all be other causes. Indeed, economic crises may be easily weathered where democratic attitudes are deep-seated. 25 per cent inflation followed by 3.5 million unemployed in the course of less than a decade does not yet (1986) seem to have impaired seriously the practice of democratic procedures in Britain. (One might well argue that religious and communal conflict in Northern Ireland have done more damage.) Yet it would be a foolhardy person who argued that no extremes of economic distress would be perilous. Would 250 per cent inflation followed by 7 million unemployed lead to rioting in all British inner-cities and then to the armed forces taking over? It is not possible confidently to answer 'No'.

As far as citizens are concerned, much will depend on how responsible they feel political leaders are for the economic situation. If they decide, as apparently British voters for the most part did at the 1983 election, that the world economic situation was responsible for mass unemployment, then they may accept economic failure stoically. If they take protestations of Keynesian management and fine tuning seriously, and if at the same time they are unaware of how their own materialistic pressures deflect the politicians from such purposes, then they may be outraged by national economic calamity. But even then, if their only response is to 'throw the rascals out', the voters are hardly the stuff from which revolutions and putsches can be fashioned.

Unless, therefore, relatively deprived groups demanding more money, higher status, fair shares, distributive justice, etc. pursue their ends in such ways as to cause the breakdown of democratic discussion, democracy is likely to survive both egalitarian and inegalitarian offensives. Adjusting incrementally to the various pressures, democratic processes should operate to ensure that no

[59] Of course, this is much more a feature of non-democratic regimes. *The Times*, 10 August 1983, reported that one of the reasons for the overthrow of General Rios Montt, president of Guatamala, by senior military officers was that the latters' wives suffered deprivation from Montt's imposition of a 10 per cent value added tax, a very unwelcome innovation with a class relatively under taxed.

irreconcilable conflicts between associational, regional, or class alignments emerge and produce the same sort of dilemma as with ethnic and cultural cleavage. An avoidance of an 'us and them' situation should be assisted by the airing of grievances and the resulting adjustments of rewards. The mixed economy is paralleled by a mixed polity, as we shall see in the next chapter.

6

PLURALISM AND DEMOCRACY

ALTHOUGH the terms are often used synonymously, pluralism is not the same as democracy. 'Pluralism' refers to a type of social and political configuration; 'democracy' describes a process of making political decisions. Yet the association between them is clear. Pluralism conveys the notion of a many-sided society, while democracy allows the expression of multi-faceted opinions.

As a concept, pluralism has not always been rigorously expounded. It has suffered from political scientists and sociologists attributing rather different meanings to it. The pluralism of political scientists, or 'political pluralism', tends to be concerned with the situation in which associational groups and political parties have freedom of action in order to bargain and appeal for support. Political pluralism is dependent on democracy. Freedom of association—a democratic right guaranteeing, for example, freedom of worship and freedom of trade-union activity—ensures that organizations can form and flourish. It is possible to imagine democracy functioning without political pluralism, though it would be rather primitive or a very small-scale democracy.

'Social pluralism', the pluralism of sociologists, has a wider connotation, assuming a society of diverse interests. Long before the democratic era, when most people had no political rights, a fairly complex socio-economic structure appertained. Even in medieval society, 'groups' of a kind would make an impact on authority. Social pluralism, therefore, is independent of democracy. The pluralism of the sociologists becomes the pluralism of the political scientists when groups are allowed to turn to conscious political action.

The problem of the relationship of groups in society to authority is relatively ancient. It has been characterized by a clash of wills in pursuit of different goals. Ultimately, the capacity successfully to coerce with effective sanctions has marked the modern state, the winner of this clash. But before political authority was strong, organizations with compelling sanctions sometimes wielded great power. Thus the pope could force the Holy Roman Emperor to go barefoot to Canossa to expiate his sins. The temporal power was coerced by the certainty of burning in Hell if penances were not completed. With this severe sanction, the Church could challenge the rather exiguous medieval state. The decline of faith made earthly power more viable.

There always have been, and there always will be, alternative sources of power to formal political authority. Although the state in modern times has become the supreme coercive force in society, there remain individuals and groups who attempt to exert power over others and who may even challenge the power of the state. Parents have always exerted power over children and employers over employees. Parents and employers have goals for children and employees, which are likely to be paramount over the objectives that children and employees may have for themselves. The wills and resources of parents and employers are likely to be stronger: the sanctions they can impose more severe. In the case of employers, their ultimate sanction, 'the sack', can deprive an employee of a livelihood and possibly a career. Some individuals and groups may use only relatively mild sanctions in the last resort in order to make people concur; others may employ relatively harsh ones.

No organization, group, or individual, however, can use sanctions as severe as those of the state. This logically follows from the role of the state as the ultimate coercive force in society. If another body can use sanctions and exert power making it inviolable to state coercion, then law and order may break down. An organization which can do this becomes, to use the familiar but apt cliché, a state within a state. If organizations, like the SA within the Weimar Republic or numerous terrorist organizations today, not only claim the right of capital punishment (a penalty no longer enforced by most states) but also have the capacity to carry it out, then the state is in peril. If citizens begin to respond to sanctions of a severity normally used only by the state but employed by some other body, then the framework of law and order is disintegrating.

In consequence, all sanctions exerted by groups and individuals in society are subject to the supreme sanctions of the state. Parents punish their children, employers dismiss their workmen and associations deal with their members within limits laid down by the state. These limits have been defined by statute law, or as a result of verdicts of the courts, and have been more and more restrictively delineated. In Britain, for example, it has become less easy to punish severely one's children, or to dismiss one's workmen, because the state has intervened in these relationships.

In modern times, however, we have democracy. Although alternative sources of power to the state existed before democracy and continue to exist after it, their situation has drastically changed. Now the power of the state is legitimized by the majority will of its citizens. Public power should more clearly than ever be supreme over private power. Indeed, one classical strand of democracy insists that no sectional wills, goals, and sanctions should exist. In this version of democracy, most vigorously asserted by Rousseau, no will should be exerted but the General Will of the people. The people is sovereign. Sectional wills are against the will of the general community and therefore anti-democratic. (Consistent with this philosophy, the French revolutionaries passed the Le Chapelier[1] law which greatly impeded trade-union activity). Institutionally, this is reflected in referendums which ascertain the views of the whole people on public issues and make it difficult for sectional groups with organized opinions to play much part in the formulation of policy. Power belongs to the majority of the people, periodically expressing its preference among options. (The implementation of decisions remains rather a vague aspect of this model.) Popular wills and goals are satisfied, while sectional wills and goals are impeded. Thus direct democracy is detrimental to pluralism.

Political Parties

Here, however, we are largely concerned with the relationship between representative democracy and pluralism and with examining the impact of democracy upon alternative sources of power within the state. As we have seen, a universal result of the introduction of civil liberties and the right of participation for everyone is the development of representative institutions and the emergence of political parties led by professional politicians. The parties will be likely to mobilize both the old pre-democratic groupings in society and the new post-democratic groupings representing the forces emancipated by the granting of the suffrage and freedom of expression.

[1] E. Shorter and C. Tilly, *Strikes in France* (Cambridge, 1974) 21.

The presence of the parties competing to steer the ship of state, as we noted in Chapter 2, produces a different model of democracy.

Political parties are so obviously associated with the practice of democracy that it may not be immediately apparent why they should ever be suspected of endangering it. But in the first place, democracy, as I have defined it, is bound to allow the expression and mobilization of anti-democratic opinions; and there are numerous examples of parties whose main objective has been the overthrow of the system which allows them freely to operate. Fascist and Communist parties, for example, in order to inaugurate a total state, intend to abolish all other parties, bringing public contestation, if not inclusiveness, to an end. They cannot allow any organized opposition to exist once they are in power but they may well compete electorally in order to attain power.

Moreover, there are people in nearly all parties who sometimes talk as though other parties have no right to exist. These are usually among the activists, the people who, often few in number, maintain the electoral organization at the grass roots. They see themselves as the guardians of the ideology of the party and, in that position, as remote from the ideologies of other parties. Their championship of the party may make them blind to its deficiencies and angry with its critics, to whom they tend not to listen. On the other hand, if they feel their party is straying from its ideological commitments (especially likely to occur if the party is governing), the activists may be among the harshest critics of the party's leaders. The latter depend on the voters for their re-election, are nearer national polit- ical problems and are closer personally in the legislature to the leaders of the other parties. Consequently, they tend to be less ideological. Unlike the activists, they are likely to be much more aware of the democratic 'rules', and if democracy is to be secure they must feel that the party's goals cannot be attained at the expense of a breach of those rules. For the maintenance of democracy, much therefore depends on the values of party leaders.

The most famous account of the internal workings of political parties is still that of Robert Michels.[2] He argued that parties were bound to be 'oligarchic', by which he meant 'not democratic'. Michels's thesis is part of the earliest wave of disillusionment with democracy. He wrote in a mood of acute disappointment with the performance of the European Socialist parties. They were supposed

[2] R. Michels, *Political Parties* (1912).

to be of the essence of democracy, he assumed, and therefore if they lapsed into oligarchic practices there was no hope anywhere for democracy. Thus he concluded that there was an Iron Law of oligarchy which would inevitably prevail in all organizational situations. His analysis identified two major factors as responsible: the 'technical' and the 'psychological'. By the former Michels referred to those institutional and organizational features of representative institutions which tend both to isolate party leaders from their followers and to make them more powerful. He perceived the leaders of socialist parties as little different from leaders of other parties in this respect. When socialist leaders attained power they were deflected from executing the mandates of 'the masses' who had put them there. The psychological causes of oligarchy, Michels asserted, lay in the nature of the relationship between the masses and the socialist leaders. The masses were by nature politically uneducated and deferential and so too easily manipulated and misled. He supported his theory with a wealth of evidence from the activities of Western European socialist parties before 1914.

Many of Michels's technical criticisms of the internal workings of organizations have never been convincingly refuted. Clearly the development of bureaucracy in large organizations, and the distancing of national leadership at the nation's capital, as well as the distractions of office, combine to make leaders somewhat aloof from followers. The psychological argument, however, is far from convincing. Michels wrote in the infant days of democracy when electorates had still not adjusted to it. In the twentieth century deference has markedly declined, and it is difficult to maintain that adulation of leadership is a common characteristic of citizens of democratic countries. Moreover, there is a flaw in his analysis which lies at the base of most of the 'betrayal' theories of democratic party leaderships. The relationship with which he deals is that between party leaders and 'the masses'; but in his use of the latter term he is either referring to party memberships, or he is conflating party members with the inevitably much larger numbers of ordinary voters. Although the relationship between leaders and members (or perhaps activists) is an important one, it is unlikely to be regarded by leaders as of equal importance as that between themselves and the voters who elect them or reject them. Moreover, intra-party pressures, as we have seen, may be in conflict with extra-party pressures. Democracy within the party may be at odds with democracy within the wider community. Thus socialist leaders, for example, may have to choose between democracy and socialism.

Many of the strictures of Michels (and others), about democratic party leaders appear to demonstrate an unawareness of the wider context within which they have to operate. For example, it is unfair to blame the Social Democratic leaders in the German Empire for their failure to carry out party policies. As we have noted, Wilhelmine Germany was not a democracy, for in spite of massive electoral support for the Social Democratic Party the chancellor was responsible neither to the Reichstag nor the electorate, but to the Kaiser, who always chose him from among the conservative elements of the polity. More generally, even within democracies, party leaders cannot be judged independently of other party leaders with whom they have to compete for publicity and votes. (See Chapter 8.)

The relationship of organized groups to each other has the utmost significance for modern society and is most marked in the case of political parties as their leaderships participate in government or in opposing governments. Any breach of the 'rules' or constitutional conventions may trigger off a process which will end in the collapse of democracy. Some of the most important rules of the game are those concerned with the transfer of power. For example, it is a convention of the British constitution that a government defeated in an election resigns and allows the new majority party to take over office. This has been accepted since 1868. A refusal to observe the convention would destroy much of the trust which characterizes the Government–Opposition relationship, thus weakening British democracy. It would undoubtedly bring about a constitutional crisis.

Hence the attitude of parties to the democratic system is a matter of the utmost significance. I have already mentioned that in all democracies there exist parties whose objective is the overthrow of democracy. Where the voting support, or legislative representation, of such parties is large there will be dangers if the other parties do not carefully discriminate between modes of activity which are legitimate in democratic terms and those which are not. For example, coalescing with parties hostile to democracy against parties which are not may well portend the collapse of a democratic regime. This may follow when the values and objectives of the anti-democratic party appear more congenial than those of a democratic opponent. Thus right-wing democratic parties may coalesce with Fascist parties because they prefer the Fascist image of the nation and conception of the nation's enemies to those of left-wing democratic parties. The latter may coalesce with Communist parties because they prefer the Communist image of international brotherhood and vision of a socialist society to the patriotism and private enterprise of right-wing democratic parties. In either case the parties which support democracy are forgetting its basis in the rules of the game and preferring the assertion of their own values and the attainment of their own ends to the preservation of democratic means. A similar indicator of loyalty to democracy can be found in the relationship with the armed forces. As Juan Linz says, 'knocking at the barracks'[3] for army support against democratic parties perceived as unpatriotic (though loyal to democracy), will arouse great distrust.

Indeed, trust between political parties is essential for democracy. What Juan Linz and Alfred Stepan describe as 'loyal oppositions'[4] will be able to distinguish between proper and improper competitive behaviour. Democratic parties in conflict will indulge to a greater or lesser extent in misinformation about their opponents, whom they may characterize as representing sectional interests against the public interest. This will be 'loyal opposition' within certain limits of fairness. 'Disloyal oppositions', however, as Linz observes, 'picture their opponents collectively as instruments of outside secret and conspiratorial groups—communism, the Masons, international capitalism, the Vatican, or foreign powers'.[5] Above all, any tendentious reporting that party opponents are plotting to subvert the rules of the game may lead to anticipating action against the democratic rights of the parties concerned. Observance of the rules, conversely, will thrive on confidence in one's opponents not breaking them.

Parties may obey the democratic rules and yet still be a source of weakness to democracy if they become out of touch with ordinary people who do nothing political except vote at elections. In a democracy there should always be people willing to initiate new parties to appeal to groups of voters and currents of opinion neglected by the old parties. Unfortunately, inaugurating new parties may be impeded by the dead weight of cultural and histori-

[3] J. Linz and A. Stepan, *The Breakdown of Democratic Regimes* (1975), 30.
[4] Ibid. 36 ff.   [5] Ibid. 31.

cal momentum. Consequently, old parties may confront one another debating worn-out themes, muttering old war-cries, and attempting to mobilize their troops of yesteryear. Their election programmes may neglect important new issues in favour of those issues which appeal to groups on both sides of old cleavages of opinion. Party conflict in this situation may become rather artificial, and new opinion-groups not catered for by the existing framework may stumble into nihilism or even anti-democratic activity. Whatever the case, democracy will be enfeebled because important issues are being overlooked, political leaders will be brought into disrepute, and voters will become cynical about the democratic process. The flexibility of democratic political parties to adjust themselves to opinion changes is therefore an important factor in favour of the viability of democracy. Both the institutional framework within which parties operate and their internal power structures are exceedingly significant in determining whether parties are flexible in this way or not.

Political parties differ from other associational forms in some obvious ways. Alone among organized groups they usually aspire to control, either alone or in alliance with other parties, the apparatus of the state. Hence they have relationships with one another and with the state quite different in their nature from those that other organizations have with one another or with the state. Because political parties alone are responsible, almost overwhelmingly, for the operation of representative democracy within democratic regimes, they are usually accorded a legitimacy not within the attainment of other groups. Even so their development, which Duverger sees as the most important political fact of the twentieth century,[6] has complicated the workings of democratic life. Each political party is a decision-making structure on its own, complete with bureaucratic machinery and collegial assemblies, a far cry from simple 'classical democracy'. As we noted in Chapter 2, political parties may distort public opinion, make ordinary citizens more remote from central decision-making, and weaken the concept of democratic accountability.

Other Organized Groups

In the web of pluralism, other groups may or may not be connected in some way with political parties. The fact that they are sometimes

[6] M. Duverger, *Political Parties* (1954) 256.

referred to as 'pressure groups' by political scientists and sometimes as 'interest groups' reveals a certain indeterminancy about their categorization. Every group and individual has certain desires about either changing or maintaining the status quo whose political manifestation may be described as an 'interest'. All entities that attempt to influence the course of events may be said to exercise pressure: pressure is what politics is all about. For this reason it is not easy to discover a group that can be described as a 'non-interest' or 'non-pressure' group. But while no group, exerts pressure or advances its interests by political means all the time, it is possible to make some distinctions.

For instance, one can distinguish between those groups whose visibility within the political arena is quite clearly defined and those who appear to have no political image at all. Trade unions and business organizations in most democratic countries are often much involved in discussing and negotiating with the government about policy. Churches, on the other hand, are not usually politically motivated, and some Christian sects (such as Jehovah's Witnesses), rejecting the things of this world, proscribe politics altogether for their members. Organized religion, as long as freedom of association guarantees its existence, may not be concerned with political objectives. If some proposed policy change or new law, however, affects its interests, a church may enter the political arena and try to exert some pressure which may be helped by its members possessing votes. Moreover, where moral values are at stake, as in the foreign policy and defence fields, church leaders have not been slow to proclaim their opinions about government policies.

Both trade unions and churches, therefore, may be involved in politics though their normal spheres of activity and *raisons d'être* are quite different. Trade unions are concerned with the material needs of their members; churches with the spiritual needs of their devotees. Both types of association only enter the political arena when necessary. Even so the quantitative difference between trade-union and church intervention in the polity is so great as to be a qualitative difference. Trade unions see a necessity to undertake political action in order to advance their objectives far more than churches do.

There are interest groups whose purpose is to overthrow democracy. Terrorist and conspiratorial groups like the Red Brigades in Italy try to disrupt the framework of the state. Their impact, though frightening, has been slight, and they have probably greatly strengthened the support Italians give to law and order. Other interests that have not always been sympathetic to democracy include the churches, some of which have seen democracy as a threat to religion. The Roman Catholic Church, for example, remained unreconciled to democracy until the Second World War. Pope Pius IX greeted the new Italian state (which had acquired his temporal realm, the Papal States, during unification), by excommunicating its ruling dynasty and threatening to excommunicate any Catholic who voted in elections. The precursors of Christian democracy tried, without great success, to heal this breach during the inter-war period. It was the threat of Communism, however, which persuaded the papacy in the end to relent, so that after World War II voting Communist became the only excommunicable political act, and even that threat has now been relaxed. While this attitude prevailed, the legitimacy of democracy was always somewhat in doubt among Europe's numerous Roman Catholics. Papal support for democracy in the last four decades has undoubtedly strengthened it.

The armed forces occupy a special position. While it might be inapposite to describe them as an interest group in the ordinary sense—they are not voluntary associations but part of the apparatus of the state—there can be no doubt that they are an 'interest' with a sense of corporate separateness. They certainly bring pressure to bear on democratic governments. Indeed, they can be one of the toughest interests with which such governments have to contend. Within democracies, pressures may relate to two areas. With their duty to defend the security of the state the armed forces may claim privileged access to the formulation of foreign and defence policies. To further these ends they will also demand funds: defence budgets comprise a considerable part of the spending of most contemporary democracies. Convinced of their own great importance to the survival of the nation it is perhaps surprising that soldiers (possessing all the guns, as Finer reminds us),[7] intervene so little, if at all, where democracy is well established. It is a fact, however, that the military so far have only overthrown democracy where it is fragile. Although the procedures and values of democracy often still strike senior military men as strange, for the most part they have not been disposed to interfere in highly

[7] S. E. Finer, *The Man on Horseback* (1962).

institutionalized and specialized societies with mature political cultures. It is thus part of their code to refrain from political activity in the ordinary sense.

To sum up: some interest groups are localized or regional and others are national. Many are recreational and cultural and little concerned with policy. Others, often called 'promotional groups', are determined to publicize a cause with a view either to initiating executive action or to stopping it. Some are highly functional and almost part of the administration. Those groups who walk in the corridors of power, who may be very informal or very formal, will use their influence, though unlike political parties they will not want to govern. Pressure groups usually pursue single issues, while parties aggregate several, attempting to reconcile them and to put them in an order of priority.

Democratic Objections to Interest Groups

Jeremy Bentham saw all private influence as exerted by 'sinister interests'. He was writing before democracy was established anywhere, but his sentiments still have echoes today. Interests that take part in decision-making outside the formal procedures of representative democracy are still eyed suspiciously by many. They are seen as whispering into important ears rather than proclaiming their arguments in public debate; or, conversely, shouting very loudly to distract attention from the weakness of their arguments and the smallness of their numbers. Other objections are because interest groups use resources such as guns or money, rather than the simple currency of the vote. The fears are that those with more organization, or more forceful personalities, or stronger lungs, will distort the impact of public opinion on rulers who will gain wrong impressions of the majority will. An even worse apprehension is that the government will know what the majority want but will be diverted from pursuit of public interest by undemocratic pressures. Those who belong to no interest group will have no chance to state a preference. Thus democratically elected governments can desert their commitments as a result of these pressures, of which one of the worst will be a powerful interest challenging the democratic state by threatening to break the law.

A more traditional objection to group activity springs from those who perceive representation in democracies valid only in geographical terms. Only communities, they argue, or their elected representatives, have a right to press their claims upon a democratic government. These champions of geographical representation assert that the spokesmen of interest groups are not only frequently unelected but also speaking for nationally organized and functional collectivities. A formal system of functional representation would not satisfy these critics; an informal one is quite reprehensible. In many ways this is a reaction against the specialized segmentation of *gesellschaft* and in favour of maintaining the values of *gemeinschaft* with its communal implications. It is not surprising that the main thrust of populist movements is against interests and pressure groups seen as too powerful by reason of their specialized knowledge, political skills, centralized organization, or privileged position in society.

The most common contemporary criticism, however, is levelled at interest groups' relationships with democratic governments, all of which consult, negotiate, and bargain with them, to a greater or lesser extent, in many different policy areas, most importantly on the management of the economy. As we have noted in Chapter 5, bargaining is not the most democratic of activities. It tends to subvert public discussion and to put a premium on stratagems, and its outcomes may not be those popular majorities would have selected. It flouts the principle of representation because governments may pick and choose with whom they bargain, and bargainers are not always elected by their followers. 'Consulting the interests concerned' is basically undemocratic even though it is a procedure which long precedes democracy. Exclusively employed it will make a travesty of democracy.

If consulting, negotiating, and bargaining with interest groups are perpetuated, it is said, governmental responsibility will be at risk. Decision-making will not really take place in legislatures but in back-stairs conclaves; governments will not easily be either dismissible or answerable, and they will certainly not be responsive to the voters. This will be because their emerging policies will not be properly known. There will be an obscurity, it is argued, about the bargains as well as how they were arrived at. This may be partly owing to the technicality of the issues; but it will largely be the result of the semi-secrecy of the bargaining process. Objections about furtiveness will be mitigated where there is fairly public and institutionalized bargaining and consultation between interest groups and the government, a feature of some democratic regimes, for example those in Scandinavia.

Even where the relationship is public, however, objections may be raised that its regularized nature is dangerous. If a highly competitive pluralism with a multiplicity of groups is seen as the ideal, then a co-operative (or perhaps collusive) pluralism might signify a movement away from democracy. If the dispersion of power is equated with democracy, as some American commentators imply, then a few large groups possessing privileged contacts with the government imply a concentration of power in policy-making and reflect an undemocratic trend. By the same criteria competitive pluralism is perceived as a basis for stability. Policy is an output which represents an equilibrium between contending forces: all majorities are shifting coalitions with not much more that 50 per cent support. Again, it is assumed that with free association everyone will be a member of many interest groups. The divisions between citizens will be numerous: everyone will both agree and disagree on different issues with everyone else. Hence there will be many cross-cutting cleavages of opinion. As a result, in spite of all the dissensions there will be overall consensus. The stability of the system will be assured because people will win on some issues and lose on others. There will be no groups that win (or lose) on every issue. Thus, competitive pluralism results from the right of free association, and the outcome is a stable democracy; where pluralism takes a different configuration—where there are fewer and larger groups and where they tend to agree on numerous issues forming regular patterns—cleavages will be deeper, dissensus will be greater, and democracy will be less stable.

Furthermore, different configurations imply corresponding attitudes and behaviour which affect the outcomes. In the ideal, highly pluralistic society there are no specially privileged people: pleasure and displeasure will be widely distributed and mixed in each individual. This will be the result of the outcomes of political bargaining being compromises. Change in such a polity will be incremental and slow, and so the great majority of citizens will be moderate in their attitudes and behaviour. They will not want radical innovations. Nor will there be any great demand for political programmes which arise from more durable coalitions of groups aggregating and rationalizing their objectives. Conversely, it is argued, where pluralism is less competitive and groups are ranged in a few larger constellations, the conflict will be more severe, policies will be more radical and less incremental, there will be more 'all-time' winners and losers, the winners will win more and the losers lose more, the behaviour and attitudes of contenders will be more extreme, and the democratic polity will be much less stable.

One objection to the idea of competitive pluralism has been the effect on group relationships where numerous organized divisions of opinion produce a perpetual round of bargainings, as mentioned in Chapter 5, emphasizing a necessity for cunning and deception in the political process. But Nicholas Miller ingeniously argues that the stratagems are a necessary part of pluralistic democracy. It is not only that everyone remains satisfied because everyone wins some and loses some. He writes: 'Precisely because social choice is *not* stable i.e. not uniquely determined by the distribution of preferences, there is some range for autonomous politics to hold sway, and pluralist politics offers almost everybody hope for victory.'[8] A most important additional point, therefore, is that losers do not lose consistently. They do not give up hope in the democratic political process because by forging alliances and trading favours they can secure the outcome they desire. In practice, this implies an electorate in which the overall majority has no strong, conscious, radical aspirations. The bargainers will be coalition-building politicians seeking majorities by rousing half-held opinions and unconscious objectives. As Miller points out, the picture is reminiscent of Schattschneider's analysis[9] of the political process.

It is not a coincidence that most of the discussion about pluralism originates in the United States. American political history has been dominated by two imperatives. The first, deriving from the foundation of the Republic, is that power must not be too concentrated. Consequently three mechanisms for diffusing power were embodied in the Constitution: federalism, the separation of powers, and the limitation of majority decision-making. Under the last device, one-third (or in one case, one-quarter), of those voting could veto proposals. As Americans came to equate their constitutional system with democracy they also equated democracy with the diffusion of power. The second imperative developed in the

---

[8] N. T. Miller, Pluralism and Social Choice, *American Political Science Review*, 77 (1983), 743.

[9] E. E. Schattschneider, *The Semi-Sovereign People* (New York, 1960).

nineteenth century: the need to integrate ethnic minorities within the American nation. Hence the ideology of harmony and stability (really small-town values, as we have noted) became part of the American ethos, the desire for consensus entered the American political culture, and democracy became associated with stability. And these values received support from the dominant group in the pluralistic competition—business. Businessmen did not want a state with strong central power but they wanted a stable society. Numerically a small group, they could only be successful in maintaining an ideology of harmony by making it acceptable to a large majority of others.

Elsewhere democratic development has been somewhat different. Other democracies, even well-established ones, have not been high-consensus societies making only incremental changes. As I argued in Chapter 1, a stable society is not guaranteed by democracy—far from it. Moreover, a system which ensures only incremental change may find itself in trouble when radical change is necessary. Robert Dahl, commenting on the mistakes of many American political scientists in making the United States their point of departure for analysing pluralism, does not feel it necessary to prescribe more stability for his country. In fact he suggests: 'If, then, the most desirable long-run solution for a low-consensus country would be to increase consensus, would not the most desirable long-run solution for a high consensus country be deliberately to foster extreme dissent!'[10] And he points out that unitary constitutions, unified political parties, and constellated pressure groups representing cleavage along class lines and producing non-incremental policies do not seem to have destabilized democracy in Sweden and Denmark.[11] Firmly held opinions and strongly pursued objectives do not in themselves endanger democracy as long as their proponents do not assert them to the point where they take precedence over the integrity of the democratic process. Indeed, it is the values groups accord to the attainment of their goals which is the important factor. Much of the discussion about pluralism and social choice, though valuable as an attempt to define elementary principles, remains abstract and arid because it makes assumptions about the willingness of groups to compromise about goals and values. Even in the

---

[10] R. A. Dahl (ed.), *Political Oppositions in Western Democracies* (New Haven, 1966), 390.
[11] Id., *Dilemmas of Pluralist Democracy* (1982), 76.

United States this cannot always be taken for granted, and in the New Deal period and later, as both Key[12] and Truman[13] demonstrate, a long-term constellation of pressure groups became associated with the Democratic Party. This was the era when class conflict was most apparent in American politics. It was also a period of considerable stability!

Interest groups are a natural element of the democratic polity. A democrat cannot object to their existence, nor to their shape and size; but the roles they have assumed in contemporary democracies may not always be accepted as legitimate. For example, strict adherents of the mandate theory would only allow them to operate politically in election campaigns: between elections nothing should deflect governments from programmes sanctified by majority support from the voters. Representative democracy, it can be argued, ought not to be welcoming to unelected people. Furthermore, even if this position is extreme—in practice governing is bound to involve consulting and bargaining with all sorts of interests—it is at least reasonable to complain about the degree to which pressure groups are involved in policy-making and the difficulties of discovering about their activities. Such obscurities increase the problems of ordinary citizens who try to understand their country's decision-making processes.

The roles of interest groups in contemporary democratic countries are by no means universally accepted as legitimate. Because pluralistic groups increase the difficulties of understanding decision-making processes there is a danger that trust and confidence in democratic regimes may be shaken. The distributive process, as we have seen, may come to be regarded as a lottery. Consultation and bargaining with interest groups may exclude citizens and their representatives from some of the arenas of decision-making. Thus their right of participation will be infringed and their facilities for public contestation will be vitiated if they do not know when and which decisions are being made.

Relations between Interest Groups and Democratic Governments

In order to test the validity of these objections we should examine the behaviour and stance of interest groups in the democratic

[12] V. O. Key, *Politics Parties and Pressure Groups* (New York, 1947), 154 ff.
[13] D. Truman, *The Governmental Process* (New York, 1951), 362 ff.

polity. It is their relations with the government, as we have noted, that gives most cause for concern. Governments for the most part formulate policies and sometimes may begin implementing them before citizens are aware. The extent of government involvement with interest groups varies greatly with time, place, and circumstances.

At one end of the spectrum there is little relationship. What Kahn-Freund called laissez faire collectivism envisages a polity in which government does not interfere in the relations between groups.[14] Dahl and Lindblom describe this as an extension of nineteenth-century liberalism from individuals to groups.[15] A. F. Bentley saw group relations in terms of competitive pluralism, a collectivistic version of Adam Smith's 'hidden hand' from which optimum outcomes would naturally emerge.[16] As this was another aspect of the diffusion of power it was often regarded, especially by American observers, as an extension of democracy. It posed no problems until democratic citizens began to demand interference with it. Although some democratic governments today, such as Mrs Thatcher's, may long for freedom from the pressures of the interests, their yearnings are bound to be in vain because freedom of association implies freedom to use collective muscle.

At the other end of the spectrum are regularized and long-standing relationships between interest groups and governments. As mentioned in Chapter 5, these often relate to the welfare state. In The Netherlands, Belgium, and Switzerland, for example, there is a system of consultation and bargaining between different cultural and/or linguistic groups. In many countries there is a particular sector of decision-making concerned with the farmers. Agricultural price supports, quotas, and subsidies are commonly negotiated in this way. Elsewhere there are examples, most striking in Scandinavia, of 'peak organizations' (confederations of similar associations,) regularly conferring with governments. In Sweden the Saltsjöbaden Agreement of 1938 for annual wage bargaining between the employers' confederation, the trade-union confederation and the government lasted for over forty years.[17]

Stein Rokkan called this process 'corporate pluralism', in

[14] O. H. Kahn-Freund, Labour Law, in M. Ginsberg (ed.), *Law and Opinion in England in the Twentieth Century* (1959) 215 ff.
[15] R. A. Dahl and C. E. Lindblom, *Politics, Economics and Welfare* (1963), 507.
[16] A. F. Bentley, *The Process of Government* (Chicago, 1908).
[17] W. Korpi, *The Democratic Class Struggle* (1983), 173.

contrast with the conventional decision-making system which he labelled 'numerical democracy', asserting laconically, 'Votes count: resources decide.'[18] The two procedures, however, cannot be entirely separated (see Chapter 7), and the duality adds to the complexity, and sometimes the unpredictability, of the situation. Voitto Helander describes as 'liberal corporatism' the situation where interest groups co-operate with one another and also have continuous access to government;[19] but it seems to differ little from Rokkan's corporate pluralism. Many other observers over the past decade have claimed to detect more significant trends. The hint that democratic capitalism is moving towards a form of corporatism such as existed in Mussolini's Italy is sometimes implicit in left-wing commentators' views on the matter; while right-wing analysts have seen sinister undemocratic tendencies at work in much of the negotiation and bargaining between interest groups and the state. Corporate pluralism, however, bears little resemblance to Fascist corporatism or classical corporatism: it is merely a pattern to be found in all democracies, though much more in some than others. The theory that trade-union leaders had become incorporated into the capitalist state, were unable to escape from its snare, and were consequently unresponsive to their followers' real needs was refuted in the late 1970s and early 1980s by the collapse of all such arrangements (including most dramatically the Swedish national lock-out in 1980).[20] The leaders of the peak organizations had retained their freedom of action. When tripartite national bargaining ceased to be profitable they withdrew from it.

Indeed, many relationships between interest groups and governments are likely to be intermittent for many reasons among which the most obvious is that democratic government is necessarily unstable. But the relationship will also be intermittent because circumstances change the needs of interest groups and governments for each other. The needs of the latter are likely to be paramount but there may be situations, such as foreign policy or economic crises, where they may be more in need of each other than at other times. Their interdependence will always be subject to variation.

[18] S. Rokkan, Numerical Democracy and Corporate Pluralism, in Dahl (ed.), *Political Oppositions in Western Democracies*, 106.

[19] V. Helander, A Liberal Corporatist Sub-system in Action: The Incomes Policy in Finland, *Tutkimus – Tiedotteita*, 1 (1979), 5. P. J. Williamson, *Varieties of Corporatism* (Cambridge, 1985), is probably the best overall survey of corporatism.

[20] Korpi, *The Democratic Class Struggle*, 159.

Numerous factors affect the pattern. As we have noted, many governments may require information from associations, especially where the government apparatus is not well informed. This may especially apply to technical matters. Helander describes how both the Finnish government and its separate ministries set up committees with interest-group representation to plan decisions;[21] and how the interest groups strengthened their position on these committees so that in the mid-1970s 59 per cent of *ad hoc* committees and 84 per cent of permanent committees had at least one group representative on them; while by 1975, 45 per cent of all committee members were group representatives.[22] Once obtaining information is regularized, interest groups become part of a consultative process. Indeed, in Finland, as in Sweden, reports of preparatory committees are sent to groups as well as to political parties, local governments, and administrators. Interest groups then express their opinions about prospective policies, and the government gathers detailed information of a specialized kind but also gauges the likely response of the electorate to new policy. In this latter circumstance the opinions of groups with large memberships will be particularly sought.[23] In Scandinavia this is called the 'remiss' system.

Governments may also need interest groups for administering certain sectors of policy. In Britain doctors are allowed to exercise some sanctions in their profession through the British Medical Association.[24] This allows them some autonomy appropriate to their corporate status while the government is saved from the embarrassment of disciplinary action. Again, quangos like the University Grants Committee (UGC),[25] a body set up to allocate funds to the universities, and supposedly representative of university teachers, may both satisfy the criterion of people making decisions about themselves and permit British Governments to avoid some responsibility for ticklish problems, an evasion helped

---

[21] V. Helander, Interest Representation in the Finnish Committee System in the Post-War Era, *Scandinavian Political Studies*, 3 (1972), 224.

[22] V. Helander and D. Anckar, Structural Corporatism in Finland. Paper presented to the ECPR Conference at Lancaster (1981) 5.

[23] D. Anckar and V. Helander, Remiss Participation and Associates. Paper presented to the IVAR/VOI conference at Brussels (1980) 20.

[24] See H. Eckstein, *Pressure Group Politics* (1960).

[25] See E. Bridges, *The Treasury*, 2nd edn. (1966), 57 ff. As educational economies have ensued in the last ten years the UGC has become conspicuously more *dirigiste* and more visibly an instrument of government.

by parliamentary questions about quangos being out of order. Similarly, American governments have developed the device of regulatory commissions. Such bodies as the Federal Trade Commission, which incorporates big business representatives into the administrative process, have been a feature of American political life since 1914.[26] Criticism levelled against such a system is hardly surprising. In recent years President Reagan's deregulation has been a response to some popular objections, as well as those from business groups not represented on regulatory boards. As with the supply of technical information, the administration of specialized areas reveals governments using interest groups in fields where expertise is lacking.

What most affects the pattern, however, is the institutional framework and how national policies are expressed by the party system. In the United States, policy in general terms is articulated very little by parties; this is the task of presidential candidates. The pressure groups have specific demands and the openness of the legislature, with the weak discipline of the parties, favours their forceful advocacy. Specific policies emerge from Congressional committee–pressure-group–executive agency 'whirlpools'[27] or 'iron triangles',[28] and much of the negotiation is in public. This process may well be considered as nearer numerical democracy because it is fairly open and elected representatives are involved. Only in the last half-century have presidents been elected on comprehensive programmes. Especially when the White House needed the co-operation of interest groups (during depression and war and for the social reforms of the 1960s), a system nearer corporate pluralism evolved which Theodore Lowi calls 'interest group liberalism'.[29]

Its assumptions are:

1. Organized interests are homogeneous and easy to define, sometimes monolithic. Any duly elected spokesman for any interest is taken as speaking for every member.

2. Organized interests represent most sectors of our lives and check one another.

[26] G. Kolko, *The Triumph of Conservatism* (New York, 1963), 265. See also J. Q. Wilson, *The Politics of Regulation* (New York, 1980).

[27] E. S. Griffith, *The American System of Government* (1954) 127.

[28] H. Heclo, Issue Networks and the Executive Establishment, in A. King (ed.), *The New American Political System* (Washington, 1978), 87–124.

[29] T. Lowi, The Public Philosophy: Interest Group Liberalism, *American Political Science Review*, 61, (1967), 12. See also his *The End of Liberalism* (1969), p. x.

3. The role of government is to ensure access to the most organized and to ratify compromises between competing leaders and claims.

Interest group liberalism is a conviction, Lowi avers, that it is both necessary and good that the policy agenda and public interest be defined in terms of the organized interests in society. For example, President Kennedy's guidelines for wage and price increases were worked out between himself, the unions, and industrial management. Bargaining between pressure groups and the executive has replaced the pressure group–Congress relationship which guaranteed open government and the rule of law. American political leaders tend to discuss functional issues rather than substantive policies because they fear political conflict and strongly desire stability. The more formally recognized groups provide much of the necessary every-day social control, and thus tend towards the creation of new privilege.[30] Hence much of Lowi's condemnation seems to stem from a characteristic American distrust of governmental power. Policy, he appears to feel, cannot be viewed in terms of popular mandates. For example, he writes, 'The abdication of Congress in the 1930s in the passage of fundamental New Deal legislation could never have been justified in the name of popular government.'[31] In other words, 'positive government' (as he calls it), bringing interest groups in its train, cannot be justified even when backed, as in the 1930s, by huge electoral and legislative majorities. Lowi wants to move to a model he believes operated in the United States before positive government. This comprises Congressional dominance, more clearly defined implementation of laws at the appropriate level of government, no delegation of decisions to the most interested parties, and the rule of law.

In practice in the United States both forms of decision-making have operated at the same time, though with the emphasis sometimes towards one and sometimes towards the other. Thus, in spite of open government, American policy-making may defy characterization by political scientists, let alone ordinary citizens. In Britain the pattern is also highly complex and even one neo-Marxist corporatist, Bob Jessop, has recently admitted:

the decline of Parliament and the rise of para-state bodies do not obviate the need for a central co-ordinating apparatus able to formulate and imple-

---

[30] Lowi, The Public Philosophy, 20.   [31] Ibid. 13.

ment the interests of capital in general. . . . The role of the Cabinet continues to be paramount here.[32]

Perhaps Grant Jordan, however, has done best in attempting to unravel the tangled skeins of British national policy-making. He describes classical British Cabinet government as an 'ideal type', citing Barbara Castle's disillusion with this model after entering the Cabinet: 'I suddenly found I wasn't in a political caucus at all. I was faced by departmental enemies.'[33] In other words at the top level of British numerical democracy, there exists, instead of a highly centralized co-ordinating mechanism, a highly segmented system of policy areas, in conflict about the allocation of public expenditure. Jordan asserts:

Decisions can be effectively made in sectors (on agriculture, defence, monetary policy etc.) before receiving perfunctory attention in the centre. Group–departmental relations are far more important than the political party–electorate focus of most cabinet government discussions.[34]

And with Jeremy Richardson he had earlier argued that policies are made

between a myriad of inter-connecting, inter-penetrating organisations. It is the relationship involved in committees, the policy community of departments and groups, the practices of co-option and the consensual style that better accounts for policy outcomes than do examinations of party stances, of manifestoes or of parliamentary utterance.[35]

Within this elaborate chaos Whitehall attempts nevertheless, in the bureaucratic fashion, 'to establish regularised and rationalised relationships approaching the iron triangle idea'. It is unusual for Whitehall to be able to impose stable rules, Jordan argues, although it did with pay policy.[36]

This analysis seems very convincing at the level of Whitehall policy-making but the problem of reconciling British corporate

[32] B. Jessop, The State in Post-war Britain, in R. Scase (ed.), *The State in Western Europe* (1980), 84. See also his Corporatism, Fascism and Social Democracy, in P. Schmitter and G. Lehmbruch (eds). *Corporatism in Liberal Democracies* (1979).

[33] B. Castle, The Loneliness of the Short Distance Runner, *Sunday Times*, 10 June 1978.

[34] A. G. Jordan, Iron Triangles, Woolly Corporatism and Elastic Nets: Images of the Policy Process, *Journal of Public Policy* (1979), 9.

[35] J. J. Richardson and A. G. Jordan, *Governing Under Pressure* (1979), 74.

[36] Jordan, Iron Triangles, 19.

pluralism with numerical democracy in its most extreme form, 'manifestoism', still remains. The facts cannot easily be disputed. Much of major British governmental policy stems from decisions made within political parties, often at party conferences, and put to the voters in electoral manifestos. Mrs Thatcher's Conservative 1983–7 government was concerned with redeeming promises of privatizing telecommunications, altering the law with regard to industrial relations, and abolishing the Greater London Council. All these measures were clearly under the heading of numerical democracy: corporate pluralism only came into it with regard to the details of the measures. Here the policy communities may buzz into activity, but it is not the most important part of the policy-making. Moreover, the Labour Party moved in the early 1980s even further towards party control over policy, with constitutional amendments smacking of democratic centralism.

Undoubtedly the configuration of political parties and their connections with interest groups has much to do with the relationship between numerical democracy and corporate pluralism. A country sectionalized by religious and/or language divisions, expressed in terms of pressure groups and political parties, may have little difficulty in accommodating the two processes. The best example of this is The Netherlands, where what Arend Lijphart calls 'consociational democracy'[37] has existed since World War I. The three pillars of Dutch life—Protestant, Catholic, and secular socialist—have been closely involved for more than half a century in 'self-regulative policies, mixed public-private committees and other manifestations of the mixed polity.' The result of this is to render the process of numerical democracy much more congruent with that of corporate pluralism, producing what Heisler and Kvavik call the European Polity Model[38] in which ideological conflict about goals has abated, the role of the legislature has declined, and the influence of the mass public has been effectively removed from decision-making. In other words, numerical democracy, the legislative–electoral process, is greatly overshadowed by corporate pluralism, the organizational–functional process which provides 'continuous, regularized access for economically, politically, ethnically and/or subculturally based groups to the highest

[37] A. Lijphart, *The Politics of Accommodation* (1975), 70.
[38] M. O. Heisler and R. B. Kvavik, Patterns of European Politics: the European Polity Model, in M. O. Heisler, *Politics in Europe* (New York, 1974), 27 ff.

level . . .'[39] New groups may be granted access by co-option, preventing the system from becoming rigid.

Heisler and Kvavik consider that Austria, Belgium, Denmark, Luxembourg, The Netherlands, Norway, and Sweden all exemplify this model: proportional representation and coalition bargaining is, to a greater or lesser extent, a feature of all of them. Accommodation in the legislature and in the process of government formation is part of numerical democracy and thus there is a congruence between both types of decision-making in these countries. In France and Italy many of the important pressure groups are divided along the lines of ideological cleavage, like the political parties. Corporate pluralism is thus weak in relation to numerical democracy. In Britain, adversarial politics is bound to be incongruent with the process of pluralistic compromise and bargaining and this may explain the difficulties of British governments in trying to steer the economy with the help of business and labour. The fact that the two British major parties are each associated predominantly with one of them cannot make the process very efficient. Of course, efficiency, as I have argued, is not necessarily very much to do with democracy; indeed, inefficiency might be the price one pays for it. But this is too easy an answer, because in some, perhaps most, of the countries of the European Polity Model there is probably more citizen participation than in Britain, and some legislatures—for example, those of Denmark, Norway, and Sweden—have retained more power than the House of Commons.

Finally, the attitude of the government itself towards various interest groups is bound to have some implications for democracy. With adversarial politics in Britain, reflecting each party being almost embarrassingly connected with a large interest group, party philosophies and attitudes become polarized. Not only the bulk of the electorate but also many independent groups, are therefore in the political centre between the parties. There has been a convention in Britain that groups who are by their nature necessarily non-political should be allowed to voice informed criticism above the political adversaries. These groups and institutions included the Church of England, the universities, *The Times,* and the BBC. In recent years *The Times* has deserted its natural stance of supporting the government of the day and become an outspoken advocate of Thatcherism. It is not without significance that the others have

[39] Ibid. 48.

found themselves under attack. The Archbishop of Canterbury incurred displeasure for remembering dead Argentinians in the national service of remembrance after the Falklands War. Later the Church was criticized by ministers for venturing into politics with its remarks about the Government's conduct of the miners' strike, or government neglect of the inner cities. In the academic world the social sciences were first assailed with the threatened closure of their research council. The severe financial economies in the universities have been accomplished through the government pushing the UGC into a much more *dirigiste* role. With university teachers feeling insecure in employment, an important source of criticism has been subdued. Uncertainty is a powerful weapon. It also affects the BBC, which receives its revenue from the purchase of licences by listeners and viewers. Increases in the licence fee must be approved by Parliament and so it is a Cabinet decision. In spite of its reputation for impartiality the BBC has been threatened by both Labour and Conservative governments hinting that additional revenue might not be forthcoming.

Of course, well-educated and informed critics are capable of saying foolish and unfair things. Moreover, all these institutions are bound to be platforms for highly disparate groups and individuals expressing controversial sentiments. Democracy, however, allows such opinions to be expressed, and vigorous responses by governments to such criticisms do not endanger democracy. It depends on the manner in which reaction is expressed. For example, relations between the British government and the BBC have been conducted in terms of a convention that while a minister could object to a programme about an area within his department's responsibility, the government would not intervene because to do so would be tantamount to control. When in November 1986 Norman Tebbit, on behalf of the Conservative Party and as its chairman, complained about the partiality of BBC reporting on the American bombing of Tripoli, people could hardly be blamed for perceiving his action as that of the government, of which he was also a minister. But it was not his objection so much as the bullying way in which it was made, and his dismissal of the argued and detailed BBC reply, which many found disturbing. It is one thing to reply sharply and firmly to critics' arguments: it is quite another to attack them with the implied threat of silencing them. In doing so Tebbit revealed an anti-democratic streak very reminiscent of those few students (and others) who endlessly shout 'Out, out, out' in order to drown the voicing of opinions they dislike.

Conclusion

Pluralism and democracy are clearly separate, though related concepts. Their relationship may take various forms, depending upon the social forces and constitutional pattern of any given democracy. All that can be assumed is that freedom of association, like freedom of speech or of the press, is a democratic fundamental, though it is bound to be more qualified than other democratic freedoms because its consequences are more likely to involve physical activity and result in a resort to law. People organize themselves, or are organized, for numerous purposes, and so associations of all kinds—corporations, trade unions, churches, recreational and cultural groups, promotional bodies—pursue a variety of objectives within a legal framework which they may attempt to change.

A democratic government, therefore, will find it difficult not to be involved with interest-group activity. Responses to the behaviour of such bodies will take various forms. In some cases administration of the law may be all that is required: in others new legislation may be needed, or regulatory bodies may have to be set up. Sometimes the associations themselves may demand new legislation, or disagreement between two or more associations may need some form of government intervention. Governments may have to mediate between different groups in the interests of society as a whole.

Governments may be most involved with pluralistic groups when concerned with social, and particularly, economic policy. In these circumstances government relationships with business and labour will be of a different nature and of greater importance than with other groups. The attitudes of these two social partners may have great bearing upon prosperity and thus affect the general political atmosphere (see Chapter 7). The fundamental problem for contemporary democratic governments is frequently that of balancing the demands of powerful groups with the electorate's view of what is in the general interest. Essentially, the situation is one in which a supervening power structure—government and its apparatus—deals with lesser, though not unchallenging, alternative sources of power. It is quite impossible for the result to be persistent stability.

Power in contemporary democratic regimes is unstable, though the supremacy of state power must be maintained if democracy and the rule of law are to continue.

Two important features of government relationships with interest groups possess great significance for the operation of democracy: their complexity and their instability, characteristics which can hardly imply clarity and intelligibility. Pluralistic structures are almost inevitably temporary and often ramshackle; the heated controversies between political scientists about them reflect their transitory natures. Our conclusion must be that this uncertainty is based on the very mixed content of policy-making procedures in all democratic states. These can tentatively be categorized in four groups, as follows:[40]

1. Universal regulation: general public policy as related, for example, to changes in government structure, ownership of industry or the educational system.
2. Specific regulation: detailed policy in specific sectors such as agriculture, commerce, industry, etc.
3. Allocation of goods and services: policy concerned with the distribution of benefits and services such as social security, education, and health.
4. Co-ordination and direction: policy concerned with control and co-ordination of all government activity and state affairs (e.g. foreign policy, national economic and financial policy).

As Jacob Buksti argues, pluralistic bargaining seems especially appropriate for (2) and (3). There are several reasons why this should be so. These are the areas for intimate clientele relations between producer and consumer organizations and ministries. Wages, subsidies, quotas, tariffs, old age pensions, family allowances, and taxation will be the sort of policy foci here. The subjects of the policies will frequently be divisible and calculable goods so that the participants are more likely to be 'sharers' rather than winners or losers. Hence negotiation and bargaining will be a

---

[40] This is a modification of Jacob Buksti, Corporate Structures in Danish EC Policy, Institute of Political Science, Aarhus University (1979), 4, quoting J. G. Christensen, Normerne for samspillet mellem den danske centraladministration og interesseorganisationerne i centraladministrativt perspektiv, paper delivered to 5th Nordic Political Science Conference, Bergen (1978). Also see T. Lowi, American Business, Public Policy, Case Studies and Political Theory, *World Politics,* 16/4 (1964), 677 ff. His four types of policy-making are: distribution, regulation, redistribution, and foreign-policy making.

feature of these lower and middle areas of social and economic policy. The tendency will be for it to take place privately because public decision-making is eschewed by business groups, which do not like to reveal their positions. ('Minding one's own business' is a businessman's maxim.) In these areas decision-making, in Britain anyway, may have gone underground, as Richardson and Jordan claim.[41] Even where, as in the United States, decisions are made publicly, such policies have tended to slip into the hands of agents of the executive and of the interested groups.[42]

With regard to (1) and (4), discussion everywhere is likely to be more public. These relate to high levels of policy-making where more important national changes are being debated, where political parties will be the main decision-making agents in many democratic countries and especially in Britain, where adversarial politics still obtains. Where intelligible issues are under discussion within this framework—Rokkan's numerical democracy—then representative democracy may operate in its familiar way. Foreign policy, for instance, which frequently arouses simple moralistic feelings, may be discussed in its essentials by a large part of the electorate. (It is usually the important sector of national policy about which the voters are most ignorant.) National economic policy, however, is so complex, not to say technical, that it is not understood, whether it emerges from corporate pluralism or whether from numerical democracy. Yet, while the electorate may not understand, it experiences the outcomes, and discerns them as of the utmost importance, as discussed in Chapter 5. The voters may not want national economic policy explained at great length but that does not stop them rewarding its successes and punishing its failures. In this area there is greater confusion, especially in Britain, between the two decision-making systems.

We saw in Chapter 2 how the nature of the competition between political parties tends to make the democratic doctrine of accountability difficult to sustain. Pluralistic bargaining and governmental involvement in it may blur even more the clarity of the image of the polity and of the responsibility of its political leadership. It becomes more difficult to discover who has done what when policy emerges from a mêlée of contending groups. The absence of lengthy legislative

---

[41] Richardson and Jordan, *Governing Under Pressure*, 191.
[42] For a lengthy statement on the American position see G. McConnell, *Private Power and American Democracy* (New York, 1967).

debate and nation-wide discussion downgrades the legislators even more. The media thus acquire more power, for they can often provide comment and question policy-makers more easily and publicly than they can elected representatives. Unfortunately, though the media have power, they do not have responsibility. A brief television grilling, however sharp, is no substitute for the process of sustained legislative surveillance and cross-examination.

Much of the distrust of policy-making outside the framework of numerical democracy stems from a feeling that the participants are favoured in some way. As Lowi says, it ordains privilege.[43] The people involved may be technocratic experts, the wealthy leaders of large corporations, or professional groups such as doctors or university teachers. Again, privilege may be given to large groups, like trade unions, whose roles in group bargaining have been established. This will leave unestablished groups with a sense of exclusion. Consumer groups, in particular, suffer in this way. Hence the principle of inclusiveness, fundamental to democracy, may be infringed. Lowi argues that access to the arenas of policy-making is granted much more readily to established interests; and that the more legitimized a group's participation is, the less voluntary is its leadership and the more necessary for the latter to demand loyalty.[44]

The bargainers and/or policy-makers who lead interest groups, many argue, become incorporated in national policy-making to the detriment of members who perceive their leaders as bound up with 'the system' and being unable to extricate themselves from it. William Kornhauser[45] says mediating groups will cease to mediate if this position is reached, and 'mass society' will ensue. His theory assumes that a straightforward relationship between leaders and masses is dangerous for democracy, and that mediating groups are essential to its maintenance. When they are unable to mediate because their leaders have defected to the 'Establishment', society moves a stage on the road to totalitarianism.

I have argued that there seems insufficient evidence to support the view that important interest groups have been incorporated into the state apparatus. Yet the disquiet about late twentieth-century pluralism springs from confusion about its form, and academic

[43] Lowi, The Public Philosophy, 19.
[44] Ibid. 21.
[45] W. Kornhauser, *The Politics of Mass Society* (1960), 76 ff.

commentators have added to the unease by their failure to agree. The controversy illustrates how much is to be learnt about contemporary democratic politics. The unease is partly caused by the secrecy and informality of the process in some countries—in turn, an intention of some of those involved—but it may also be a result of the bewildering floods of information modern organizations disgorge. If policy makers are so overloaded with data that making a judicious assessment is difficult, how much less likely are ordinary citizens to be able to do so. The result may not be corporatism, but it may render responsive and responsible democratic government rather problematic. On the other hand, as we noted in Chapter 5, it is possible to agree with Lindblom that pluralistic bargaining, where it is relatively open to the public, may enhance accountability.

As far as governments are concerned, it is often a case of balancing efficiency against democracy. More efficient legislation and administration may depend on technical knowledge which can only be obtained, especially at short notice, from the interest group concerned. A democratic government, however, should attempt to discover whether there are any other viewpoints among the electorate at large. (Sample survey techniques now make this easy.) It should endeavour to look at problems with perspectives different from the interest groups involved. Electoral expedience, if nothing else, is likely to dictate this course. None of the important interest groups enjoy overwhelming popularity with the voters. Hence careful governments will want to sort out the value-judgements of interest groups from the information they provide. Again, the influence of producer groups can be balanced by encouraging consumer groups to organize.

Thus though not all the objections to interest groups can be sustained, there can be little doubt that they are the cause of confusion about the nature of the present democratic system. To a greater or lesser degree, in all contemporary democracies there is a discrepancy between the ideal version of the political system and its actual performance. The decision-making process produces doubts about roles and responsibilities. Dahl has recently written: 'I do not believe we have yet found an altogether satisfactory way of resolving the tension which exists, both in theory and practice, between pluralism and democracy.'[46] The problem is greatest where, as in

---

[46] R. A. Dahl, Polyarchy, Pluralism and Scale, *Scandinavian Political Studies*, 7 (1984), 238.

Britain, it is the conventional wisdom that political parties and interest goups have very different roles. A party's classical roles are governing, or aspiring to govern, or to share in government; mobilizing voters through electoral organization; nominating candidates for legislatures; and articulating and co-ordinating general policy. Interest groups classically possess only one role: articulating specific policy and representing a sectional interest. A majority party government in Britain will make a strong claim to have the sole right to formulate national policy. In contrast stands consociational rule where no party can make this assertion: all parties represent sectional interests. With American 'exceptionalism' it is questionable whether parties exist at all in terms of the above definition.[47] (Many American political scientists seem unaware of this.) In these latter two instances, because bargaining about policies is so much a feature of numerical democracy, it is much more congruent with corporate pluralism, the other decision-making process. The incongruity is sharpest in Britain, as we have noted, where the two forms are least reconciled and the problem least recognized. Thus is Britain, both in theory and practice, the tension is greatest.

Obviously, resolution of this tension in order to assure good government and the maintenance of democracy is a major task. To confront the problem much more information about the internal procedures and external relations of pluralistic groups is needed. Only then can they be made more accountable to the voters and to their elected representatives.

[47] American parties do not govern or aspire to govern; nor do they articulate or formulate policy. Presidents and presidential candidates do so. Voters usually nominate candidates through the primaries. Electoral mobilization is done largely by the *personal* organization of candidates and they also collect personal campaign funds. Other money for candidates comes from the Federal exchequer. For the most part the Republicans and Democrats do not have individual party members.

7

DEMOCRACY AND THE SOCIAL PARTNERS

IT will have already emerged that among other pluralistic relationships, the one between the state and business and labour organizations, first called in Austria the 'social partners', is both unusual and singularly important. In many ways it might be regarded as the outstanding problem confronting the democratic state. It is not only a relationship of great intricacy and complexity, it also varies with time and place. Moreover, there are difficulties, which do not exist to the same degree with other interests, in reconciling the activities of business and labour with the theory and practice of democracy.

At first sight the differences between the social partners are enormous. Capitalists and capitalism preceded democracy, whereas organized labour normally flourished only after the winning of free association and universal suffrage. (This was not so in Britain, where many working men were voting in trade-union elections before obtaining the right to do so in national elections.) Business, therefore, has a normality and a legitimacy which unions lack in the eyes of many, in spite of the small numbers which businessmen bring to the count in numerical democracy. In this respect they are swamped by millions of trade-union votes, enough to put businessmen out of action altogether if used for that purpose. But this has not occurred; to a great extent because business fears union power with an intensity that trade-union members do not feel for business power. The disparity is reflected in differing modes of activity: business hopes to influence those in political power by informal consultation. Trade unions may also proceed in this way, but more often they will rely on a deployment of their main resources—organizational strength and numbers. The resources of business and industry lie in wealth which they may use to contribute to party funds or, occasionally, in advertising campaigns aimed at the electorate. There is a conflict of interests at the shop floor level because trade-union objectives of better pay and conditions and, less explicitly, some measure of control over industry, are not easy to reconcile with employers' desires to keep down costs and to retain autonomy for management. With their contrasting styles business may often escape notice whereas trade unions, as I have already noted, are very visible.

Although the dissimilarities between the two sides of industry are painfully obvious there are, nevertheless, reasons why conflict is not the most common outcome of their relationship. They are partners in a very real sense, and co-operation in the productive process is the most common everyday expression of the partnership. Neither can proceed towards their objectives, in a democratic situation, without taking account of the other. Some employers might wish that the unions could be abolished; but they are hardly likely to persuade the electorate that this should be done, however much the voters distrust the unions. Some trade-unionists believe that private capital should be abolished, but the public ownership of most industry seems a remote possibility—again, voters nowhere favour it—so in practice union leaders, however revolutionary their beliefs, are forced to negotiate with the employers. On both sides for the most part there is a common interest in the prosperity of their own industry. Profits will normally imply higher wages: bankruptcy results in unemployment.

The activities of both interests, as well as their interrelationships, have obvious implications for the operation of democratic procedures. Corporate pluralism, I have argued, has a rather dubious democratic validity. When it involves two of the most powerful groups in society it is bound to arouse suspicion. The triangle—business, labour, and the state apparatus—has been subjected to a good deal of analysis. It is a common formation because, as we have noted, laissez faire collectivism is not often to be found, however much contemporary governments may yearn for it. Governments may often want forewarning about the intentions of both partners; they may need their expertise about industrial matters. Regular negotiation and consultation may sometimes suit all three parties, and sometimes not.

It is when governments need to bargain with the partners, however, that a regular relationship often becomes desirable. This circumstance has arisen in recent decades when governments have proposed national incomes policies. Trade unions and employers' associations in these situations become regular clients of governments whose reason for adopting this relationship is easy to discern: their desire for a prosperous economy. For example, keeping wages stable for a period enhances the possibility of a standstill in employers' costs and so removes an element of unexpectedness from forward planning for industry. On its side a government can persuade private employers to bargain (sometimes by its own performance as a public employer); can make promises about taxation and financial policy; and can also stabilize farm prices by bringing farmers into the bargaining. It is less easy, however, to perceive what trade unions can gain from national incomes policies; but if governments can deliver stable price levels and welfare benefits, then trade-union leaders and members (for both have to be persuaded) may agree to bargain. Clearly, the possibility of galloping inflation or mass unemployment might help to draw both unions and employers into national wages bargaining: it depends on how much they see these as threats. Again, this will depend on the degrees of knowledge, rationality, and economic literacy among the parties involved. Hence we shall examine government relations with business and organized labour below in more detail.

Relations between Business and Government

Business is sometimes seen as a threat to the proper working of democracy because its impact on decisions is far in excess of its numbers. It is an alternative source of power, and unlike trade-union power, it existed before the democratic state. Like the apparatus of the state, business has a pyramidal hierarchy which is bound to place it in a challenging stance. Its leadership tends to be more stable than democratic political leadership, which is liable to be dismissed at fairly short notice. There has, in all democracies, been constant adjustment between business and the democratic process. This readjustment has varied from one democracy to another, partly because business practices vary, but largely because the forces that range themselves against business have differed greatly as between different societies.

Because they are vastly outnumbered, businessmen are unlikely to respond instinctively to numerical democracy. Hence their efforts have been concentrated on informal consultation and bargaining, to which business is, by nature of its own command structure, a good deal more sympathetic. The more elitist practices of small numbers of people conferring about decisions (in Britain usually privately), is something that business understands. Especially where the matter to be decided lies within the sphere of the economy, corporate pluralism is likely to strike businessmen as more natural than numerical democracy.

One can overestimate the power of business, however, if one sees it as a united, coherent force challenging the decisions of governments elected by democratic majorities. Businessmen are seldom, if ever, united: always there is the fact of business competition. In the Confederation of British Industries (CBI) there are divisions between public and private industry and between big and small business. There are also disagreements between different industries. Moreover, in Britain there is the very significant divide between manufacturing industry and the City, always believed to be a particularly strong influence on the economic policy of British governments. Wyn Grant and David Marsh remark on the suspicions of British industrialists about 'what they often see as undue influence exerted by City interests on government'.[1]

The fact that business is not, as some would see it, a solid, unified force is bound to weaken its power in relation to the state, the ultimate coercive power in society. The sanctions of businessmen against the state may not be great. 'Peak organizations' of business, such as the National Association of Manufacturers in the United States, or the CBI in the United Kingdom, can never rely on the whole-hearted co-operation of their members. They thus tend to avoid controversy by not taking up public positions or, when they do so, choosing rather peripheral sectors of governmental policy in which to participate. In fact in both countries, large corporations have always preferred to deal individually with governments.[2] They have not felt comfortable in using intermediaries. Indeed, Big Business has often been well-informed enough to be aware of its unpopularity. Political leaders, even of right-wing parties, have not usually been anxious to be identified with Big Business. Consequently the latter has preferred informal approaches to top leaders as the best way to proceed politically.

The picture of Big Business threatening a left-wing government

[1] W. Grant and D. Marsh, *The Confederation of British Industry* (1977), 69.

[2] G. K. Wilson, The Changing Role of Business in American Politics. Paper presented to the 1980 conference of the Political Studies Association at Exeter, p. 29; Grant and Marsh, *Confederation of British Industry*, 55. See also G. K. Wilson, *Business and Politics* (1985).

with an 'investment strike' seems rather far-fetched. The idea that a business firm would deliberately forego a profitable investment in order to weaken a social democratic government appears as unlikely as one knowingly undertaking an unfavourable investment. It is not in their nature to do such things. Indeed, the possible sanctions of a reforming government may well cause business to act warily. Few governments will be as dramatic as President Kennedy, sending FBI agents to question steel executives about a price rise;[3] but pressures against business in the contemporary democratic state are a fact of life. Investment is likely to slacken under a left-wing government, not because business is trying to bring the government down, but because the rate of return almost inevitably will diminish. As Lindblom says, 'If spokesmen for business predict that investment will lag without tax relief, it is only one short step to corporate decisions that put off investment until tax relief is granted.'[4]

There is more plausibility in the idea of a flight of capital, deliberate action by bankers and financial business in order to weaken left-wing governments. Finance capital is distinguished from industrial capital by its much greater fluidity and mobility. It can change its nature and move its base of operation very rapidly. It has none of the problems industry has with the labour and few of the difficulties associated with the productive process. Michael Moran, writing about 'the inventiveness of the banking markets', refers to the problem of monitoring their activities. He says:

The special problems created by financial markets lie in the markets' capacity for innovation, usually prompted by the effort to circumvent regulation. Innovation creates new institutions and new financial instruments; in so doing it continually changes the nature of the economic data.[5]

Capital flows to the most profitable markets as water to the lowest point. Socialist governments usually provide rather unfavourable opportunities for finance capital, and only regulation may prevent a flight of capital from a country after a left-wing government comes to power. This may be a strong sanction though not necessarily a very deliberate one. It may merely be part of an instinctive reaction

---

[3] T. C. Sorensen, *Kennedy* (1965), 443 ff.

[4] C. E. Lindblom, *Politics and Markets* (New York, 1977), 185.

[5] M. Moran, Banks and Politics: An Anglo-American Comparison. Paper presented to the 1983 conference of the PSA at Newcastle, p. 22. See more recently his *The Politics of Banking* (1984).

to move from less favourable to more favourable investment situations.

Finance capital may be in its strongest position *vis-à-vis* government when loans are required to offset public debt. Here the terms drawn up can affect policy. In such cases, however, it is usual for the loans to be provided by foreign bankers. Thus the British Labour government in 1931, faced with rising unemployment and increasing debts, appointed a Committee on National Expenditure under Sir George May, former secretary of Prudential Assurance, with four other businessmen and only two representatives of labour.[6] It recommended increased taxation and increased economies, of which two-thirds were to be found by reductions in unemployment expenditure. The May Report caused foreigners to withdraw funds from the City of London, and set in train a financial crisis which led to the bankers telling the government that unemployment benefits must be cut. C. L. Mowat rejects the idea, however, that this was a 'bankers' ramp', arguing that the financiers' advice was orthodox advice, accepted by an orthodox Chancellor of the Exchequer: to blame the bankers for giving it, is to blame them for lacking a belief in economic theories which only became fashionable later.[7] In the end after J. P. Morgan and Co., American bankers, sent a telegram saying they were only willing to make good the deficit if Parliament enacted economy legislation, eleven members of the Labour Cabinet accepted a 10 per cent cut in unemployment benefit while ten were opposed. The Cabinet then broke up. It is possible to argue that the loan was only offered on terms known to be unacceptable. On the other hand, the cut in unemployment benefits was opposed by the TUC, to whom its rejection was a matter of fundamental principle. The Labour government of 1929–31 was therefore on the horns of a desperate dilemma. Anyway, it did not have a majority in the House of Commons. Probably no British government in the twentieth century has been in such a weak position.

Another Labour government in a predicament with some similar features, faced in 1976 with burgeoning public expenditure and reluctant to increase taxation, decided to approach the International Monetary Fund (IMF) for a loan. Denis Healey, the chancellor of the Exchequer, could only succeed in negotiating one on IMF

---

[6] C. L. Mowat, *Britain Between the Wars* (1955), 379 ff; R. Bassett, *Nineteen Thirty One* (1958), 54 ff.   [7] Mowat, *Britain Between the Wars,* 383.

terms which involved giving certain assurances about cuts in the public sector borrowing requirement and in money supply growth, and accepting some monitoring of the loan's implementation.[8] This also could in no sense be adjudged a bankers' ramp, but it demonstrated that governments in need of financial support, like individuals in the same position, cannot be regarded as entirely autonomous.

Hence it is difficult to deny that the impact of business, especially Big Business, on the democratic decision-making process, is far in excess of its numbers. But the reasons for this impact may lie in reasons which have some democratic justification. Capitalism existed before democracy and democracy had to come to terms with it. In the course of doing this, democracy was able to curb capitalism's more unpopular manifestations but unable, in most countries anyway, seriously to attack it because democratic governments need economic prosperity in order to stay in power. Thus there is a tacit mutual acceptance of business by democratic governments. It has a privileged position. On the other hand, as Michael Moran, G. K. Wilson, and David Vogel argue, there is regulation of capital, including finance capital, and it is not as perfunctory as Lindblom appears to maintain. Michael Moran says of the United Kingdom and the United States: 'In both countries regulation does far more than ratify or amend (Lindblom's words) the decisions of bankers: it pervades markets, shaping industrial structure and development.'[9] Public control of the banking system has influenced greatly, sometimes unexpectedly, industrial and financial structures; but in general, 'those who argue that market capitalism gives business men a special kind of power are right.'[10]

It is, of course, especially Big Business which wields power. Oligopolistic corporations, as J. K. Galbraith has maintained,[11] fix the prices of their products mainly to promote the attainment of their planning goals. In times of rising prices and prosperity they may have little difficulty in maintaining their profits by passing on wage rises in the form of price rises. In so doing they will be exerting a strong influence upon the economy, affecting government policy, and therefore also intervening in the polity. On their side,

[8] Chris R. Milner, Payments and Exchange Rate Problems, in P. Maunder (ed.), *The British Economy in the 1970s* (1980), 234.

[9] Moran, Banks and Politics, 2,

[10] Ibid. 25.

[11] J. K. Galbraith, *The New Industrial State* (1967), 186 ff.

governments in the twentieth century have extended the polity in order to regulate areas of the economy. Some large economic actors have become so controlled that their power over the economy has been transformed into political power as they negotiate and bargain with governments.

The reluctance of business to be controlled may be exhibited in lack of respect for the rule of law—for example, it is sometimes alleged that not only is industry evasive about old laws relating to safety and health standards in factories, but also about new laws concerned with pollution. Other laws, such as those about seat belts or lead in petrol, whose introduction was inevitably opposed by manufacturers, are not hard to administer, and it has not been possible to avoid them. Much depends in such cases on the quality and quantity of inspection. But there is also the question of penalties and punishments. Successful wealth-creators are naturally objects of envy, and people become suspicious of the activities of top businessmen. So it is not uncommon for accusations about the inviolability of business to prosecution to be bandied about in democratic countries. If wealthy bankers and manufacturers do influence politicians and administrators of the law in order to procure their own immunity, then the rule of law is being threatened.

Such allegations may have a basis of credibility in the fact that politicians and political parties depend on money, especially for electioneering, and contributions by business to political funds are one of the facts of political life. There is no democracy in which this is more pronounced than the United States: primary election candidates must often find their own funds, with the result that fund-raising is a major political activity. The need for President Nixon to finance his re-election campaign in 1972 led to his turning an unconstitutional blind eye to certain large corporations who might have been sued under the anti-trust laws.[12] The terms of the campaign acts of the 1970s, allowing for public funds to be paid to presidential candidates with the intention of diminishing the power of money, also legalized Political Action Committees, providing a channel for business funds to be directed to pliable candidates. While only a minority of PAC money comes from business, media

[12] US Senate Select Committee on Presidential Campaign Activities 93rd Congress. 1st Session, *Watergate and Related Matters, Phase III Campaign Financing*, 5405, quoted in Wilson, *Business and Politics*.

attention has resulted in campaign spending by business being viewed as a classic symbol of outsized corporate political power.[13] Indeed, money talks much more loudly in all democracies at election times when, as in Britain, large private corporations quietly donate money to the fighting funds of the party they most favour. As Big Business does not have a vote-winning image (rather the opposite), this is almost certainly its best strategy.

Finally it is often believed that business frequently succeeds in evading the tax laws. Small businessmen do this by not revealing their transactions: large businessmen do it by using their fluidity of resources and their legal expertise. Hence, it is argued, businessmen subvert the rule of law while other people with much less wealth make a point of paying all their taxes. The complaint has become much more politically significant since large proportions of democratic electorates, even quite a high proportion of manual workers, pay income tax to the public revenue. In France it is commonly believed that everyone who can avoids paying tax. The British ITV programme World in Action recently claimed that tax evaders were 30 times less likely to end up in court than those falsely claiming social security benefits.[14] This sort of allegation is widely accepted. Whatever the truth, it did not help confidence in the rule of law at a time when much zeal was being expended in the pursuance of 'social security scroungers'.

For business, of course, all taxation is a diminution of profits and all regulation a restriction on entrepreneurial freedom. Other citizens may perceive businessmen as a small minority with disproportionate wealth and therefore power out of all proportion to their numbers; businessmen, on the other hand, are likely to perceive themselves as a small minority paying a quite disproportionate amount of both national and local taxation and motivating industry and commerce despite being subject to crippling limitations. It is not surprising, therefore, that businessmen frequently find themselves out of harmony with the choruses of democratic citizens.

Furthermore it is argued that business, as a privileged minority with an undemocratic internal hierarchy, is likely to support those elements in society with undemocratic aspirations and values. Earlier I observed that the structures of business and politics are not

---

[13] D. Vogel, The Political Power of Business: Is It an Issue in Need of Management?, *Public Affairs Review* (1983), 8.   [14] *The Times*, 8 Jan. 1983.

dissimilar: both are pyramidal, both need a few leaders and many followers. On turning to functions, however, the similarities diminish. The democratic state, especially, is by nature unstable. It depends on a chain of command system only in as much as once decisions are made they are usually executed. But the commanders are frequently under attack from the troops, and liable to be replaced by opponents; and before decisions are finalized everyone is liable to be involved in the arguments. This is a situation which industry and commerce could never tolerate. Business needs stability, security, and discipline to a degree that democracy can never attain.

In these circumstances one must ask whether businessmen, as businessmen, actually regard democracy as the best form of political regime. It would seem that a mildly authoritarian regime. favourably disposed to business but unfavourably disposed to trade unions, might provide the best political environment for secure and stable investment. And, indeed, in most parts of the world, businessmen operate in some such context. German businessmen adjusted, for the most part, to the Third Reich; and business in Chile, Argentina, and Brazil (to name only a few South American countries) has frequently allied itself with military dictatorships in preference to democratic leadership which it has not found so congenial. True, business has not fared too badly in adapting itself to democracy; but if democracy was threatened in those countries where it seemed firmly established, would the industrial and commercial leadership hasten to their aid? Are they likely today to echo the cry of some French businessmen in the 1930s, 'meilleur Hitler que Blum'?

Lindblom summed up the position in what has become a famous comment: 'The large private corporation fits oddly into democratic theory and vision. Indeed, it does not fit.'[15] Big Business, as we have noted, is not made to feel welcome in the democratic debate, though its informal influence may be considerable. It is much more likely, however, to have a bureaucratic, rational–legal ethos, which makes it more acceptable in the corridors of power than small businesses. Small business may feel it is much more in tune with democracy because its values will tend to be populistic. Small businessmen will be much less comprehending of bureaucracy and much more likely to opt for overt political pressure. Thus in certain circumstances small businessmen can swing to Poujadism,

[15] Lindblom, *Politics and Markets*, 356.

especially where changes in taxes or subsidies suddenly alter their conditions of economic operation. Whereas Big Business inclines to the rational, small business may turn to the irrational. Neither of these attitudes is intrinsically democratic—an authoritarian regime can be highly rational or highly irrational—but the values of Big Business are likely to be much more intellectualized and, therefore, to be more acceptable superficially to democratic political élites.

The extent to which businessmen give support to democratic regimes is bound to vary from one country to another and to be dependent upon the position of business in each case. Businessmen support democracy where and when they believe democracy is supporting business. Where the conception of democracy implicitly includes competition, free enterprise, or capitalism, as so often in the United States, anything that limits entrepreunerial freedom may be regarded as undemocratic. As David Vogel writes, 'In no nation have the principles and practices of democracy and of the free market been as intrinsically connected as in the United States.'[16] American businessmen are often staunch supporters of the American Constitution because the government power it fragments and decentralizes is highly advantageous to American business which is probably more powerful, both at a national and local level, than in any other country. There is one feature the American political system possesses, however, which runs contrary to business practice. The American way of making decisions publicly is not congenial to the business desire for secrecy; and this may partly explain why the group which has disproportionately benefited from government policies has such an underlying suspicion and mistrust of government.[17] Yet at the same time American business idealizes the Constitution: consequently it has seen successive administrations, especially in the last half-century Democratic administrations, as essentially subversive of democracy. The idea of popular power exercised through majority mandates is not even now a familiar American conception.

Elsewhere, in most other democracies, business has had to come to terms with the phenomenon of workers' power. Almost alone among its counterparts, American business has not had to face the countervailing force of politically organized labour. In Scandinavia

---

[16] D. Vogel, Why Businessmen Distrust their State: The Political Consciousness of American Corporate Executives, *British Journal of Political Science*, 8 (1978), 59.

[17] Ibid. 58.

and Britain the strength of social democracy has produced an inured business leadership, always without the prestige of its American counterpart. On the other hand, European businessmen have been able to avoid the public scrutiny and inspection that characterizes American democracy's open decision-making. Thus, European business has been less identified with the rhetoric of democracy but has become more accepting of the social and economic outcomes of universal suffrage, implemented by a highly centralized power.

Of course, in all countries where democracy has persisted for some generations, democratic values have become firmly rooted, and many categories of people by their nature disposed not to favour them—such as military men and business leaders—may well be deeply imbued with the need to preserve public contestation and inclusiveness. Particularly, Big Business leaders will often be involved in the cultural pursuits of democratic nations, and their educational backgrounds may inculcate within them the same values that pervade the rest of society. (It has often struck the author how relatively strongly Scandinavian businessmen are committed to communitarian values.) Hence their exasperation with left-wing governments will not lead to alienation towards democratic ideals. This has not happened with senior soldiers and sailors in any long-standing democracy, so it is scarcely likely to occur with leading financiers and industrialists in normal circumstances.

It is not possible to say how Big Business would behave in abnormal circumstances. A summary of the previous argument would suggest that most businessmen are not totally committed to democracy as I have defined it, though they are more favourably disposed where they see it as guaranteeing the existence of private enterprise. This consideration, however, is not completely fulfilled in any contemporary democratic state. For the most part businessmen adjust to the instability of democracy as they adjust to any other type of political regime that permits their existence. On balance, where democracy is well established most businessmen appear to prefer it, especially as the mixed economy (inevitably, as I have argued, the economy of modern democracy) has not proved to be a mixture in which public enterprise has become too dominant.

To sum up: it is indisputable that the influence of business is quite disproportionate to its numbers. Governments are often concerned with the prosperity of business because they see their fates interlocked. How undemocratic the concessions made to business will be depends, in the last resort, on how the electorate views such privileges, and here one has only the circumstantial evidence of the majority's mood varying. Perhaps a common popular attitude, towards Big Business especially, is one of grudging tolerance tempered by suspicion, rarely changing to a mood where the existence of business is threatened. As we saw in Chapter 5, all democracies to a greater or less extent have capitalist economies. We are therefore entitled to assume that business is accepted, though acceptance is conditional upon its willingness to be controlled.

Relations between Trade Unions and Government

Like business, organized labour is often perceived as a threat to democracy. Viewed as solid monoliths—which they seldom are—trade-union movements rank as easily the largest interest groups with which democratic governments have to deal. Trade unions have two main sources of power in industrialized democracies. Firstly, they are strong in the currency of democracy, votes; they represent the interests of what is still the largest group in society, manual workers; and, increasingly, they also represent the interests of white-collar workers. Secondly, in the great and growing interdependency of modern society they have the ultimate sanction of withdrawing their labour, causing great inconvenience to the public and considerable loss to industry. It is not unsurprising, therefore, that they are sometimes regarded as an alternative source of power to the government, and there are those among the middle classes who fear them obsessively. This is partly an atavistic dread of 'the masses' and partly a dislike of powerful groups. Powerful groups, however, as we have noted, have a right to exist in a democracy as long as they accept the rule of law.

For the most part trade unions do not break the law. Within democracies they operate inside a framework of law which, occasionally, they infringe, especially by industrial action. The right to strike, however, is upheld with qualifications in all democracies. The law is broken by strikers, if, as with other legal activities, strike actions are undertaken in an illegal way. Assaulting people while striking is illegal; but, then, assault is always a breach of the law. So is intimidation which can arise with picketing, a form of activity usually legal though it has been very much qualified by legislation and by verdicts in the law courts. In itself, picketing—the practice of waiting outside a strike-bound works in order to inform people entering of the reasons for strike—seems relatively innocuous; but when hundreds of people, including those not involved in the dispute, take part, it is difficult to uphold a legal right of entry. If the police are also unable to do so then there is a breach of the rule of law. The incident in the British miners' strike of 1972 when Arthur Scargill, leader of the Yorkshire miners, used massed pickets to prevent the use of the Saltley coke depot, is an example of the rule of law breaking down.[18] This is not because it was secondary picketing (which it was)—British law did not then explicitly outlaw secondary picketing—but because physical force was used by the pickets to prevent people going about their lawful business. The border-line between physical and moral intimidation, however, may be very difficult to draw in such situations.

A British example, illustrating the attachment of a trade union to the law, can be taken from the steel workers' strike of January 1980.[19] This action, unusual in an industry with very good industrial relations, was provoked by the rationalization exercise undertaken by Ian MacGregor, the new head of the union, the British Steel Corporation. Towards the end of the month those men employed by privately owned steel works decided to strike. The employers obtained an injunction from the Court of Appeal under Lord Denning declaring the strike illegal. The executive of the British Iron and Steel Trades Confederation, and its secretary, Bill Sirs, himself a justice of the peace, then ordered members back to work. They obeyed while he appealed to the House of Lords. The Law Lords, meeting unusually on a Sunday, overruled the judgment of the Court of Appeal, and on the Monday Bill Sirs called his members out again. This was an example not only of collective discipline but also of collective intent to avoid breaking the law.

Another objection is that the unions are so powerful that they are able to restrict the freedom both of their members and the general public. It is alleged that not only do trade unions as monopolies interfere with people's freedom of economic activity through collective bargaining and the closed shop, but also that they interfere with democratic freedoms. It is sometimes argued that in

[18] M. Crick, *Scargill and the Miners* (1985), 52, ff.
[19] *The Times,* 26 Jan.–2 Feb. 1980; Bill Sirs, *Hard Labour* (1985), 97 ff.

factories or localities where unions are very strong, people are afraid to speak out against declared union policy. No doubt there is some truth in this allegation, as everywhere it needs moral courage to oppose the majority. Yet clearly many trade-union members are not afraid to speak out, or vote, against their union's policies (there are many examples from the recent history of the British miners to support this statement). On the other hand, many trade-unionists do not hesitate to contract out of the political levy to the Labour Party.[20] Such manifestations must be proof of the fact that most trade-unionists feel themselves protected by the state against liberty-denying sanctions that their union's leadership might exert upon them.

A more convincing complaint against the unions, in this context, relates to those associated with the mass media. In general, trade unions in the newspaper industry, or associated with radio and television, have a strategically responsible position for the maintenance of democracy. If the unions in these industries were to set themselves up as censors, then freedom of the press would be in peril.[21] The best-known episode is that of the *Daily Mail* compositors who, at the beginning of May 1926, refused to set up the editorial, For King and Country, which claimed patriotism lay on the side of the employers in the industrial crisis. Thus began the General Strike.[22] The editorial was, in the circumstances, irresponsibly provocative; but the freedoms of speech and of the press allow people and organizations, including trade unions, to make irresponsible and provocative statements. Trade-unionists who, for the most part, are as strongly in favour of freedom of speech and of the press as anyone else, often feel that the media are biased against them, and indeed it is difficult to see how in Britain this cannot be true. There is no British daily or weekly identified with the trade-union point of view. The newspapers devote little space to industrial relations and seldom treat strikes seriously, frequently omitting details of pay and conditions. Consequently, there is a good deal of resentment against the media in the British trade-union movement, and attempts by unions in the media to censor anti-union opinions are possible. This underlines a weakness in

[20] Comparing the 1985 Labour Party and TUC reports, the proportion contracting out in that year was 30.7 per cent.
[21] Where trade unionism is repressed the unions may agitate for a free press. See J. J. Linski, *KOR: A History of the Workers Defense Committee in Poland 1976–1981* (1985), 477 ff.
[22] H. M. Pelling, *A History of British Trade Unionism* (1963), 175.

democracy. It is dependent on freedom of expression, which is dependent on the media, yet the media's criteria are often commerical. If the people who run the media, employees and employers alike, are dominated by monetary considerations at the expense of a free exchange of opinion (a not unlikely situation), then democracy is that much weaker. But neither is it strengthened by media censorship, including that threatened, and occasionally exercised, by unions in the newspaper industry.

Much of the threat which the unions are supposed to pose to democracy, however, relates to their alleged ability to hold society to ransom (as it is often put). The most dramatic expression of this capacity is the general strike. The advocacy by Georges Sorel[23] and Michael Bakunin[24] of this way of overthrowing capitalism has given it revolutionary overtones. Yet most general strikes have neither seriously shaken democratic societies, nor the democratic process itself. Indeed, some general strikes have had democratic motives. In 1893 in Belgium, and in 1902 in Sweden[25] there were successful general strikes in order to secure the extension of the suffrage. On other occasions a nation's workers have struck to prevent the overthrow of democratic regimes by would-be military leaders. The German unions in 1920 and the French in 1961 struck to forestall respectively the Kapp putsch and the generals' revolt in Algeria.[26] Moreover, none of these strikes were characterized by much violence. Nor was the Finnish general strike of 1956, or the Australian general strike of 1976.[27] Clearly one can be far too pessimistic about the consequences of general strikes.

General strikes might be regarded as undemocratic, however, when they are directed against democratically elected governments. Klaus von Beyme argues that in Germany any strike interfering with the legislative process must be 'regarded as illegal because it takes away the sovereign rights of the people and the organisational power of the unions is used to suspend the principles of equality of opportunity for everyone in political life.'[28] Thus all so-called political strikes (and it is argued all general strikes are political) must be undemocratic because they are opposed to the public will as represented by a democratic and elected political leadership. But

[23] G. Sorel, *Reflections on Violence* (Paris, 1906).
[24] See M. Bakunin and A. Lechring (eds.), *M. Bakunin: Selected Writings* (New York, 1974).
[25] K. Von Beyme, *Challenge to Power* (1980), 196.
[26] Ibid. 193.   [27] Ibid. 149 ff.   [28] Ibid. 195.

suppose a democratic government does not have any electoral mandate for its policy, and/or suppose its policy is not embodied in any statute. This will be the case with much national economic policy, which is often conveyed in the homilies of ministers in Parliament or the media. A good deal of wages and prices policy, and Keynesian management generally, during the last thirty years has not been statutory. Both individuals and groups in democratic countries frequently act contrary to government policy without behaving illegally. (For example, the bulk of the British athletics team went to the 1980 Olympics in Moscow in spite of the prime minister's expressed wishes to the contrary.) The act of striking is not in itself a breach of democratic principles, yet striking may be rightly described as political where it is directed against the government, as when public sector workers strike for higher wages from their employer, the government; or when workers protest against national incomes policies by withdrawing their labour. Thus in few democratic countries are all political strikes illegal. Quite legal actions, however, could sometimes be a threat to democracy. The important question raised by this discussion is to what degree is it undemocratic to oppose the unmandated policy of an elected government collectively and in an organized way by actions that are not illegal in themselves?

The answer must depend on the context. Where there is no democracy, as for example with the Russian strikes of 1905,[29] as I have argued, it can hardly be claimed that democratic criteria are infringed. Where democracy *is* installed, however, then one must agree with Leslie Macfarlane: 'The unpalatable truth that needs to be asserted is that coercive industrial action against the Government in furtherance of directly political objectives is a danger to the democratic political system'.[30] Thus if a trade union deliberately sets out to overthrow a legally constituted government it is behaving in an undemocratic way even if it is not acting illegally. As we have seen, there have been few general strikes, let alone other smaller strikes, in which directly political objectives have been sought, although the British miners' strike of 1984–5 does partly qualify for this category. It is true that its main objective was to save what was sloganized as 'pits, jobs, and communities'. But the miners' leader, Arthur Scargill, on more than one occasion spoke

---

[29] Ibid.
[30] L. J. Macfarlane, *The Right to Strike* (1981), 164.

about bringing the government down: in other words he was usurping the functions of the electorate, Parliament, and Her Majesty's Opposition. Probably some people in his union and the wider labour movement accepted this strategy, though for the most part the strikers' motives and those of their sympathizers were economic. The contest was to some extent personalized, in that the prime minister justifiably perceived Scargill as an inveterate opponent of all her economic policies, someone who had to be defeated, while the miners' leader suffered from hubris as a result of what he believed to be his success in bringing another Conservative government down in 1974.[31] Quite commonly held, this belief is largely invalid. Two factors make it unacceptable. Firstly, Prime Minister Edward Heath dissolved Parliament in February 1974, hoping to profit electorally from public reaction against the strike. Secondly the agency of the voters was needed before the government could be forced to go. It was overthrown by the normal democratic process. There was a good deal of sympathy with the miners, and the government probably was held more to blame for the situation. Ten years later everything was different. The economic and political climate had changed greatly and the miners were perceived by the bulk of society as an importunate and troublesome pressure group, an impression much derived from the behaviour and opinions of Scargill himself. The 1974 miners' strike was a wage strike, and the political implications of it arose quite indirectly. The 1984–5 strike was partially political.

Any serious strike, however, is likely to have some political implication; and this makes answering the question exceptionally problematic. The example of the 1926 general strike in Britain, already referred to, illustrates the complexity of the question. In its origins it was a wage strike: in fact, the Trades Union Congress, anxious to avoid Sorelian terminology, persisted in calling it the National Strike. J. H. Thomas, the railwaymen's leader, declared in the House of Commons, 'I have never disguised that in a challenge to the Constitution, God help us unless the Government won.'[32] The circumstances of the strike arose from the Conservative government's change of economic policy when, in the 1925 Budget, it returned to the gold standard and appreciated the pound, thus damaging all export industries including coal. This completely

[31] Accounts of these can be found in G. A. Dorfman, *Government Versus Trade Unionism in British Politics Since 1968* (1979), 76 ff.

[32] *Hansard Parliamentary Debates,* 3 May 1926, 5th ser., vol. 81, c. 195.

unmandated policy—the Conservatives under Stanley Baldwin[33] had won the 1924 general election on 'safety first'—was suggested by an unelected, unrepresentative body, the Bank of England, and only reluctantly accepted by the chancellor of the exchequer, Winston Churchill. He had no great understanding of economics, but was advised by Keynes, among others that the policy would lead to even greater unemployment and industrial troubles.[34] And so it did. In order for industrial costs to be reduced, wages had to be lowered. An employers' offensive followed, with the coal-owners, who needed a decrease in the price of coal, taking the lead. Although Baldwin was a pacific man whose declared aim was industrial peace, he was forced to ally himself with the employers, announcing in July 1925, 'all the workers of this country have got to take reductions of wages to help put industry on its feet'.[35] He postponed the confrontation, however, by giving the mining industry a subsidy. This expired at the end of April 1926. When the coal-owners began a lock-out, the vast mass of workers under the organization of the TUC came out in sympathy with the miners.

Thus in essence the 1926 general strike was that familiar feature of trade-union activity—a wage strike. All workers were justified in fearing that their wages would be reduced and that the miners were merely first in the queue. The strike was not intended to challenge elected and constitutional authority: it was a defensive action in face of the employer counter-offensive, itself induced by unexpected and inappropriate government economic policy. Although the violence and disorder in the strike is sometimes underestimated, it was a relatively peaceful affair. On the other hand, the suppression of normal productive and distributive activities for nine days might eventually, even against nearly everybody's wishes, have resulted in great public disorder and finally a revolutionary situation. This must always be the fear with comprehensive strikes, though as experiences of general strikes in democracies demonstrate it is a much exaggerated fear. In long-standing democracies with highly organized union movements such apprehension is almost certainly unjustified. Violent, disorderly strikes are much more a characteristic of early industrialization and weak trade unions struggling for recognition.

More pertinently the 1926 general strike might be interpreted as

---

[33] Mowat, *Britain Between the Wars*, 187.
[34] P. J. Grigg, *Prejudice and Judgment* (1945).
[35] *Daily Herald*, 31 July 1925.

a powerful pressure group in contest with the Government and usurping the role of the Opposition. (The Parliamentary Labour Party maintained an embarrassed reticence.) If one believes that elected governments are unaccountable between elections, then any opposition, beyond verbal opposition, is undemocratic. With this premise, any oppositional *action*, even if legal in itself, is against constitutional rules and therefore undemocratic. Thus a strike in these circumstances, if it leads to an impediment to government policy, is undemocratic, even if the policy in question has not been sanctioned by electoral mandate. In practice it is a restriction on the right to strike. Conversely, the view that policies not mandated at election time have less legitimacy, and that no legal action can be undemocratic, would lead to an interpretation that the 1926 general strike was only indirectly political and no threat to democracy. Powerful pressure groups, by this argument, as long as their actions are not directed to political objectives, can impede unmandated economic policy without acting undemocratically as long as their actions remain within the legal framework.

There is a difficulty in laying down any strict principles in the field of economic policy. This arises because, like foreign policy, its decision-making is often influenced by external events over which governments have little control. Surprising changes of circumstance may lead to governments sharply deviating from their declared intentions, and it is not always very reasonable, in these fields, to expect firm adherence to electoral mandates. Indeed, the wisest politicians may make few promises about these matters. The sudden rise of oil prices in 1973 forced democratic governments in many countries into sharp changes in economic policy. (Of course, in Britain, 1926 is an early example of the results of a U-turn). In contemporary societies there is much greater specialization and interdependency of functions. Quite small groups might make life unliveable, and governments could hardly avoid intervening in order to maintain essential services like water, sewage, electricity, and food distribution in operation. This is generally recognized even by the unions concerned. In some countries such as France certain public sector workers are forbidden to strike.[36] Thus vital services for life as well as for industry are meant to be guaranteed by these prohibitions. Governments feel strongly the responsibility of keeping them functioning and small groups which cause trouble,

[36] Von Beyme, *Challenge to Power*, 198.

especially in the transport services, are very unpopular. Reducing a country to industrial chaos is much easier than it used to be, and though there is no example of this leading to great public disorder it can hardly improve standards of civility and tolerance. Greater interdependency implies a greater capacity to harm and the need for greater responsibility on the part of all groups if life is to remain pleasant. Where all groups become more selfish and less caring it is possible that anti-democratic forces calling for social discipline and harmony about national objectives may emerge. Pluralistic complexity may then be replaced by monolithic simplicity.

It is the interdependency of trade unions with business and government in economic policy-making, however, which provides the most difficult problem. The capacity of a trade union to harm will relate not only to the employers, other unions, and the public generally, but also to the government's programme and hence possibly to its electoral chances. A union might do this either by refusing to co-operate in some all-embracing 'social contract', or by taking part and then withdrawing at a crucial stage. In these situations governments may not be legislating for, but 'guiding' and 'steering' the economy. How damaging is it to democracy if unions refuse to be associated with such a system? Does freedom of association, which must also include freedom not to associate, extend to freedom not to associate in what Rokkan called corporate pluralism? Is refusal to bargain and negotiate with the government, when it is harmful to the national economy, an anti-democratic position? The answer, I think, must be that such a rejection of co-operation can only infringe democratic criteria when there are statutory requirements defining the system.

Trade unions, then, pose no great threat to democracy, in spite of the gloomy prognostications of some critics. Their leaders strongly favour lawful rather than revolutionary activity. For the most part they are concerned with controlling capitalism rather than overthrowing it. One of their advantages—the ability to mobilize large numbers of people—may strengthen their position in the political field as well as the industrial field: on the other hand, it may give them an exaggerated view of their political strength. They may see themselves as the expression of the popular will: but even when able to mobilize millions in industrial action, they have no guarantee that their unity will be maintained in support for parties with trade-union sympathies at election time. (For example, in

Britain the display of solidarity in the general strike was followed by large proportions of the manual workers refusing to vote for the Labour Party in any general election until 1945.) Trade unions are manifestations of democracy; but their own views of it are coloured by their need to show a solid front against employers. Hence they may be intolerant of minorities in their ranks and inclined to enforce as their conception of democracy a rather simple majoritarianism. Their own internal arrangements are also democratic, to a greater or lesser degree, and have often afforded ordinary working people the opportunities to learn administrative and political skills. In some countries they practised democratic procedures, including voting, before they obtained the franchise for their own parliaments. A good indication of their democratic bona fides is the hatred all totalitarian dictators have shown towards them in the twentieth century.

Much of the apprehension about trade-union movements lies in the belief that their power is not legitimate. This is not only held by business men, who fear the threat to their profits and to their decision-making autonomy, but also by much of the wider public, including many trade-unionists. It is a reaction to the inflation of the 1960s and 1970s and to public service strikes, which inconvenience nearly everyone and, inevitably, cause disorder. Hence unions come to be perceived as a threat to the rule of law as well as national prosperity. Thus the simple assertion that their power must be legitimate where it is exercised legally neglects the changing moods of public opinion which have led in the last forty years in all democracies to trade-union law being frequently revised. The most striking instance is that of Britain, where in the eight years between 1975 and 1983 the legal position of the unions changed from traditional voluntarism to a tightly defined and relatively crippling legal framework. The many doubts about the unions' legal position (which is not clear anyway without cases being tested in the courts) reflect the uncertainties of public opinion. The restriction of their legal power followed from uncertainties about their legitimacy. Such instability of legal status is an example of the operation of democracy where large collective forces are involved.[37]

Thus the uncertain relationship between large unions and the democratic state is partly a reflection of changing public attitudes to trade unionism, and these in turn are partly a reflection of changing economic circumstances. The situation has varied greatly, however,

[37] See above, p.19.

between one democracy and another. Factors such as the degree of unionization, the relationships with political parties, the amount of public ownership, the extent of the complexity of union structure, and national values all affect the nature of trade-union power; and it is likely that this is always exaggerated. Firstly, because the unions can hardly be constructive. Launching policy initiatives tends to be the prerogative of political parties; it does not come easily to unions. Secondly, in many countries trade-union movements are too sectionalized to co-ordinate strategies. In Britain, for example, the TUC General Council presides over a fragmented organization: its general-secretary is a classic case of responsibility without power. Thus trade-union power may often be limited to obstructing government economic policy. It tends to be negative.

Numerical Democracy and Corporate Pluralism and the Social Partners

Neither business nor labour are the threats to democracy that they accuse each other of being. None the less they both present problems to democratic governments. Their relationship with each other must be a matter for concern, because if it is bad a country's internal and external trade will suffer. As retention of power may well depend on overall economic performance, democratic governments should favour industrial harmony. It is true that left-wing governments may carry anti-employer values with them into office; but once there they discover that their electoral prospects will suffer from discontented private industry. Similarly, right-wing governments are likely to soften an anti-labour stance, dependent as they will be on some votes from manual workers. Thus numerical democracy does exert a general, overall pressure towards good industrial relations.

Although dualism in decision-making applies to many policy sectors, and although corporate pluralism may have a regularized pattern in some sectors (e.g. health, agriculture), it is in the field of economic policy making that it has been most criticized as detrimental to democratic procedures and values. The academic controversy about corporatism is an indication of the concern. What, then, are the factors which have encouraged corporate pluralism in national economic policy-making? And how has its relationship with numerical democracy in this field evolved in modern democracies? To answer one needs to consider two groups of factors—the economic and the political. The political factors, already considered in Chapter 6, relate to institutions and the pattern of party conflict. Economic circumstances and theories about managing the economy have also played a major part in influencing the pattern of interrelationship between the two policy-making processes. Indeed, the formulating of national economic policy has in many democratic countries been the salient factor in swinging the balance of national decision-making away from numerical democracy and towards corporate pluralism. Where Keynesian fiscal policy is adopted it may prove difficult, Gerhard Lehmbruch argues, 'to reconcile effective political management of the business cycle with the parliamentary process of consensus-building'.[38] Price and wage freezes may fail, either because they cannot be ratified and made law by a parliamentary majority or because business and labour may not comply. Hence bargaining between large, or 'peak', associations and the government will tend to be favoured. Lehmbruch also points out how the time perspectives of electoral politics may clash with the imperatives of economic policy-making:

Economic policy decisions often have a strong short-run component, and the pressure of time may be high. Political parties, then, either are incapable of building sufficient consensus within a short time span or they produce irrational decisions. This may induce the decision-makers to shift responsibility for consensus-building towards the subsystem of interest associations.[39]

There may be a tendency for political parties to avoid the discussion of specific economic policies at election time in any save the most general terms. They then avoid commitment to particular economic policies which may be very difficult to explain to the electorate anyway. So the parties may claim little more than that they will manage the economy better than their opponents. Consequently, if elected to power, they may shift responsibility for short-term policies to a bargaining structure.

Inflation was the economic situation in which, from the late 1960s if not earlier, democratic governments sought the co-operation of both business and labour. In times of rising prices, trade unions are most militant and employers most ready to yield to wage

[38] Lehmbruch, Liberal Corporatism and Party Government, *Comparative Political Studies* 10/1 (1977), 97.   [39] Ibid. 100.

demands. The temptation for both social partners to avoid the embrace of political authority is therefore great. With recession they will both look for help from the government and will be much more disposed to political action though governments may need their co-operation for economic policy-making less. The success of the famous tripartite model in Sweden may lie in the fact that, unlike many of the others, it was initiated not only in deflationary times but also in a Keynesian context. If a monetarist creed prevails with an ideology of reliance on market forces, as with the present British government, trade-union leaders may find themselves not even consulted. Indeed, one may speculate that one of the reasons for favouring a monetarist policy is the autonomy it restores, or appears to restore, to government economic policy-making.

Conclusion

The problem of summarizing the relation between democracy and the social partners is one of great variety within time and space. In any one country and as between different countries we confront a changing pattern. This is not surprising because, as I have already remarked, democracy implies instability.

One result is that both business and organized labour operate within a context that may in theory and in practice be modified at any time. This applies to the legal framework as much as anything. Changes in the law with regard to both business and the unions are usually as controversial as they are important. Thus in Britain the legislature ushered in an age of free trade with their repeal of the Corn Laws and Navigation Acts in the mid-nineteenth century. By the 1930s protectionism had returned. In the United States the successful demands for a tariff by businessmen were mostly a reaction to British competition. In the early twentieth century the anti-trust acts further altered the rules. After World War II both countries moved some way back towards free trade. Entrepreneurial autonomy, so much greater in these two examples of early industrialization, is very much more restricted by the state in other democracies. Where labour movements are very strong, as in Scandinavia, business may feel the legal balance heavily weighed against it.

Similarly, the legal position of trade-union organization is subject to alteration everywhere. Freedom of association is not absolute; its limits can be defined by the state. In Britain the recent pattern is for successive governments substantially to change the law. In the nineteenth century the lack of legal regulation of British trade unions was admired by other countries where there was no such freedom, but in the twentieth century trade unions have tended to benefit from laws which restrict arbitrary action by employers. They have also been much more inclined to trust the courts. Von Beyme distinguishes three types of European labour law systems.[40] First, as in Ireland and Britain, where collective agreements are not legally binding. Second, where there is a differentiation between individual and collective disputes with the latter subject to concili- ation or mediation procedures, as in Italy, France, or Belgium. Third, where obligations to keep the peace are legally binding, or where legal sanctions are possible when contracts are infringed. This last obtains in Germany, Austria, Switzerland, and Scandinavia. But there are several other criteria for categorization besides the standing of contractual agreements. Other avenues of change include bargaining rights on the shop floor, the legal status of officials, and laws restricting the employers' right of lock out. But none of these legal frameworks necessarily determine the nature of industrial relations. For example, in Australia and New Zealand, where there are extensive systems of industrial arbitra- tion, union militancy has sometimes been quite marked.

Indeed, systems of industrial relations depend as much on the nature of parties concerned, and on what one might call the 'indus- trial culture', as on statutes which are often intended to counteract these factors. William Gamson describes how even after the Supreme Court had validated the Wagner Labour Relations Act, Chicago police in 1937 shot seven strikers dead at the Memorial Day massacre during the Bethlehem Steel strike. He remarks on the common practice of American employers at this time of stocking arsenals of weapons and tear gas in anticipation of labour disputes.[41] Half a century later US industrial relations are no longer as savage, but remain violent when compared with many European systems. Shorter and Tilly, however, note the relentless hostility of French employers and their reluctance to bargain with their workers.[42] The authors see this as peculiarly Gallic. Although these

---

[40] Von Beyme, *Challenge to Power*, 213.
[41] W. A. Gamson, *The Strategy of Social Protest* (Homewood, Ill., 1975), 1.
[42] E. Shorter and C. Tilly, *Strikes in France 1830–1969* (1974), 34.

two systems might resemble one another in physical violence (and both have a low proportion of organized trade unionism) in many other features they contrast markedly. To American business unionism, the function of the strike has long been as part of the collective bargaining process. In France it needed the events of May 1968, with nation-wide sit-ins, before most employers would concede collective bargaining at all.

Of course, as business and organized labour are so much involved with each other, they have, inevitably, shaped one another's behaviour, strategies, attitudes, and values. But, intervening in the relationship through legislation, the state completes the critical triangle which has been so important to modern economies. Each social partner, therefore, has to contend with two other forces. Each will want to ally itself with the government, if possible, and use its resources against the other social partner, or, if alliance is impossible, it will want, other things being equal, to avoid the unpleasant consequences of not being allied. In general, there are several varieties of the relationship.

Walter Korpi believes that though the working class is subordinated to capital, it can through its political and trade-union organizations diminish its relative weakness; and he distinguishes five categories of strength.[43] In the lowest group of democratic polities is the United States, where there is no labour party and unions are excluded from national economic policy-making and are weak in mobilization. In France the trade-union position is not much stronger; the lack of unity because of ideological divisions, the infrequency of left-wing governments, and union ineffectiveness in the planning system induce a general feebleness. In Britain and Belgium, labour parties are sometimes in power and there is a high level of mobilization. In Sweden, Norway, and Austria governments sympathetic to labour are frequently in power and mobilization capabilities are at their greatest. Significantly the ranking order for business would probably be reversed. It is strongest in the United States, a little weaker in France (perhaps because of the tutelage of the state) and weakest of all in Scandinavia.

Thus relatively successful economies can be found where there have been highly formalized (though not permanent) triangular relationships as in Scandinavia; and where, as in the United States, there are only tenuous links between the social partners and the

[43] W. Korpi, *The Democratic Class Struggle* (1983), 41.

state. Economic success, therefore, whether in the steered or unsteered economy, is not dependent on the industrial relations system and its connections with the state apparatus. Indeed, I have already contended that efficiency in the economic sense is unlikely to result from democratic institutions. Mancur Olson argues that pluralism, in particular, and especially the complex collusions it has brought in its wake, reduces efficiency, makes political life more divisive, retards decisions in business and politics, and increases the role of government, as well as reducing the clarity and intelligibility of national policy-making.[44]

Thus when pluralistic structures and their relations with government are relatively simple, where, using Olson's term, 'encompassing' interests are involved, this effect would be less. Where there is Byzantine complexity, as in Britain, Olson's hypothesis of consequential low growth and political conflict would seem to be validated. Countries like Norway, Austria, and Denmark, found by Korpi to have high indices of class voting,[45] are given the highest ranking in corporatism by Schmitter.[46] As we have noted, they possess very institutionalized bargaining systems, well-structured peak associations, and some of the highest standards of living. On the other hand, other countries, like Canada and the United States, also have very high standards of living, combined with low indices of class voting and a low ranking on the index of corporatism. The former group of countries have strong labour movements; the two North American countries have strong business. Yet both groups have a relatively low rate of growth between 1953 and 1973, and all would probably be regarded as very stable democracies. Thus the argument might be as below:

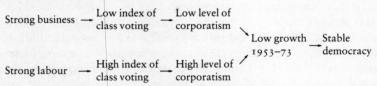

Clearly, the chain of causality could be set out in other sequences.

[44] M. Olson, *The Rise and Fall of Nations* (1982), 74.

[45] Korpi, *The Democratic Class Struggle*, 55.

[46] P. Schmitter, Interest Intermediation and Regime Governability in Contemporary Western Europe, mimeographed (1977). Paper for the Annual Convention of the American Political Science Association at Washington, D.C. By corporatism he meant corporate pluralism.

Olson's thesis is by no means disproved by this illustration, but it does not seem to indicate any obvious linkage between consensual pluralism (or 'corporatism'), economic efficiency, and a healthy democracy.

These variables may affect the nature of democracy, but none of them are necessarily more or less congenial to its continuance. Cultural factors shaped often by early experiences of industrialization play a large part in determining the character of the triangular relationship. But a very important determinant is knowledge of one's own economy, society, and polity—what one might call 'literacy in the social sciences'. Ronald Dore comments on the consensus about both facts and values in Japan producing a broadly shared appreciation of the national situation and how this contrasts with Britain, where there can be disagreement between public bodies about basic economic facts. He concludes: 'Japan is a consensual technocracy and Britain is . . . ruled by politicians in a competitive party-ocracy containing two class-based parties, both capable of electoral victory.'[47]

Perhaps, therefore, clarity of thought and consensus about facts among the chief bargainers, the 'political class', is the essential component for both efficiency and the proper conduct of democratic debate about national economic policy. It is again not a case of dismissing irrationality as unforgiveable, or of unrealistically refusing to face up to the fact that every individual and group is self-interested, but of realizing that self-interest needs a deeper imperative: that of understanding the nature of the problem under discussion. Rationality aids democracy not because it assists a more efficient conduct and disposal of public affairs (though it does), but because knowledge and logic are needed before people can be aware of their long-term, as well as their short-term, interests. Of course, their view of their long-term interests may still not lead to efficiency in the economists' sense, because their costings may put a higher value on leisure than material rewards, or on tranquillity as against the nervous exhaustion of contention and argument.

In economic policy-making rationality is complicated, as we have already observed, by the fact that it crosses so many border-lines: between the polity and the economy; and between authoritative

[47] R. Dore, Industrial Policy and How the Japanese Do It, *Catalyst*, 21 (1986), 51.

allocation, voting, and bargaining. Hence the perceptions of those who inhabit this no-man's land are liable to be somewhat distorted. Consensus about the facts will undoubtedly help; a long history of conflict about them will lead to distrust about motives.

As I have argued, neither business nor organized labour pose a great threat to the democratic state. Yet there are democracies where each sees the other as a possible menace. The unions perceive business as hierarchical, lacking in patriotism and concern for the wider community, and basically undemocratic. Business sees the unions as irresponsible and as subversive of discipline, common sense, and the rule of law. Essentially, they hold different conceptions of the nature of democracy. The unions have a majoritarian one and tend to identify themselves with 'the people' or popular majority. Businessmen tend to see it as something to do with morality, harmony, and legitimacy. They identify it with 'our way of life,' a consensual norm spoilt by trade-union recalcitrance. Hence though they may have to accept the legality of union action, they never feel it is legitimate. Roger Scruton echoes this attitude when he enquires 'is the establishment of the labour movement complete, even at the civil level? Nobody seems to have a clear and coherent answer.'[48] This may well be. In Britain, and numerous other democracies, trade unions have never been accorded complete legitimacy. But, then, like democracy, the unions are much more recent than commerce and industry. Indeed, unlike business, which preceded democracy, they exist by virtue of democracy itself.

The relationship of industrial relations to economic policy-making, and of both to national economic success, is bound to be an important preoccupation of the contemporary democratic state. Business and organized labour cannot be denied the right of association, because without pluralistic freedom democracy cannot exist. Yet freedom of association, like any other democratic freedom, cannot be absolute. It is bound to be defined by the courts and limited by law. The social partners are the two most powerful forces in most democracies, aside from the government itself and the apparatus it controls. Hence their exercise of power is likely to be constantly under review. Because democratic governments often need their co-operation in policy-making, however, they will be chary about challenging union or business power, though pressures to modify their status will always exist to a greater or lesser degree. As

[48] R. Scruton, *The Meaning of Conservatism* (1980), 176.

both maintain, to some extent sincerely, that they have little power (meaning they cannot attain many of their objectives), although everyone else believes they have great power (because they seem to be so successful in impeding others' aims), the capacity of business and labour for feeling unfairly treated and relatively deprived is great. As demands to weaken their power will probably always exist they will always operate in a milieu of some uncertainty. How they react to these pressures may well depend on how governments handle the situation. There is no problem of modern democracy needing wiser and more careful reflection.

8

LEADERSHIP AND DEMOCRACY

AT first sight, leadership and democracy are contradictory notions. Leadership presupposes hierarchy and discipline, whereas democracy is supposed to connote equality and liberty. As Sartori writes of leadership, 'We are here confronted with inequality, disparity, superiority—all the things that are repugnant to the democratic ideal'.[1] And especially in recent years, dislike of leadership of all kinds has become fashionable among radicals of all varieties, the dirtiest word in their vocabulary often being élitism. It seems that an underlying assumption of those with such ways of thought is that, in any situation, super-ordination (to use the ugly technical word) is of necessity undemocratic.

The logical consequence of such a belief, asserted by radical anti-élitists, is that nowhere has democracy ever appertained. They only need to point to the fact that authority is everywhere conspicuous, even in those modern states purporting to be democratic. Hence the overthrow of the *ancien regime* and its replacement by represent-ative institutions was a sham. Ordinary people are still not in control of the circumstances which shape their lives. The subordin-ate are destined to remain subordinate whatever the type of regime.

One implication of this argument can certainly be accepted. Authority is as much a feature of the modern democratic state as it was under feudalism. A situation in which the few lead and the many follow is the pattern wherever in the world any form of polit-ical organization exists. In fact, this last sentence is tautological: organization necessarily assumes control by the few over the many. It is a situation which the many usually accept. Perhaps one basic reason for their acceptance is that authority is so much more famil-iar to them than democracy and so much easier to understand.

Democratic states, therefore, are bound to have authority and leadership, because authority and leadership are the inevitable features of states and lesser organizations. As Benn and Peters

[1] G. Sartori, *Democratic Theory* (Detroit, 1962), 98.

remark, 'We accept authority because most social enterprise would be hopeless without it.'[2] And Sartori urges, 'Let us immediately settle a preliminary point by admitting that democracy is not anarchy. This means that in accepting democracy we agree to solve the question of power and command in a positive fashion.'[3] He implies that the political equality of democracy relates to the suffrage and to the opportunity of becoming a leader, but it does not extend to the sphere of authority. All cannot be leaders at once, that would be anarchy; it is difficult to imagine a situation where there are more leaders than followers. The few must lead and the many must follow. This is one of the simplest of maxims in political science and it holds for all types of regime, including democracies.

Having made this admission it still remains a reasonable conclusion that leadership in a democracy is very different from leadership in a non-democratic state. Democratic leaders operate under different conditions, are subject to different pressures, have different relationships with followers, and are a different type of person, from autocratic, or hegemonic, or aristocratic leaders.

Characteristics of Democratic Leaders

What sort of leader, then, is produced by the democratic turmoil of criticism and competition? He or she is likely to be a person with certain skills and resources, of a limited range of personality types, predominantly from certain backgrounds and characterized by some traits that distinguish him or her from people who are not politicians.

One of the facts of modern industrial society, not entirely attributable to the coming of democracy, is the increasing specialization and professionalization of occupations. This trend has even affected politics; today the typical democratic leader is a professional politician. It has been present in all democracies though in some, like Britain, where the aristocratic tradition was strong in parliamentary politics before the inauguration of universal suffrage, it may have been delayed. In a sense the professionalization of political leadership is as rational as any other form of specialization: it allows those who do not wish to lead to specialize in something else.

[2] S. I. Benn and R. S. Peters, *Social Principles and the Democratic State* (1959), 2.
[3] Sartori, *Democratic Theory*, 96.

The main difference between amateurs and professionals is that the latter are paid. The rise of the professional politician has been indicated by the introduction of salaries for legislators. Opposition to the concept was strongest in Britain; paying MPs was postponed until 1908, and the feeling that people ought to want to do it for nothing has lingered on, maintaining parliamentary salaries at a lower level than in comparable countries. Again, professional occupations are full-time, and increasingly this is what constituents have demanded of their representatives, although no political career can be as secure as other professions: defeat at the polls is a possibility politicians often have to face. Only a few occupations, such as being a lawyer or free-lance journalist, can easily be combined with being a national legislator. Finally, professional people have a sense of vocation, and most politicians feel called to their trade. There is little doubt (in my mind) that there is an identifiable state of being a professional politician which has the uniqueness associated with a separate calling.

Not that politicians are so different from other professions in their socio-demographic backgrounds. Preponderantly they are men, predominantly recruited from non-manual backgrounds. A very high proportion are lawyers and teachers.[4] Those who are from manual occupations have nearly always graduated through leadership in working-class organizations like co-operatives or trade unions.[5] Quite a high proportion have served as representatives at the state, regional, or municipal level. There is thus something like a ladder of promotion in the vocation of politics, or at least a common order of progression. Few people enter politics at the national level without some earlier organizational experience. This is because the resources and skills needed are by no means possessed by everyone.

One obvious resource is money. One cannot become a leader in normal circumstances without an electoral campaign, involving the expenses of advertising and hiring halls and people. A leader with a

[4] D. C. Matthews, *The Social Background of Political Decision-Makers* (New York, 1964). Id., *Senators and their World* (Chapel Hill, 1966). B. Zeller, *American State Legislatures* (New York, 1954). For Britain, see A. Ranney, *Pathways to Parliament* (Madison, 1965), 194 ff, for France, see M. Dogan, Political Ascent in a Class Society: French Deputies 1870–1958, in D. Marvick (ed.), *Political Decision Makers* (1961).

[5] W. E. Paterson and A. H. Thomas, *Social Democratic Parties in Western Europe* (1977).

power base is at an advantage because he can rely on corporate funds to finance him. Most would-be leaders find their way to the top with the help of the wealth and organizational muscle of political parties. Democratic leadership usually means party leadership. Where parties are weak and unable to provide enough money and organization, as in the United States, the political leaders may have to provide these resources themselves. Television time, especially, can be immensely expensive, and the tendency arose in the 1950s and '60s for aspirants for nomination for the presidency to be millionaires. Nixon was a relatively poor man, and in his corrupt dealings with ITT and the Milk Marketing Association we see the effects of the necessity to accrue campaign funds. The Federal Election Campaign Acts of the 1970s, allotting federal funds to recognized candidates were introduced to alleviate these problems (not without success).[6] Where political parties are not organized for electoral campaigning, personal wealth becomes important to leaders, giving them a certain independence. Less wealthy leaders may be more dependent on political parties and the compromises associated with this dependency.

Another important resource is time. Shortage of time most frequently explains why so few people are willing to undertake democratic leadership. This can be gathered from local politics, where leaders tend to be people with the time to spare.[7] The high proportion of retired people, women, and those in occupations with flexible hours, like insurance agents and university teachers, among political leaders demonstrates that one needs time to be even a part-time politician. Politics at a national level is usually a full-time business which only those with strong leanings to public life will want to pursue.

Motives for Becoming and Remaining a Leader.

How do we explain, then, the instances in which people do become democratic political leaders? To answer the question we must distinguish between those who become political leaders almost unintentionally and those who are motivated by political ambition. Today it is probably only at a local level that political leadership is

---

[6] H. L. Le Blanc, *American Political Parties* (New York, 1982), 247 ff.
[7] An analysis of people's motivations at the local level can be found in Frank Bealey and John Sewel, *The Politics of Independence* (Aberdeen, 1981), 201 ff.

assumed without deliberate political aspirations. Leaders of social and cultural interest groups, especially those who have had the confidence and initiative to set them up, may become involved in the political arena through the force of circumstances. Moral responsibility, a sort of *noblesse oblige,* may propel them towards political activity. Sometimes members of families with a tradition of public service may enter politics, almost casually, in this way.[8] At a national level this may still be the case where there is an aristocratic political tradition; but, in general, democratic politics is detrimental to automatic assumption of leadership.

Most democratic political leaders, however, are motivated by ambitions of some kind. They may be completely selfish, wanting to exert power over others in order to win fame, glory, and wealth, or they may be altruistic, yearning to pursue goals for the good of mankind. Both of these types, however, have one thing in common which distinguishes them greatly from their fellow citizens: they have selected themselves for political careers. But while they have surmounted the first hurdle—self-selection—which most people never do, many have no very precise idea of the nature of political life. Remaining a leader implies a process of adaptation which many will not survive.

At the next stage other people may be involved in the selection of leaders, and factors other than sheer ambition becoming important, many potential leaders may be discouraged. They may not be successful or they may find they dislike politics.[9] If they are at first unsuccessful in obtaining recognition, much will depend on their tenacity. There is a lot of evidence to support the view that so few people ultimately want to be leaders that those who persist in spite of early setbacks may in the end realize some of their ambitions. Perseverance and resilience in the face of failure are qualities all professional politicians require. Others, even if they are initially successful in politics, may find its demands distasteful and drop out of political life. This process of elimination is a very common feature of the workings of democracy.

[8] There is some evidence of people whose parents have been prominent in politics becoming subject to pressure to enter politics themselves—e.g., the Kennedys and Gandhis. L. Moss and S. R. Parker, *The Local Government Councillor:* An Enquiry for the Committee of Management in Local Government (1966), 42, say that of English and Welsh councillors who were recruited informally over a third had family associations with council work.

[9] P. W. Buck, *Amateurs and Professionals in British Politics 1918–1959* (1963), 13, describes how more than half the candidates for the House of Commons in this period were unsuccessful and never stood for office again.

Those who leave politics at an early stage probably do so for two main reasons. They dislike obeying the imperatives of bidding for support and tolerating public criticism. Appealing for votes implies projecting oneself on a larger stage: selling oneself as a packaged commodity in modern public relations terms and subjecting oneself to the scrutiny of the mass media. It will mean listening to ordinary people's problems for, in modern democracies, as we have noted, people expect politicians to find solutions to their problems. It will involve, in order to remain successful, calculating the electoral consequences of one's statements and actions by a sort of mental arithmetic that in time may become automatic. Canvassing for support privately may call for other qualities of a more diplomatic nature. The ability to be pleasant to those one dislikes is very important when engaged in committee work, coalition-building, or bargaining. The self-indulgence enjoyed by so many men (not so many women) of putting people in their place should not be practised by the politician who wishes to be successful. This may partially explain why women are so often better at committee work. The democratic leader who wants to survive must try to suffer fools gladly.

The successful political leader in a democracy must therefore learn to criticize, if at all, in a very gentle way, while at the same time turning the other cheek to criticism of the harshest kind. Only very tough people are likely to survive this process. The stress of remaining restrained in one's response when one is totally misrepresented and of enduring the spotlight of searching publicity on one's every action may be too much for normally sensitive people. Democratic leaders become encased in a resistant shell. To remain rather touchy, like, it is said, Ramsay MacDonald,[10] will put one at a disadvantage. (Of course, one can find numerous examples of top leaders reacting touchily, but this must be set against the enormous criticism they suffer.) Insensitivity may be *the* mark of the professional politician, though this may be a handicap when it comes to assessing others' reactions. Certainly toughness is needed to acknowledge responsibility once office is attained, especially as the politician out of office can easily lay the blame at the door of political opponents. The ordeal of public accountability could be enough to drive the average citizen to tears.

Few citizens, however, as I have already noted, want to be leaders. In fact, there is quite strong evidence that the aspirations of

---

[10] D. Marquand, *Ramsay MacDonald* (1977), 408 ff.

some to high political office may spring from a need to compensate for emotional deprivation. Lucille Iremonger first remarked on a pattern of childhood bereavement among British prime ministers from Perceval to Chamberlain—a period of a century and a half.[11] Hugh Berrington added that they were two and a half times as inclined as peers to have lost a parent as a child.[12] James Barber, in his study of Coolidge and Hoover, mentions that both suffered as children from losing a parent. Hoover lost both.[13] Both were shy and nervous loners. Hoover was terrified at the opening of every speech. Both also had difficulties in establishing personal relationships. These characteristics, frequently associated with emotional deprivation, are not uncommonly found among top political leaders. This explains their low self-esteem, driving them by way of compensation, Barber argues, to undertake a role which does not seem to attract many well-balanced, emotionally undeprived people. (People of abnormally high self-esteem may be either apolitical or ideologues, according to another interpretation,[14] depending on how they perceive the complexity of their own personalities.) Richard Neustadt exhorts us to beware of the insecure,[15] but it appears that national political leadership may have a particular attraction for people with personality problems. The implications, as Berrington points out,[16] may be that quite unsuitable people are likely to become prime ministers and presidents. We may think democratic leaders should be good mixers, of robust temperament, and free of neuroses. In fact, there seems to be a tendency for them to be rather neurotic, lacking in a sense of proportion, and enjoying political authority as a substitute for success at face-to-face relations. Hence one of the supposed drawbacks I have mentioned of being a politician—the need to be two-faced, or friendly to those one dislikes—does not affect this type of person so much. Dahl's suggestion that 'in spite of his appearance of friendliness and

[11] L. Iremonger, *The Fiery Chariot: A Study of British Prime Ministers and the Search for Love* (1970).

[12] H. Berrington, Review of *The Fiery Chariot, British Journal of Political Science*, 4 (1974), 345–69.

[13] J. D. Barber, Classifying and Predicting Presidential Styles: Two Weak Presidents, in A. Wildavsky (ed.), *The Presidency* (Boston, 1969), 97 ff.

[14] R. C. Ziller, W. F. Stone, R. M. Jackson, and N. J. Terbovic, Self–Other Orientations and Political Behaviour, in M. G. Hermann (ed.), *A Psychological Examination of Political Leaders* (New York, 1977), 174–204.

[15] R. E. Neustadt, *Presidential Power: The Politics of Leadership from FDR to Carter* (New York, 1980), 183.   [16] Berrington, Review, 362.

warmth, the professional may in fact carry a cool detachment that many citizens would find it impossibly wearisome to sustain.'[17] supports this analysis (though it is about leaders generally). Indeed, it may be that the manipulation of others for political ends, distasteful to the average person, comes easily to the emotionally deprived leader. Of course, such a personality type may be even more common in non-democratic regimes. In democracies the voters can at least reject them if they have the ability to sort them out.

Thus the successful professional politician in a democracy is likely to be an unusual personality type. Striving to identify with the voters, to be the common man (or woman) writ large; subjected to intrusion on privacy to the extent that, at the top, private and public existence can scarcely be distinguished; and constrained to behave in ways which are alien to many people's instincts and inner disposition, democratic leaders may develop personality problems even if they do not have them to begin with. A survivor of such experiences may find it difficult to claim a true self. The real self has long ago disappeared, as with actors, under the layers of roles memorized for different performances. The political personality may be the end-product of a process of denial of one's integrity. It may be an abnormality difficult for a normal person to admire. It is not a persona with which many will be anxious to identify: democratic political leadership is not a role which people rush to assume. It seems not only that too many regard it as a thankless job, but also that they view it as a rather dubious occupation. Democratic politicians are by no means universally ranked as people of high status. The circumstances under which they work do not encourage either high recruitment rates or general approval.

Circumstances of Democratic Leadership

A democratic leader, particularly at the national level, is the target for public criticism of the most outspoken kind. Free speech and a free press do not imply a hundred per cent concentration on politics: indeed, much criticism may be reserved for sportsmen,

---

[17] R. A. Dahl, *Who Governs?* (New Haven, 1961), 298. R. Christie, in R. Christie and F. L. Geis, *Studies in Machiavellianism* (1970), 3, sees the political operator as relatively lacking in empathy for others, unconcerned with conventional morality, fairly free of neuroses and psychoses, and pragmatic rather than ideologically committed. A good summary of theories of the psychology of leadership is L. Etheridge, Hardball Politics: A Model, *Political Psychology* 1 (1979), 3–26.

novelists, and ballerinas. But freedom to criticize is bound to include freedom to criticize authority and, under democracy, authority lives in a perpetual condition of repelling attack.

Public criticism of democratic leaders in newspapers, on radio and television, and in meetings takes several forms. Sometimes there may be statements alleging that the politician in question is not personally fit to be a leader. Sexual or business morals are the stock-in-trade of this kind of criticism which is a feature of all democracies but which is most common where populism and puritanism prevail; and where individual, as opposed to collective, leadership is part of political culture. When aristocratic values still permeated political life, as in nineteenth-century Britain, a sexual peccadillo might not be electorally damaging. For example, Disraeli was afraid that Palmerston, at the age of 79, would win the next general election as a result of Tories publicizing the allegation that the latter had committed adultery with the young wife of a radical Irish journalist.[18] On the other hand, in twentieth-century Britain where more middle-class values, as well as universal suffrage, are predominant, the Macmillan government in its later years was shaken by the revelations of the Profumo scandal. In the United States all three factors coincide: puritanism is often in association with populism, and the executive is an individual who is elected by nation-wide vote. It is scarcely surprising that the sexual and business morals of presidential aspirants and candidates have been scrutinized in presidential campaigns. The Democratic Party was thought to have been very daring in nominating Adlai Stevenson, who was divorced, as its presidential candidate in 1952 and 1956. In both years he was heavily defeated, and some believed this confirmed their prognosis.

The scrutiny which the private morals of democratic leaders undergo can easily be dismissed as the obsession of prurient humbugs. Yet underlying it is the value that democracies should be led by irreproachable people; leaders should set an example to the led. With the increase in permissiveness a more tolerant attitude to sexual shortcomings has probably developed (for example in 1980 no great outcry was raised about Reagan's divorce), but attention to the ethics of politicians in other ways is probably as great, if not greater, than ever. The vigilance of journalists, as President Nixon's experiences after the Watergate episode demonstrate, can be a

[18] J. Ridley, *Lord Palmerston* (1972), 532.

powerful deterrent to unethical conduct. Nixon's resignation in 1974 might in future come to be regarded as the high-water mark of the power of investigatory journalism. Whatever the case, it is hardly likely that the personal record of leaders will ever cease to be a subject of interest for the free mass media of the democracies.

Of necessity, however, the public statements and actions of democratic leaders receive most criticism. National leaders expecially will have to face numerous forms of attack, extending sometimes to abuse, contradiction, misrepresentation, and outright calumny. At local levels criticism will often be muted, especially in small communities where there is a widespread feeling that conflict should be avoided; but no such sentiment characterizes national politics, where political leaders exist in an environment of verbal hostility which occasionally extinguishes their political lives. Leaders in power are naturally a target for criticism; but those out of power will not escape, particularly if they are prominent and especially if they have at one time held office. Much of the criticism of leaders' actions will include exhortation to pursue a different policy. Some of it, as in the popular press, may be snappy and unthinking; but in certain political weeklies, and in the quality press, alternative courses of action may be argued at great length, with force, clarity, and command of detail. Democratic leaders are never short of advice, informed and misinformed. To both varieties of counsel, even in the moment of rejecting it, they need to show restraint and courtesy. Successful democratic politicians are often those who never appear dismissive of criticism.

This follows from the nature of democracy. The leaders have to bid for support from the voters who take advantage of the position. At the local level the representative may find himself approached by individual voters, or small groups of constituents, who demand favours in return for votes. A reputation for neglecting such solicitations will not stand the politician in good stead, though faced with conflicting pressures it will be impossible wholly to please everyone. Hence politicians may endeavour, by compromise, to avoid as much displeasure as possible; but there are bound to be those who complain that downright decisions have not been taken. Voters' criticism may not be the sharpest and best informed that politicians have to face but it may well be the most telling. Presidents and prime ministers sometimes find it necessary to explain their positions directly to the voters.

Criticism from the media takes several forms. Newspaper criticism differs from broadcasting and television interviews because the politician cannot immediately answer back. Occasionally, it is true, politicians reply in the letter columns but this is very rare. Interviews on television, a development of the last twenty years, are yet another potentially dangerous hurdle for the inexperienced politician to surmount. The fact that most of the nation can see the politician under interrogation revolutionizes democratic procedures. If the interviewer is skillful, knowledgeable, and determined, he can subject a politician in office to a cross-examination about motives and objectives such as would be impossible for a member of the House of Commons at question time, let alone a newspaperman, while an ordinary voter could never hope to be in such a situation. Of course, an adroit and well-briefed minister can turn an interview to his own advantage, using it as a vehicle to explain policy, to counter criticism, and to suppress ill-founded rumours about his intentions. The effect of the television interview, especially with ministers in office, is to give television considerable power as an institution to which political leaders are, in a sense, accountable. It is very difficult for them to refuse to be interviewed.

The most severe criticism of democratic politicians is likely, however, to come from democratic politicians. Democracy presumes a competition for power among leaders. To accept this one does not have to agree with Schumpeter that it is a central theme. In this context the rule is frequently 'No holds barred!'. Moreover, at the highest level of political activity especially, criticism may come from all sides. Naturally, democratic leaders of one party expect to be criticized by leaders of other parties with whom they are competing for governmental power. But they will also be criticized by people contending for various positions within their own party. Indeed, competition within one's own party may be fiercer than that with one's opponents. Intra-party conflict is particularly embarrassing for political leaders; but it is inevitable in view of two factors which are well-nigh universal. In the first place the number of offices in any organization or institution is limited. There can only be one president of the United States or France, and one British prime minister. Organized party being as strong as it is, the way to such positions is, to a greater or lesser extent, through party. Consequently competition among leaders in any particular party is bound to be severe. Secondly, people who are active in political parties but who do not aspire to be leaders nevertheless feel it is part of their role to hold the leaders to account. The activists often want to exercise some influence over policy, and they also see themselves as the guardians of the ideological purity of the party.[19] In aggregating enough votes to maintain the party in power, the national leaders may well stray away from their party's ideological objectives by making promises that compromise these aims. Hence leaders of a democratic party in power, in responding to voters' criticisms, may well lay themselves open to attack from their activists. Other leaders in the same party may well take advantage of this. Examples from the British Labour Party are too numerous to need quoting.[20]

Types of Political Leadership

To answer the question, 'How do people lead?', let us examine leadership in general. I have argued earlier that leaders often have quite different personalities from other people. So categorization in psychological terms may be appropriate to begin with.

B. M. Bass, concerned with leaders of all kinds, divided them into three groups.[21] Self-oriented leaders are motivated by strong power drives: they attempt to become leaders independently of any expectations of achieving group success. Such leaders may not be at all good at solving the problems of their followers, indeed, they may be handicapped by an incapacity to assess their own abilities. Task-oriented leaders will not suffer from this sort of neurosis. They will be pragmatic people concerned with specific objectives they feel they can attain: under their direction, groups are much more likely to attain their goals. Interaction-oriented leaders are most concerned with the inner state of their group: they will be most likely to attempt to lead when they feel relationships are less than satisfactory, believing they have the skills to resolve internal difficulties.

Democracy should normally have little time for self-oriented leaders. One might suspect that they would only gather large followings at times when people are easily deluded about the

[19] M. Duverger, *Political Parties*, 109 ff.
[20] See, for example, R. T. McKenzie, *British Political Parties* 2nd edn. (1963); R. Miliband, *Parliamentary Socialism* (1961).
[21] B. M. Bass, *Leadership, Psychology and Organisational Behaviour* (1960), 148.

solutions needed for their problems (but see below, p. 242). Self-oriented leaders are often totalitarian leaders who tend to emphasize their unique leader-like qualities. Democratic leaders, on the other hand, may be anxious not to appear different from their constituents. This especially applies to interaction-oriented leaders who may emerge in committee discussions where there is much friendly exchange of information and opinion in an ambience of corporate harmony. They may become bargainers and brokers concerned with exchanging favours for votes, what James Burns calls transactional leaders.[22]

These psychological types may bear some resemblance to the familiar trinity of authority characterized by Max Weber.[23] What he called charismatic leadership, where authority is legitimized by certain personal qualities of the ruler, has some affinities with self-oriented leadership. Charismatic leaders emerge in time of transition when traditional values are weakening. They tend to assert their own values. Although they can be found in any sort of regime, like self-oriented leaders they are clearly least likely to flourish in democracy. Traditional leaders, most characteristic of a pre-democratic era, are associated with hereditary, personal, and perhaps, spiritual rule. Legal–rational leadership, on the other hand, is clearly congruent with democracy, esteeming law and procedural rule. But it does not necessarily ensure democracy. Both task-oriented and interaction-oriented leaders could be either traditional or legal–rational rulers; but they are obviously most suited to polities where rationality is the main legitimizing feature.

Leaders may also be perceived in terms of class origins. Marxists see bourgeois political leadership in democracies as a reflection of capitalist dominance of the economy. They are doomed to be overthrown by the revolutionary activities of proletarian leaderships. With the advent of socialism this will give way to no leadership at all. At a more pedestrian level many studies have demonstrated that leaders are predominantly middle class, a fact which is largely a function of recruitment and the skills needed to be a politician. As the middle class are supposed to favour democracy this is an example of a self-perpetuating situation. Legal–rational leadership is likely to be upheld by professional and managerial people, those classes to whom the observance of rules is

---

[22] J. M. Burns, *Leadership* (New York, 1978), 4.

[23] H. H. Gerth and C. W. Mills, *From Max Weber* (1948), 245 ff.

most important. Although it is obviously not inevitable that democratic political leadership should be largely a middle-class activity there are reasons why the working class find leadership hard to attain. As Duverger says: 'For the patrician leader power results from his natural superiority: for the plebeian leader the superiority is the result of his power.[24] He believes aristocratic and middle-class leaders more naturally rely on their status and persuasive skills, whereas proletarian leaders have more faith in discipline which is necessary to their organizations. Robert Michels asserted: 'In all countries we learn from experience that the working-class leader . . . is apt to be capricious and despotic. He is extremely loath to tolerate contradiction.[25] He argued that one important reason why such leaders were autocratic was the adulation heaped on them by their followers. It would, however, be confusing leadership style with ideological principles to infer from this that working-class leaders are necessarily a threat to democracy. Samuel Barnes recalls that the most effective leaders of lower-status citizens in the United States were the city bosses whose leadership style was not democratic and he concludes that 'democracy on the systemic level is quite compatible with non-democratic . . . styles of leadership in intermediate organizations.'[26] Moreover, 'toughness' may go with clear, firm allegiance to democracy, just as 'tenderness' and unautocratic leadership may conceal muddle, irresolution, and a misunderstanding of what democracy stands for.

Finally leaders may be categorized by what one may call their 'political personality'. This is a compound of their personal character, their conception of what roles high office demands, and their political style, by which I mean their ways of approaching their relationships with both the public and with their colleagues in government.

A simple and rather deterministic typology of political personality was provided by Vilfredo Pareto who divided leaders into two categories, 'lions' and 'foxes',[27] terms he had borrowed from Machiavelli. They represent different methods of dealing with people and circumstances. Lions are temperamentally conservative, anxious to preserve the status quo and firm in doing so. Foxes are

[24] Duverger, *Political Parties*, 171.
[25] R. Michels, *Political Parties* (1914), 318.
[26] S. H. Barnes, Leadership Style and Political Competence, in L. J. Edinger (ed.), *Political Leadership in Industrialised Societies* (New York, 1967), 79, 82.
[27] S. E. Finer (ed.), *Vilfredo Pareto: Sociological Writings* (1966), 256 ff.

cunning and prepared to adapt to innovation by manipulating the masses. Sometimes one, sometimes the other, will be predominantly in power. Thus Pareto saw political personality largely in terms of the personal character of the leader. Élite characteristics, or 'residues', were scarcely affected by other factors. Pareto, however, had no interest in democracy. He conceived of democratic leaders as little different from other leaders.

A rather more complicated categorization of leaders, though one which still perceives personal character as the crucial factor, is expounded by James Barber.[28] (He writes only of American presidents but his analysis is applicable to other government leaders). Barber sees early experience as highly formative. He uses two spectrums to define his subjects: the *active–passive* which stretches from energetic to highly lazy, and the *positive–negative* which extends from those presidents who enjoy the office to those who find the exercise of power depressing and burdened with anxiety. The product of these two variables is a configuration of four presidential types, each with differing reactions to the experience of national leadership. Barber examines the early family relationships of eleven presidents in order to prove his point (see above, p. 232). The argument is supported by a wealth of scholarship, and is of absorbing interest; but it is difficult not to agree with Alexander George that explanations based predominantly on private personality are not enough and that the political philosophy of the president, as well as the political context, must be taken more into account when assessing presidential performance.[29]

Therefore I would argue that democratic leaders' perceptions of their roles, and their political styles (both of which may obviously be affected by personal character), are the most important differentiating features; and these will be influenced by the political institutions and the political situation with which they have to deal. For example, with American presidents, the image they have of the presidential role is bound to be significant. Eisenhower thought the president should be a unifier and above politics, and this clearly explains the way he so often distanced himself from domestic problems such as McCarthyism. He was 'the good man above politics', in the style of George Washington, Robert Neustadt

[28] J. D. Barber, *Presidential Character* (Englewood Cliffs, 1977).
[29] A. L. George, Assessing Presidential Character, *World Politics* 26 (1974), 234–82.

comments;[30] but when fundamental constitutional precepts were under threat, as at Little Rock, he had to intervene. Woodrow Wilson, as an academic, argued that Congress was the centre of power[31] and perceived the presidency as bound to follow. When he became president, however, he quickly emerged as a forceful leader. Indeed, emphatic personal leadership is much more likely in democracies in war time. In the United States, the president's function of commander-in-chief of the armed forces is naturally enhanced at this time allowing him to proceed relatively unimpeded by Congress. It is no coincidence that Lincoln, Wilson, and Franklin Roosevelt, all war-time presidents, have been hailed as great leaders. In Britain, where Cabinet secrecy tends to favour the private exercise of political power, the opportunities for dramatic leadership have almost never been in peacetime. As Erwin Hargrave writes, 'The great periods of heroic leadership by Prime Ministers in British history have been in wartime.'[32] Lloyd George and Churchill naturally come to mind. It does not follow, however, that all democratic wartime leadership is heroic. The examples of Asquith and Chamberlain are a refutation of such an assertion.

One might conceive of a dichotomy between heroic leaders and humdrum leaders. Collective executives and Cabinet government are more likely to favour the latter: individual executives and presidential government are more likely to encourage the former. Cabinet government emphasizes compromise and brokerage. It does not put a premium on drama. Where features of the political culture as in Canada, make brokerage imperative, humdrum leadership will be at a premium. Great Canadian prime ministers, Hargrave asserts, can never be heroes.[33] The country's leaders are forced to be pragmatists, mediating between the French and British communities, so ensuring the survival of the Dominion. Mackenzie King was adjudged an ideal leader because he managed to solve problems without involving the public. Under the Third and Fourth Republics French political leaders were also in the humdrum mould. This was partly a reaction against Bonapartism, but mostly the result of a strong legislature and coalition governments putting a premium on broker politicians. As in Britain, heroic leadership

---

[30] R. Neustadt, *Presidential Power* (1960), 266.

[31] W. Wilson, *Congressional Government* (Boston, 1885).

[32] E. C. Hargrave, Popular Leadership in the Anglo-American Democracies, in Edinger (ed.), *Political Leadership*, 217.   [33] Ibid. 169 ff.

was only likely to be successful in wartime. Clemenceau in World War I is the obvious example. In peacetime such leaders fared badly, as the case of Mendès-France illustrates. Indeed, the institutions and values of the Third and Fourth republics inculcated routine leadership so much that only non-politicians were likely to jolt it. In France, Stanley Hoffman opines, 'Heroic leadership is the statecraft of an outsider.'[34] Humdrum leaders have no time for grand gestures or theatrical politics. They avoid, as far as possible, becoming committed to controversial goals.

Heroic leaders, on the contrary, strike dramatic poses and proclaim national aspirations. They believe very often that their own destiny accords with that of the nation. Heroism is ascribed to them not only by the public but also by themselves. For example Eisenhower, Neustadt informs us, genuinely thought himself the hero others thought him.[35] Though he had never been under fire, he *was* a heroic leader, both publicly proclaimed and self-regarded. Of course, being a heroic leader is different from being a leader who is a hero. Truman and Attlee were both heroes of World War I, but they were not heroic leaders. They did not see themselves as such, and the public saw them as humdrum, rather pedestrian little men. Heroic leadership, therefore, is very closely associated with rhetoric, style, and charisma. It may be connected with important changes which do not conform with the prevailing political culture, and/or which signal its reorientation. Thus de Gaulle, both a hero and a heroic leader, possessed a political personality well suited to the crisis produced by the collapse of the old institutions and routines in 1958. The Fifth Republic inaugurated the visible rule of one man, untrammelled by the restraints of a powerful legislature. Although analogies were naturally drawn with the Bonapartes, the heroic leadership of de Gaulle, who had long believed he was destined to rejuvenate France, did not break the rule of law or the rules of the democratic game largely because the hero himself was concerned that this should not happen. Thus heroic leadership can be consistent with democracy, though strains may develop if it persists for too long.

The typical democratic leader, then, is a humdrum power-broker who is committed to legal–rational authority. On the other hand, there are numerous exceptions to this archetype. In surveying top

[34] S. Hoffman, Heroic Leadership: The Case of Modern France, in Edinger, *Political Leadership*, 123.   [35] Neustadt, *Presidential Power*, 165.

politicians one is struck by the variety of personality types amongst them. Yet they display numerous common characteristics, especially the possession of many skills and qualities not found to a great extent among ordinary citizens.

Skills of Democratic Leaders

If the resources needed to be a democratic leader are not in abundant supply, the skills are even less widely distributed. To some extent they are born with people, though to a greater extent, perhaps, they are learnt. But they cannot be learnt without practice. Consequently if one does not have the opportunity to learn some of the skills through success in politics, relative failure may dog one's political career.

One skill which may be a matter of congenital temperament is the ability to think and speak on one's feet. The gift of the gab may be given to some and not to others. It is not easy for those who feel they are not good public speakers to advance far in politics. This is, perhaps, nowhere more so than in Britain, where an aristocratic tradition encourages young undergraduates to think they can lay the foundation stone of a political career by learning to speak in public. Often debates in British student unions are modelled on the House of Commons with the vague implication that political reputations can be initiated in debating chambers. And this in turn derives from an out-dated impression of a talking and debating Parliament as the main decision-making arena of the nation. Legislatures in the contemporary world are more 'working' than 'talking' bodies so that opportunities for oratory in them, may be very limited indeed, as in the American House of Representatives. But public speaking is still important in getting elected, though it is probably no longer the most telling of political skills.

Those skills which relate to making a favourable impression are partially innate. Most successful politicians are, to some extent, actors, and the ability to act is only partly learnt; a great deal of it is born with one. All the actor's instincts and skills—a sense of theatre, a capacity to learn one's lines, a feeling for an audience, and an instinct for timing—are useful for politicians. Harold Macmillan was probably more conscious of this than most politicians. He actually used the metaphor of the old actor on whom the curtain had rung down to describe his retirement from the political stage. Both he and Stanley Baldwin were businessmen but felt it was important, as Conservative prime ministers, symbolically to identify themselves with the countryside. Hence Macmillan culti-vated a grouse-moor image and Baldwin, a Midlands ironmaster, enjoyed posing as a Worcestershire squire. Thus the humdrum type of democratic leader without colourful histrionics can play a role reassuring and commanding enough to up-stage rival leaders.

With more heroic leaders, political theatre is even more import-ant. American presidents, as I have noted above, by the nature of their position, may often be thrust into heroic roles. John Kennedy, who had a penchant towards dramatic action, became a 'hero' figure, Orrin Klapp argues,[36] through a series of historic confronta-tions such as his successful encounter with the United States Steel Corporation. (He forced the industry to cancel its price increases.) On the other hand, Richard Nixon, despite his acting ability, was still handicapped by image trouble. With neither Kennedy's good looks nor his political charm he suffered, as Kennedy profited, from the advent of television which accentuated all his handicaps. As a result, after his early defeats, Nixon decided that his image had to be manufactured, and he put himself in the hands of professional public relations experts.[37] The modern national political leader has become as a result of television a celebrity willy-nilly; and so, perhaps, we may be entering an age when the heroic leader will be a necessity. Hence Ronald Reagan, an actor turned politician, was a natural. Hardly a hero, he had the clean looks and upright bearing of one. He also had confidence in his own powers of charming the populace, probably the essential foundation for presenting a favourable image. Scarcely a heroic leader by my definition he showed signs of aspiring to be one, and the American citizens seemed anxious to claim him as one.

Private skills, however, as I have already suggested, may be more important than public skills for the democratic leader. All those activities which are combined in the concept of the 'committee-man' are relevant to the contemporary democratic politician. An ability for sustained argument and discussion, for patient but tenacious advocacy combined with persuasiveness and mastery of detail, for not becoming excited or angry but exercising restraint, and for procedural cunning—these are the qualities of the success-ful negotiator. To a significant extent, political life is concerned

[36] Orrin E. Klapp, *Symbolic Leaders* (Chicago, 1964), 79.
[37] J. McGinnis, *The Selling of the President 1968* (1979), 35 ff.

with negotiating with people holding different views and conflicting objectives. Outwitting an opponent at the bargaining table is facilitated, as we have noted, by an ability to conceal one's preferences, goals, and knowledge of the situation while at the same time discovering one's opponent's preferences, goals, and knowledge. Thus one should aim at appearing to make serious concessions when one is conceding little. The committee room is very different from the hustings and calls for very different qualities, but the modern democratic politician, to be successful, must learn to operate in both situations. His public stance should serve well his private political activities and vice versa.

Linking private and public political domains is the role of power broker. It is difficult for the modern democratic politician not to play this role in some sense and to some degree. At its most dramatic, power-broking is illustrated by the activities of the old-fashioned American city boss who carefully balanced his tickets with the candidates of numerous ethnic groups in order to obtain a majority of votes and political power. At a higher level, at the Democratic Party's 1932 presidential nominating convention James A. Farley aggregated enough bundles of bosses' votes to nominate Franklin Roosevelt, whose campaign he was managing.[38] Brokerage can also be appropriate at the level of legislative seats. The *Guardian* of 10 October 1979 recorded the activities of Gosta Bohman, 'power broker'. As leader of the Swedish Conservative Party, he threw his weight behind Thorbjorn Falldin, leader of the Centre Party, rather than Ola Ullsten, Liberal Party leader, thus ensuring that Falldin became prime minister of the coalition government of the three parties. As an occupation, brokerage demands great knowledge of the commodity being traded—political support. Power brokers hope to obtain power for themselves by procuring power for someone else. This not only calls for skills in bargaining but also acute knowledge of how much all sides to the deal are willing to compromise their stated goals. Shrewdness and judiciousness as well as tact and discretion are essential for power-broking. The skills required by the successful democratic politician are thus varied and extensive; and it is unlikely that all will be practised by any one person with great proficiency. But most successful leaders are likely to possess many of them.

I have argued that two general categories of political skill are the public and private. More extroverted people are likely to excel in

[38] H. Eaton, *Presidential Timber* (1964), 325 ff.

public skills and more introverted with private. Whatever the case, most citizens either do not possess them to a high degree or, if they do, choose not to use them. Only a few people enter political life, either at a part-time or full-time level, which is hardly surprising in view of the circumstances under which democratic leaders operate. Requiring a wide range of rather diverse skills, the rewards the job offers are not those that appeal to the vast majority of people, while the costs are usually considered prohibitive.

It is not totally far-fetched to regard being a politician as one of the 'dirty jobs' in our society. These are occupations, we are told, that people are reluctant to undertake because the rewards are not commensurate with the risks and drawbacks, because the hours of work are inconvenient and bad for home life, the conditions unpleasant, and because the activity itself is not highly regarded by the community and so confers low status. Dustmen, street sweepers, sewage workers, and bus conductors are among the jobs categorized in this way. Yet they are all necessary occupations without which the economy and society could not easily survive. And the question may well be asked, how long could we continue without political leaders? They are constantly criticized, often abused, sometimes underpaid (as in Britain), frequently overworked, and with little time for home life. (There is a high rate of marriage breakdown among politicians.) Yet they are necessary for democracy. It is hardly surprising that so few people wish to become politicians. The wonder is that any still do at all.

A Crisis of Democratic Leadership?

It is common to say that at no time have politicians been less respected than in the present. This assertion, however, needs careful examination. Those who remember the world between the wars are less likely to concur because a world in which the frail German and Italian democracies were overthrown by Fascist dictators, in which the French Third Republic tottered to its downfall, in which presidents Harding and Coolidge in the United States and prime ministers Baldwin and Chamberlain in Britain, were in power, can hardly be described as one safe for democracy. It was also a period when democratic politicians were savagely attacked for their inability to solve the problem of mass, long-term unemployment. The experiences of Roosevelt's twelve-year leadership in the United States, Britain's war-time egalitarianism, the achievements of the post-war

Labour government and the return to prosperity in the 1950s, successful restoration of democracy in West Germany and Italy under highly regarded leaders, and the successful introduction of it in Japan to a large extent dissipated this mood. By the mid-1950s only in the French Fourth Republic were democratic politicians widely held in disrespect. (Though unfairly, Philip Williams argued: the French had better politicians than they deserved.[39]) Hence the post-war trend was one in which, to a great degree, democratic political leadership recovered some of its self-respect.

Thus I would argue that it is wrong to envisage a gradual decline of the quality of democratic leadership in the twentieth century, though as the century has progressed both societal and political factors may have contributed to the formation of such an impression. Basically the misunderstanding stems from the increasing salience and public awareness of the apparent paradox which is the central problem of the contemporary democratic state. There is a call for better and stronger hierarchy; it is said the authority of democratic leadership should be more emphatically asserted. At the same time there is a growing demand for wider and more intensive participation: there is an increasing inclination on the part of some to insist on their right of democratic activity. (This is not inconsistent with falling electoral participation rates.) It might therefore seem that validating the equation 'more democracy equals weaker and poorer leadership' requires little effort. There are some easily identified factors in the modern world apparently indicating that leadership is in crisis.

New forces in society have challenged established hierarchies with demands for more control over individual life-chances. People in superordinate positions—managers in industry, heads of schools and colleges, and cadres of all kinds in other associations—have faced demands for accountability. Generational conflict has extended far outside the democratic world as in the Chinese Cultural Revolution. Whether the instability resulting from this trend is more damaging to democratic or non-democratic leadership is difficult to discover. Almond and Verba might argue that a crisis in the family and the schoolroom resulting in wider participation by the young[40] would enhance civic competence and so strengthen democracy. Eckstein also argued that congruent types

---

[39] P. Williams, *Politics in Post-war France* (1954), 402.
[40] G. A. Almond and S. Verba, *The Civic Culture* (Princeton, 1963), 346 ff.

of authority pattern are good for the stability of democracy. Those furthest removed from the polity, however, least need to be democratic.[41] Undemocratic authority exerted in family and classroom might not favour the maintenance of democracy in the polity; but as the relationship between democracy in the schoolroom or family and in the wider polity is bound to be tenuous, it will have little effect on democratic stability.

The industrial sphere is clearly nearer to the political. A prosperous and productive industry with good relations between employers and employees is important for the success of governments. Where the failure of industry to perform well in this sphere is attributed to governments (and, as I argue elsewhere, this is commonly the case in many democratic countries), then governments must be concerned with the challenge to industrial leadership posed by shopfloor indiscipline, strikes, low productivity, and absenteeism. Yet it would usually be contended that in a democratic country the practice of democracy is buttressed by industrial democracy i.e., the institutionalization of shop-floor pressures on management. It is not only that industrial productivity is stimulated by participation within the work place, but also that democracy at the top is enhanced by the presence of democratic procedures and values within any arena near to it. Clearly industry and industrial relations are often the concern of national policy-makers. Therefore, industrial democracy may be regarded as a support for, and a corollary of, democracy itself. But conversely it might seem, as I argued earlier, that democracy in industry is detrimental to effective economic policy-making.

Consequently we seem to have a dilemma. Democracy at the workplace, structurally close to the national policy-making arena, seems both detrimental to, and a favourable influence upon, the wider democracy of the nation. In organizing the division of labour and the productive function, once goals and strategy have been laid down managerial directives must be obeyed. But determination of goals, strategies, and decisions about working conditions may be open to prior discussion and bargaining. The paradox is only apparent. Good leadership and democracy in industry can be reconciled.

When we turn to those associations nearest the centre of the

[41] H. Eckstein, *Division and Cohesion in Democracy* (Princeton, 1966), App. B, A Theory of Stable Democracy, 225 ff.

polity—political parties—we should expect to find leadership both responsive and responsible to followers. Where party leadership cannot fulfill its leadership function, democracy may face a crisis. Again, with both parties and pressure groups, mass participation is not necessarily detrimental to firm leadership. What leadership wants is a decision-making process which allows policies to be debated and to be decided fairly. What the membership requires is that agreed objectives should be articulated clearly and implemented, implying a competent and honest leadership. When the rank and file does not know what it wants, however, the leadership may be faced with either doing nothing or itself composing and implementing party policy.

In general, since democracy arrived in the nineteenth century, the tendency has been for political parties to become mass parties and more national in scope. This has affected the relationship between leaders and members. Leaderships, as Michels maintained, have become more bureaucratic, more remote, and less like their followers. But as discussed in Chapter 6, there is no iron law of oligarchy in democratic parties. Party members have rebelled against this situation in order to install new leaderships with different values and styles. Such a succession of power, however, is scarcely damaging to democracy within the party; indeed, it is a consequence of it. It is only where and when no leadership is allowed to consolidate that a crisis of authority might arise, and this only happens when the revolt of the rank and file is against leadership *per se:* when they are unwilling to accept *any* leadership. Then organization may begin to break down, and with it procedures which are necessarily part of democratic government.

A more likely cause of instability of party leadership stems from the fact that mass participation is uncommon within 'mass parties'. A small proportion of party members are concerned to be party activists. Consequently, the activists are also not representative of the membership; but in many parties they recruit the leaders from amongst themselves. Therefore they may tend to choose leaders not representative of the membership, still less of the electorate. This type of leadership may well be responsive and responsible, in its values and policies, to the activists; but hardly to the voters, until it has to face electoral competition and, ultimately, governing the country. In these circumstances the flexibility both of the political leaders and of the party activists will be tested. Where the political party tends to be like a church or sect—that is, where it is most wedded to its doctrine—the leaders will find it difficult to depart from the party line in order to be responsive to the electorate. On the other hand, a political party without strong dogmatic attachments may exert very little pressure on its leaders, either in or out of office.

Doctrinal parties and doctrinal leaders are not in themselves detrimental to democracy. For doctrine, however, the democratic process provides a testing ordeal. If the electorate is well disposed to doctrine then it may support leaders propounding doctrine; but in contemporary decades the voters have seemed less and less inclined to favour anything that smacks of ideology, and ideological parties have been forced to adjust to this shift. For example, in 1958 the German Social Democratic Party, as a result of repeated electoral failures, drew up at Bad Godesberg a party programme excluding public ownership.[42] From that time forward its electoral fortunes improved until it was able to take power. The British Labour Party, on the other hand, has not been able to develop in the same way and at times has shown a tendency to move nearer to a restatement in its electoral manifestos of its basic doctrine of common ownership summarized in Clause 4 of its constitution.[43] This has provided great problems for its leadership.

Leaders may realize that if a party moves too much to the right, or left, it will lose favour with the voters, however much the movement satisfies the activists. Leaders of doctrinal parties, therefore, may have to be ideologues within the party, but pragmatists with the voters, a difficult manœuvre to execute. Where wooing the voters becomes paramount then doctrine is less important and activists are neglected, giving leaders more power. This is the case with aggregative or catch-all parties of which the Gaullists are often quoted as the prototype. Otto Kirchheimer, however, sees the role of the leader as hardly heroic in this sort of party which attempts to imbue the electorate with an image 'analogous to that of a major brand in the marketing of a universally needed and highly standardised article of mass consumption'.[44] The leader of such a party must suit his behaviour to standard requirements. As the catch-all

[42] K. Sontheimer, *The Government and Politics of West Germany* (1972), 90.

[43] P. Whitely, The Decline of Labour's Local Party Membership and Electoral Base, 1945–1979, in D. Kavanagh (ed.), *The Politics of the Labour Party* (1982), 119 ff.   [44] O. Kirchheimer, *Politics, Law, and Social Change* (1969), 362.

party is concerned with electoral success above all else, the techniques of electioneering are very important to it. Thus its leaders will be subject to public relations techniques, and its policy will be influenced by the results of public opinion polls. Television performance and personal characteristics will be important. The process may produce not a de Gaulle but a Reagan: not a heroic leader, but a quasi-heroic one.[45] Once elected his managers may be concerned to keep him as far away as possible from the voters. The leader may be a problem for the party rather than, as in doctrinal parties, the party being a problem for the leader.

Therefore the relationship with the electorate, or at least a large section of it, should most concern democratic leaders. Identifying issues to place on the political agenda, for example, can only occur where the politicians have a view of what support the electorate is likely to give them. More frequently, of course, political leaders are solicited by groups of voters to adopt certain issues, and the leaders' problem is whether, or how, to respond. The discovery or choice of marketable issues by democratic politicians may depend on the length and sensitivity of their political antennae. For the most part they respond to opinion rather than arouse it; but the most able democratic leaders may be capable of articulating what the inarticulate cannot express. As Burns says, 'The leader's fundamental act is to induce people to be aware or conscious of what they feel—to feel their true needs so strongly, to define their values so meaningfully, that they can be moved to powerful action.'[46] The leader mobilizes feeling and values to use in the interests of followers' aspirations for political power. In more clearly identifying their objectives for them, he identifies himself with them.

Informing followers and explaining the development of the debate on the issues will be another important role of the democratic leader. The successful leader educates followers, through speeches and writings, sometimes by rhetoric and sometimes by patient argument. He also does it by his actions. Sometimes leaders may have to undertake action which they know to be impracticable in order to demonstrate that fact to their followers. This is a case of leaders following followers in order, later, to lead with more conviction. Opinion polls show that voters

---

[45] In his 1980 campaign, quoting another quasi-hero frequently, Reagan said 'Duke Wayne did not believe that our country was ready for the dustbin of history.' See E. Drew, *Portrait of an Election* (1981), 336.   [46] Burns, *Leadership*, 44.

are much more influenced by political action than by political propaganda.[47]

Democratic politicians are also expected to achieve credibility by solving problems. Some of these will be known and widely accepted by the electorate: others the politicians must identify, convincing voters of their existence and explaining and evaluating them. It is doubtful, however, whether many serious problems can be solved without acts of creative imagination. This may often involve seizing on compromises not hitherto evident to any side in an argument. The introduction of power sharing in Northern Ireland by Willie Whitelaw, the British minister for the province, and Brian Faulkner the Ulster prime minister, bringing Protestant and Catholic leaders together in the same Cabinet, is an example of a remarkable political achievement, though in this case imagination outstripped reality. Politicians of vision define long-term national problems and suggest solutions, something that most other people are incapable of doing. If democratic politicians do not do this the country may either languish or turn to non-democratic leaders. The danger within contemporary democracies is that as problems become more complex, people expect more from their governments, and more imagination is needed from political leaders. In the end the strain may be too great for them.

Another danger is that solutions to problems are proffered in a hurry, probably a feature of much policy-making by contemporary democratic governments. This springs from a perception that we are living in a crisis: crisis measures are therefore needed. (Proper crisis management might decree otherwise.) The general effect is an atmosphere in which 'hand-to-mouth' decisions are made because leaders have not time to think. For example, Helmut Schmidt, the Social Democratic chancellor of West Germany, said in March 1977[48] that he spent 85 per cent of his time in justifying decisions, 10 per cent in administration and implementation, and only 5 per cent in reflection about policy and making it.

The degree to which such leadership behaviour indicates a real

[47] F. V. Cantwell, Public Opinion and the Legislative Process, *American Political Science Review*, 58 (1946), 932, says events are more important than statements of Congress or the president in shaping the direction of public opinion.

[48] W. E. Paterson, The Chancellor and His Party: 'Political Leadership in the Federal Republic', p. 8 in id., and G. Smith (eds.), *The West German Model* (1981) quoting *Frankfurter Allgemeine Zeitung*, 26 Mar. 1977.

crisis and the degree to which it is a consequence of their own misperceptions of crisis is incalculable, so closely connected are leaders' decisions with the situation within which they operate. Summit diplomacy in the post-war world, however, has obviously increased the visibility and paramountcy of heads of government. Indeed, for this and other reasons there may be a drift to concentration of power in the hands of top leaders. More important than summitry is the need for an arbiter and co-ordinator between the warring spending sectors of the modern state. Only the head of the executive, and possibly the finance minister, can give coherence to policy where there is competition for resources. Harold Seidman has written: 'The struggle for power and position has contributed to fragmentation of the executive branch structure and proliferation of categorical programmes.'[49] It is to counteract this trend that heads of government have striven to assert control and to impose an overall policy. This has led to a sharpening of the cone of responsibility, especially under parliamentary government, where a gap has opened between prime ministers and senior colleagues. It is probably not a coincidence that France has, since 1958, moved to a strong presidency, while German chancellors and British prime ministers have been accused of adopting presidential styles and behaviour.

The latter argument is a very confused one, partly because it is assumed that 'presidentialism' implies greater executive power, whereas the American presidency with which the analogy is perceived is an example of a weak executive. Perhaps the intended contrast is between collective and individual executives, with the implication that increasingly the world's democracies are moving towards the latter. It is usually argued that elected individual executives result in a perception of politics much more in terms of personalities than issues. As Robert Lane wrote nearly thirty years ago, 'it is clear that the main source of emotion for most people in recent American history is not the issues *per se* but rather the political leaders (seen, it is true, against a background of issues) . . .'[50] The attention given in more recent years to the personalities of top politicians almost everywhere in the democratic world is often attributed to television. This may have coincided with a decline in

---

[49] H. Seidman, *Politics, Position and Power* (1970), 34.
[50] R. E. Lane, *Political Life* (New York, 1959), 130.

interest in issues, or it may have partly caused it. Whatever the case, for all these reasons, it does appear that there is a trend towards associating policy and direction with top individual leadership.

If this is so, appeal to personality may become a more marked feature of political behaviour. The implications of such a development for democracy were also spelt out by Lane: 'displacement of emotion on person is easier for most people than displacement upon groups or issues, or even symbols, a phenomenon which, if true, could help to explain the personalisation of politics both in the United States and abroad'.[51] Lane saw the root cause of this trend in the yearning for relief from responsibility, a characteristic of our time, he believed. He condemned appeals to personality, complaining:

They indulge the citizenry in the gratification of immediate psychological needs at the expense of any long-term improvements in their situation. They confuse the import of elections and virtually eliminate the meaning of an electoral 'mandate'—not a very clear meaning under the best of circumstances.[52]

In short, he perceived democracy as weakened by a trend to personality politics: and, if this *is* so, its materialization (perhaps, caused by, or linked with, television), may be an indication that electorates are taking their democratic regimes less seriously.

Unfortunately, today's democratic leaders need much more than charm, charisma, guile, and a ready wit. Democracies benefit from leaders with intellect. They also need leaders willing to work hard, with the education (which may not necessarily mean formal education) to understand difficult briefs and complex problems. A proper understanding of the contemporary world must include a sense of history—important for comprehending the values and likely behaviour of different groupings within society, as well as foreign nations—and sociological and economic knowledge, enabling one to avoid being bamboozled by experts, and to develop perspectives for the future within which present events can be given direction. Dag Anckar, in rejecting a view of the democratic leader as 'largely a reactive agent guided by the collective wisdom of the group', commends the three components Walter Carlsnaes thinks necessary for democracy: 'an enlightened and critically reflective public, a corps of politicians sufficiently well-informed not to be the pawns of experts and professional bureaucrats, and a dynamic area of

---

[51] Ibid. 139.   [52] Ibid. 355.

public debate not beholden to any particular—private or public—interest'.[53] Ideally one wants more rational leaders *and* more rational followers.

If there is a leadership crisis its causes may be numerous. For example, it might be a reaction to grass-roots protest movements that have no particular significance for the operation of democracy. It is hard to deny, however, that at the top levels of the democratic state there is cause for concern. Matti Wiberg among others has shown that trust in democratic politicians is not great.[54] Democracies, even though they may breed people and values distrustful of hierarchy, need leadership like any other sort of regime. The anti-politician cult exemplified by *Le canard enchâiné* and *Private Eye,* or by programmes like 'Spitting Image' on television, flourishes where political leadership is losing legitimacy. Whether this is caused by poor performance by leaders or the expansion of a highly educated and sophisticated public with higher standards is difficult to judge. Perhaps both factors are at work. Whatever the reason, a considerably larger group of citizens expects better decision-making and is much more critical of its leaders. At the same time the latter have lacked the qualities needed to be successful, particularly of enterprise and imagination. Too many top leaders have chosen only aides who agree with them whereas, as Roosevelt demonstrated,[55] argument and disagreement assist policy-making. Too many, like Nixon, have distanced themselves from contentious issues and people.[56] As any kind of formal training for top politicians seems wildly impracticable, the only possible suggestions are that voters should be both more careful about those for whom they vote and less expectant about their abilities.

Whether there has been a crisis of democratic leadership or not, it does appear that a rather different species of politician has emerged in the years since the Second World War. Social change and, perhaps, intellectual fashion, have stimulated criticism of authority in all walks of life. There is less deference and people are more inclined to dissent from accepted ways of thought, a tendency

[53] D. Anckar, A Definition of Democracy, in D. Anckar and F. Berndtson, *Essays on Democratic Theory* (Tampere, 1984), 29, quoting W. Carlsnaes, Foreign Policy and the Democratic Process, *Scandinavian Political Studies*, 3 (1981), 81–108.

[54] M. Wiberg, Wrong Persons are Making Good Decisions Without Hearing Us; Paper given to the ECPR joint workshops at Barcelona, March 1985.

[55] A. S. McFarlan, *Power and Leadership in Pluralist Systems* (Standford, 1969), 200.

reflected in the organization of certain pressure groups, or militant sub-groups in political parties. At the same time there has been no marked increase in political participation. The voters have been inclined to leave the solution of problems to their leaders, though they have been always willing to throw them out of office. It could be argued, in fact, that there is as much a crisis of followership as of leadership.

Conclusion

Robert Dahl has recently posed the problem for democratic theorists as follows: 'To portray a democratic order without leaders is a conspicuous distortion of all historical experience; but to put them in the picture is even more troublesome ... the superior influence of leaders violates strict criteria for political equality.'[57] Indeed, there is a certain unnatural element in the position of democratic political leaders. They are subjected to continual criticism and unlike most people in positions of authority—fathers or mothers, professors, surgeons, employers, judges—they are liable almost summarily to be dismissed by their subordinates. Their situation is not one to be envied and it is not surprising that there are few contenders for their places. The competition for office evokes a great deal of biased reporting and downright misinformation. The struggle for power in democracy is characterized by an unusual lack of physical harassment and intimidation (compared with the non-democratic world), but there is little restraint on what opponents say about each other.

The relationship between different sets of political leaders is of the greatest importance for democratic society. It is no exaggeration to affirm that the maintenance of the democratic rules of the game depends on leaders' respect for them. This also includes respecting the rights of abusive opponents. The atmosphere of trust so important for the smooth operation of democracy very much depends on democratic leaders not giving even the merest suspicion of tampering with constitutional conventions.

In their relationships with the voters, successful democratic leaders are likely to be both responsive and responsible. They are inevitably sensitive to the feelings of at least more than half of their constituents, and the more successful politicians will be searching

[57] R. A. Dahl, *A Preface to Economic Democracy* (Berkeley, 1985), 152.

for popular policies to espouse. These will seldom arise spontaneously from the electorate. As Gerald Pomper says, 'Initiatives in a democratic system lie not with the voters but with politicians.'[58] This is especially true if it also includes grass-roots leaders, local politicians whose activities are often directed to transmitting issues, either through party structures or members of the legislature, to the centre. National politicians will place, or not place, issues from the grass roots on national agendas (assuming that they have this freedom of choice). Depending on how they judge such issues as vote-winning possibilities, and how they can deal with the pressures, they must make up their minds whether to back them or not.

Hence the best politicians will be sensitive to issues but wary about responding to them. Whether they approve or disapprove further pressure may follow. Once a commitment has been made, politicians will be held responsible for actively supporting the issue. As democratic politicians will be under pressure from numerous, often conflicting, quarters, they will be reluctant to commit themselves strongly. Thus leading politicians may often find it useful to find a formula, a few 'weasel words', which can be manipulated to appear as either a commitment or not. For this reason, among many others, mandates are often far from clear. This would be inevitable anyway because the most practical (and therefore the best), politicians realize that so many unpredictable variables can intervene to impede the most promising schemes.

Leaders can only be understood, as I have argued, in terms of their relationships with followers. Democratic leaders are usually party leaders and therefore they have to lead their party as well as seeking to lead the country. Hence local party activists as well as voters are followers to be taken into account. These complexities demand leaders of great versatility in skills, considerable adaptability in roles, and a wide range of qualities. To make the most obvious point: the personal characteristics and accomplishments needed to secure election are quite different from those needed to lead a party or direct a government. Being a successful democratic politician is not possible without long experience, one might almost say training, only there is no formal training and there is not likely to be.

Nevertheless democratic politicians are, in some senses anyway,

[58] G. M. Pomper, *Elections in America* (1968), 216.

'professional'. They are paid, they usually have some sense of vocation, and they are in a highly specialized occupation. Unsurprisingly, in spite of predominantly being men from middle-class backgrounds, they are rather apart from other people. Temperamentally, leading politicians tend to be thick-skinned, egotistical, and rather ruthless. This sets them apart from the majority of humanity who do not want power and the responsibility and publicity that goes with it. Again, the practice of politics tends to give representatives an unusual combination of characteristics—conversational wariness, calculative resourcefulness, and an obsessiveness about other people's reactions. The glare of publicity is bound to accentuate these traits and for national leaders the advent of television has been especially important in this respect. Indeed, 'no good on television' is now reckoned to be a damning comment to make about any aspirant for political leadership.

The yearning for publicity coupled with the need for circumspection provides a dilemma for all democratic leaders. None too happy about media criticism, politicians wish only to deal with it on their terms; but that is completely impossible in a free society. While most democratic politicians would like to bring pressure on the media, merely the suspicion of doing so may lead to unpopularity. Fortunately television interviews rarely take long, and most politicians have enough skills to avoid being forced into unwanted commitments or undesired revelations. National political leaders particularly welcome occasions, such as for example the D-day anniversary of 1984, which project their images without opening them to censure. Even mediocre leaders can emerge with glamour from such ceremonies.

Nearly forty years ago, Duverger wrote that two essential facts dominated the evolution of parties in the twentieth century: the increase in the authority of political leaders and the tendency to personal forms of authority.[59] Both trends were related to the 'rise of the masses'. Written so soon after the catastrophe of Fascism, his analysis could be regarded as backward-looking. Yet it would be possible to argue that an evolution towards personal leadership in democracies is still in progress. This could be supported by the supposed trend towards 'presidentialism' in some Western democracies, with a parallel movement away from policies and towards preferences for managerial styles as vote-

[59] Duverger, *Political Parties*, 168.

winning factors; and a similar tendency towards aggregative rather than articulative parties. These alleged developments could all be regarded as threatening for democracy. The charismatic, heroic leader coming to the fore in a time of crisis might, as a result of success through demagogy, warns Sidney Hook,[60] become contemptuous of the voters and end public contestation.

Memories of Lenin in 1918 ordering the suppression of Russia's first democratically elected constituent assembly, or of Mussolini and Hitler shutting down their parliaments, are likely to be ineradicable wherever democracy is valued. Heroes will be at a disadvantage because people with democratic traditions are suspicious of charismatic leaders. As James Margach illustrates, British prime ministers[61] do not like to relinquish power; but in well-established democracies normal procedures, as well as death, seem to have prevented too sustained a rule by one person. Yet ultimately only vigilance and an electorate that takes political issues seriously and responsibly can guarantee against one person retaining power undemocratically. A participating electorate, if it is sensibly aware of the roles of leaders and shrewd in evaluating the quality of its leadership potential, should choose leaders who look to the future and anticipate difficulties; who reflect on and diagnose the country's ills; and who co-ordinate and guide the flow of national business. Electoral competition, however, is hardly the most rational of processes. Whether a democracy gets such a leader or not may often depend on an element of chance.

[60] S. Hook, *The Hero in History* (1945), cited in M. W. Fisher, Nehru: the Hero as Responsible Leader, in R. L. Park and I. Tinker (eds.), *Leadership and Political Institutions in India* (Princeton, 1959) 64.

[61] M. Margach, *The Anatomy of Power* (1979), 34 ff.

9

CONCLUSION

THERE are at least three reasons why people have been confused about what democracy implies. One of these is familiar and alluded to frequently at the popular level: democracy is associated with the 'good', and so even undemocratic regimes are anxious to claim association with it. A second is the fact that democracy, historically speaking, is quite a recent phenomenon. The strictest application of my criteria would date it from 1918 in the United States, 1928 in Britain, 1946 in France and Italy, and 1972 in Switzerland. (The dates of the inception of universal adult suffrage.) Other entities I have discussed in this book, such as the state, bureaucracy, and capitalism, all preceded democracy by some centuries. When democracy arrived on the scene, as it were, it had to come to terms with them; they have all persisted and to many people they still remain more familiar than democracy which has modified them. The third reason for confusion is that democracy is often discussed in terms emphasizing only the differences between democratic and non-democratic states, though many of the same problems and political relationships exist in both types of regime. For example, state power coerces in democratic as in authoritarian countries, merely the terms under which it operates are different. Democracy is certainly not a system in which everyone's wishes are fulfilled: one can be as frustrated and disappointed as in any other sort of regime. The difference with democracy is that it allows one to express disappointment very loudly. For some people this may not be much of a boon.

The long connection of democracy with liberalism also misleads people about its true nature. There can be little dispute that democracy and liberalism developed conjointly. Public contestation, inclusiveness, the rule of law, and responsible government can all be regarded as liberal ideas. But liberalism was also linked with nationalism, egalitarianism, libertarianism, and economic individualism. None of these can be regarded as necessarily identified with democratic regimes. Viewed as objectives they are matters for democratic decision. Mid-nineteenth-century liberalism, with its belief in the perfectibility of man and man's capacity, with education, to reach a higher plane of reason, anticipated democratic institutions achieving a high level of rationality. The late nineteenth-century revolt against reason portended the twentieth-century rebellion against democracy. Liberals became disappointed with its achievements and exasperated by its failure to produce quickly those liberal objectives and values to which they aspired. They underestimated the natural conservatism of ordinary people and the irrationality of collective social forces. Above all they did not face up to the fact of power.

Democracy, however, cannot abolish hierarchy and power. These are too necessary for the functioning of any political system. Politics is about power. What democracy does is to change the context and conditions in which power and hierarchy operate. The decision-making process in a democratic regime bears only a faint resemblance to that of a non-democratic regime. In the former there are conflicting leaderships, the leaderships are subject to criticism and find it necessary to bid for followers, and the followers can become leaders. Leaders are dismissible and answerable. The process is slow and complex. Procedures are governed by rules. Hence leadership in democratic regimes will tend to be legitimated by legal–rational criteria. Nevertheless, democratic citizens will be as subject as any others to control by authority.

Another difficulty for the liberals who promoted democracy was that rationality decreed that a liberal polity would pursue efficiency. Democracy and efficiency were therefore often seen in the same light: authoritarianism and inefficiency were perceived as partners under the *ancien regime*. Perhaps the roots of this idea sprang from the analogy between consumer sovereignty and universal suffrage. Yet democracy is hardly likely to be very efficient, as I have argued, in terms anyway of conventional economic and organizational theory. The managers are always being changed, as are the firm's objectives. (No business enterprise has ever chosen to make its decisions under such conditions. If it did it would be hardly likely to maximize its profits.) Of course, it is only fair to say that classical theorists like Mill did not see the democratic state intervening such in the economy. It is ironical that electoral pressures have brought about mixed economies in which prosperity becomes the important criterion for assessing the popularity of governments.

Thus the rulers of a country with an inefficient economy can be held to account for not being efficient.

The relation of efficiency to democracy reaches a crucial point when seen in the light of power. Fundamentally, in democracy the majority of the people are in power; but many millions of people cannot make a judgement efficiently regarding the application, for example, of Keynesian management techniques. There is a transmission of power by representative institutions. Hence the complex problem of responsible power. How much responsibility should the voters accord to their elected governments? If they want to accord little they may plump for direct democracy, but as we have seen this may be very inefficient. If they want to accord much then they should do nothing but vote at elections for candidates who proffer no policies, the 'trustees' mentioned in Chapter 2. Turning over responsibilities to representatives may be either efficient or inefficient, depending on the competence of those elected; but it certainly does not allow for great upward control. Moreover, it does not escape the dilemma because, even if individual voters do not press governments, organized interests will do so. Consultation and negotiation with the interests concerned have always taken place and also ante-date democracy. But in Britain, Samuel Beer suggests,[1] although pressure groups are important, the reasons for stagnation derive from the programmatic parties. Perhaps British parties have been relied on too much by their supporters.

Whatever the case, pluralism is an inevitable adjunct of the democratic state. Mass political parties and most interest groups are offsprings of democracy. The complex relations between them are difficult to define and anyway vary from one democracy to another. The outputs of their bargaining with one another, and with their governments, can scarcely just be measured against the majority will. A mixture of values will have gone into the process. At one point it may be the rationality of the technocrats pushing for the 'correct' solution; at another an attempt of some group, strategically placed, to affect the final outcome in their own interests; and at yet another the electoral calculus of the politicians, partly influenced by the distance from the next election. In some democracies the procedures will be largely private, in a few they will be more public. It can be argued that policies produced by such

[1] S. H. Beer, British Pressure Groups Revisited: Pluralistic Stagnation from the Fifties to the Seventies, *Public Administration Bulletin*, 32 (1980), 16.

processes are associated with certain political leaders who will take responsibility for them at the next election. In this way democratic legitimacy is assured.

This apologia does not take into account citizen participation. As we have seen, what Rokkan calls corporate pluralism bargaining between groups and government, operates in parallel with numerical democracy, the more conventional system of decision-making through elections and representative institutions. It is true that in some interest groups (though scarcely at all in business, the most powerful in proportion to its numbers) ordinary members may have the opportunity of a good deal of active participation (this especially applies to trade unions, though even their internal democracy is somewhat attenuated). In general, however, democratic citizens obviously can no more participate in consultation, negotiation, and bargaining between interest groups and governments than they can in the deliberations of their Parliaments. But with regard to numerical democracy, two qualifications must be made here. In the first place all citizens can join political parties and take part in their discussions about party policy. Secondly, the debates of Parliaments and discussions of political parties can be reported in the media. But no reports, in any detail anyway, are made of discussions under corporate pluralism. The secrecy, lack of clarity, and unintelligibility of the process in many democracies can scarcely be accommodated with any model of the democratic ideal. Thus one important reason why the citizens cannot participate is that they do not know what is going on. Where outcomes satisfy this will not necessarily lead to distrust of corporate pluralism, but where there is relative deprivation people may become suspicious of the whole democratic process. When a political system is very different from the conventional view of what it is, there is at least a possibility that it may become unstable. If people's expectations of democracy are disappointed then they may turn against it.

A recurring theme in this book has been that without knowledge democracy is flawed. Not only participation in institutional decision-making but also popular discussion and controversy is hampered where certain information is not known. The knowledge required for satisfactory democratic activity is of three kinds. Firstly, a government proposal to privatize a public utility cannot be debated rewardingly without technical knowledge about both the service and its financial position. One might need at least some understanding of both engineering and accountancy. Secondly, knowledge is required about the history of the issues and personalities involved. Awareness of how the argument has proceeded to date is a great advantage. Thirdly, knowledge about contemporary democratic processes is needed and, as I have argued, it is not widespread. Even highly educated democratic citizens are often quite unaware of the difference between what the system is supposed to be and what it is in reality. Either the myths of traditional civics texts encrust like barnacles the minds of some who should know better; or, with others, ideological controversy distorts the image of how democracy operates. All these short-comings will be detrimental to the formation of public opinion through informed debate.

Knowledge about issues is, for the ordinary citizen, difficult to obtain, for two reasons. In the first place democratic politicians naturally misrepresent one another's positions. In the struggle for votes they conceal their real motives and distort information to make it favourable to their own case. Secondly, the mass media are not a very reliable source of information for several reasons. Newspapers, in particular, frequently have connections with parties and politicians and therefore their judgements and even their selection of facts are likely to be biased, unfortunately often widely so. Moreover, the press and television may primarily be interested in commercial profits and therefore the provision of trustworthy political comment is not a primary concern with them. In many democratic countries much of the media has sunk as low as extreme trivialization.[2] Indeed, serious coverage of domestic and foreign political news seems increasingly in short supply. This is especially the case with the daily press in Britain,[3] while television and broad-casting are more and more devoted to entertainment. Hence serious democratic discussion of issues by the public, it often seems, becomes less and less common in spite of rising standards of education. The argument that this is an outcome of consumer preferences, and consequently resembles democratic choice, is not acceptable because people can only make rational choices between options they are informed about. If the media do not set the agenda

---

[2] See N. Postman, *Amusing Ourselves to Death* (1985).

[3] J. Curran and J. Seaton, *Power Without Responsibility: The Press and Broadcasting in Britain* (1981), 128, quantifies the great decline in public affairs news and features in popular British daily newspapers between 1936 and 1976.

of political debate, as some imply,[4] they surely restrict and impoverish it.

The problem is a serious one for contemporary democracies. Freedom of the press remains an under-used right where the press does not inform the people. Many important issues, for example fiscal and economic matters, require a good deal of explanation. Even if the finer points are beyond the average citizen, what she/he wants to know is what impact the policies will make. Hence there is great scope for people who can explain the options in simple and impartial terms. (It may be objected that no one is impartial; the point is that it is not difficult to find expositors who are a good deal less partial than politicians.) Raising the general standard of education is bound to increase understanding though not, perhaps, as much as is often thought; because the issues have become more and more technical, inevitably involving consultation with experts. So even the educated public remains in something of a fog. It seems likely that politicians and civil servants take advantage of this confusion.

What is needed is a comprehensive and detached source of news, in addition to partisan comments, so that people can make up their own minds. Unfortunately, it is not easy to envisage such a source that is not publicly owned; and public ownership carries all the dangers of governmental pressure. Even the BBC, long regarded as an unprejudiced disseminator, so that in other countries the statement 'I heard it on the BBC' is accepted as proof of veracity, has in recent years unfortunately come under criticism and pressure from governments of different complexions. (This in itself is a gauge of its neutrality.) Generally speaking, therefore, it may be difficult to find an absolutely detached source of political information.

Knowledge about the background of decisions is especially important for people involved in decision-making. It is not easy to draw up strategies without being aware of where certain groups or a representative cross-section of individuals stand on an issue. Groups and individuals who have had a long history of involvement may be at a great advantage in making assessments about other's motivations. Ignorance about such matters springs from secret decision-making (common in Britain) or decision-making in which the proceedings, if not secret, are not widely reported.

[4] See T. H. Qualter, *Opinion Control in the Democracies* (1985), 165.

Citizen groups who are unaware of the agenda and timetable of decision-making may find themselves faced with *faits accomplis*.

Finally, we turn to knowledge relating to the workings of one's own democratic system. We have noted the complexity of the dualistic decision-making structure with corporate pluralism rivalling the traditional structure, numerical democracy. While there may be a misunderstanding of the implications of some of the traditional aspects of democracy, such as freedom of speech, there will be almost total lack of grasp about the mixed polity. Trust and tolerance may give way to distrust and intolerance when people find the system cannot easily be understood. People may accept losing the game with good grace when they have understood the rules and believe they have been applied fairly, but they may be much less sportsman-like if they think the rules have not been interpreted clearly or have been rigged. Whether people become alienated or only apathetic, democracy may be endangered. One assumption of democracy—that criticism is of value to those in authority—cannot be fulfilled where citizens withdraw from participation. When a popular view prevails that 'something is going on out there and they are making decisions we will not like in ways we cannot hope to understand', a mood in which democracy can prosper is lacking. This emphasizes how important it is for the political system to be examined critically, explained, and understood. It does not help when leading social scientists are in dispute about some of its specific processes, though such controversy does indicate how remote and obscure, as well as how complex, the policy-making system can be.

Hence there may appear to be a paradox. People's knowledge about political issues and decision-making may be declining in a period when society is becoming more knowledgeable. Robert Lane describes a knowledgeable society as one in which to a greater degree than in other societies people inquire into the basis of their beliefs, are guided by objective standards of truth, and at the upper levels of education devote considerable resources to scientific enquiry, constantly try to extract further meaning from it, and employ this knowledge to illuminate their values and goals as well as to revise them. He believes that in this type of society abstract thinking will result in differentiation of ego from inner world and from environment. Imaginative thought becomes possible. The knowledgeable society is characterized by flexible thinking, making it congruent with the democratic society. Lane contends: 'More than this, the members of the knowledgeable society are endowed with the capacity to tolerate ambiguity, conflict and dissonance.'[5] Those who will tend to make policy in this society will be professional people with tendencies to allocate responsibility for knowledge domains. They will not operate on the criteria of immediate political advantage but on their own standards. Politics will not be eliminated from policy-making, but problem-oriented scientists will have more say. Ideology and dogmatism will decline, replaced by knowledge as the mainspring of policy.

Lane's analysis does not entirely refute my previous picture of the lack of good information about public issues. Indeed, it can easily be accepted as complementary. Basically he describes a society in which technocrats have become much more important. Significantly, he implies a sectionalization of expertise at the same time as total specialized knowledge in the sciences and social sciences has vastly increased. Lane's analysis does not conflict in any way with a decline in political interest and knowledge among democratic publics. Indeed, the rise of the technocrat is one of the factors associated with less citizen involvement. A faith in techniques is a feature of our times, and the temptation to leave judgement and action to those who know better must always be present. This mood will hardly be dissipated by the soporific effect of the media, especially television, which Neil Postman describes as 'a medium which presents information in a form that renders it simplistic, non-substantive, non-historical and non-contextual: this is to say, information packaged as entertainment'.[6] As Ronald Reagan has affirmed, politics is 'just like show business'.[7] The new technology of information can be enlightening politically: conversely it may be used for misinformation.

A great deal of the misunderstanding about decision-making in the modern democratic state arises from problems of economic policy. Some types of issue lend themselves well to democratic methods, others are not so suitable. For example, where the main purpose of the state is to mobilize for battle, the main issues will be national defence and security; immediacy and secrecy in decision-making will be the dominant values. When the issues are simple and

---

[5] R. E. Lane, The Decline of Politics and Ideology in a Knowledgeable Society, *American Sociological Review*, 31 5 (1977), 649–62.

[6] Postman, *Amusing Ourselves to Death*, 141.   [7] Ibid. 125.

lack urgency, so that they can be explained easily and nearly everyone can have time to understand them, democratic decision-making should prosper. Economic policy-making, often perceived by governments as like defence policy, has been one cause of the decline of legislatures. Politicians say it is too technical to be explained. One of the problems, of course, is that many politicians do not understand it. Others think it will bore the voters. Better therefore, many democratic leaders may argue, to obfuscate somewhat. It is well not to be too long-winded and didactic in one's electoral addresses. Television producers certainly emphasize this approach. Politicians also object that there is no mileage in it: the rewards for sound economic policy-making will be enjoyed by the next government but two, in the way that the success of economic policy in the Fifth Republic is said to have been based on the Monnet Plan sponsored by the politicians of the Fourth Republic de Gaulle so despised.

Indeed, some economists have argued that the ability of governments to manipulate the economy in the short run to their electoral advantage, contrasting very ill with their neglect of it in the long run, points to the iniquity of four or five-year governments. There are no votes to be won by acting with economic responsibility. What is needed, therefore, is elections every ten or twelve years, a period in which long-term economic policies, such as research and development, can be evaluated in relation to their sponsor's promises. There are two favourable outcomes suggested for this change—it will make for more responsible government because the effects of policies will be more evident, and it will improve democracies' economic performances. The bad practice which has developed in Britain, for example, of governments relaxing controls on the economy as a general election approaches, has produced what is called the 'political business cycle'.[8] (Where governments have a right to dissolve the legislature, the attraction of this manipulation is enhanced.) Hence fewer elections and longer parliaments and restriction of the number of times a citizen is allowed to cast a ballot for or against the government will improve the

---

[8] Articles on this include four in *Political Studies*: C. A. E. Goodhart and R. J. Bhansali, Political Economy 18 (1970), 86; B. S. Fry and H. Garbers, Politico-Econometrica: On Estimation in Political Economy, 19 (1971), 316; W. L. Miller and M. Mackie, The Electoral Cycle and the Asymmetry of Government; and S. S. Nilson, Politometric Models, 21 (1973), 263 and 280.

efficiency of the economy and the efficacy of democracy. Unfortunately, it will not do much to improve the quality of democracy!

A familiar contemporary view is that democratic governments are doomed to inefficiency, and therefore instability, because they try to do too much. Franz Lehner and Ulrich Widmaier define the dilemma of 'government overload' in stark terms: 'The political institutions of Western democracies are historically the political institutions of a liberal society and have not been designed to manage high demands on government.' If the economy is to be steered there must be a high degree of consensus between different interests, but

The representative institutions of government, mainly elections and parliament, can only integrate a rather low number of issues and can hardly provide a systematic and consensual government programme. This inevitable selectivity involves a strong tendency to cyclical and inconsistent interest aggregation.[9]

Furthermore overloaded government may lead to segmentalized decision-making (as noted in Chapter 7), and this also encourages conflict between interests, rendering both management of the economy and (more importantly for our purposes) accountable and successful government very difficult.

Lehner and Widmaier declare that institutional reforms are needed in democracies to help government resist pressure from organized interests and at the same time to increase government's capacity to deal with conflicting demands. They feel that efforts to set up neo-corporatist structures are a first step in the right direction. Other familiar options relate to dismantling such structures and 'unloading' government. This might be done by weakening important interests by legislation or other means, by cutting or abolishing expenditure on public services, by government withdrawing from relationships with interests, or by various combinations of these methods. Another option would be to take neo-corporatism to its logical conclusions and to institutionalize completely the processes of corporate pluralism. The French Economic and Social Council is an example of this line of action.[10]

[9] F. Lehner and U. Widmaier, Market Failure and Growth of Government: A Sociological Explanation, in C. L. Taylor (ed.), *Why Governments Grow* (1983), 255.
[10] See J. E. S. Hayward, *Private Interests and Public Policy* (1966) for a study of this body.

To what degree an economic and social parliament relates to other legislatures is a problem in itself. It is significant that such assemblies to date have only been consultative; but it may be that their most important function is to provide a forum at which the economic and social problems of the nation are openly and lengthily discussed by, among others, representatives of the interests involved. Through such an institution the country might be better informed of the issues. On the other hand, if the economic and social parliament is excluded from decision-making, the same objections about lack of accountability will arise. One ultimate conclusion could be that major economic strategies which require a high level of rationality cannot be reconciled with democracy. Attempts to pursue such strategies will only endanger democracy.

The degree to which democracy is directly threatened in the contemporary state can be exaggerated. An assessment of the matter involves examining the present condition of those identifying features which were categorized in Chapter 1. Public contestation has not been seriously impaired in any well-established democracy: if anything, it has somewhat increased during recent decades though the needs of national security and the expansion of government espionage are present threats. Inclusiveness has been extended. In most democracies, during recent years, the qualifying age for the suffrage has been lowered to eighteen. There are no convincing threats to restrict this right in any of the well-established democracies. Consequently it is only accountability, or upward control, which can be perceived to be not operating properly. Democratic governments are only accountable in that they can be dismissed by electorates; they are often not accountable in the sense that voters can exercise much control over them in between elections. Moreover, the fact that during election campaigns they give so few accurate and comprehensive accounts of their activities hinders the voters from properly assessing their performances, so that 'throwing out the rascals' cannot proceed as judiciously as it should. Lacking basic information it is not easy to choose between the more rascally and the less rascally politicians.

The trend towards less accountability of democratic governments emanates from several sources. Clearly the growing propensity of bureaucrats and technocratic experts to make policy does not enhance citizen control. Where even elected representatives may not be involved in policy-making, the fact that they can be questioned and even censured about the policy once implemented gives them only ritualistic responsibility.[11] The more policy formation is in the hands of the unelected, the more accountability is threatened. This may apply also to interest-group leaders who may or may not be responsive and responsible to their followers, and with whom governments may strike bargains not reported to legislatures. Furthermore, the media, which certainly hold politicians accountable in one sense, can never be substitutes for the supervising of elected legislators. Media commentators may cross-examine politicians about specific issues; but are not so well suited to examining broad policies either in the process of formulation or implementation. Thus the media may occasionally score a great triumph for democracy, as with Watergate; but their concentration on sensation and on personalities tends to distract citizens from the humdrum issues about which their everyday experiences should make their opinions most valuable.

Politicians must also bear a share of the trend towards less accountability. In the first place this is hardly surprising, for the avoidance of responsibility is a human failing and politicians are called upon to bear more responsibilities than most. The pressures of electoral politics force them into numerous evasions, and particularly where information is complex and technical it may be easy to transfer the blame to political opponents. The complexities of issues and their increasing volume lead elected representatives to rely on bureaucrats and technocrats; and the decline of legislatures has emphasized the roles of a few leaders at the top. The increase in the power of executives in well-established democracies in the twentieth century reflects a concentration of steering in the hands of a few. They have greater power than ever before. Sectional struggles within executives over expenditure have tended further to confirm presidential-type powers in the hands of highly visible leaders, thus emphasizing personalities rather than policies and even more lessening accountability to the voters. The voters cannot consciously control policies where they attach more importance to personality traits. The attention paid to leaders as trouble-shooters—often fostered by the leaders themselves—leads to an emphasis on specific and immediate issues. Social and economic policies, seldom of this nature, need more of an effort to understand. Yet it is the outcomes

[11] D. F. Thompson, Bureaucracy and Democracy, in G. Duncan (ed.), *Democratic Theory and Practice* (Cambridge, 1983), 240.

of such policies which affect the voters most. Thus a good deal of upward control stems from politicians' anticipations of voters' reactions.

Finally, democratic voters must bear some responsibility for the trend against accountability. Majority pressures have shaped many of the ways in which democratic governments behave, encouraging the evolution of positive government and the rise of programmatic parties. Their voters have inclined these parties to the welfare state, Keynesian management, and social reform. In time such programmes have necessitated the great extension of the state apparatus, the centralization and concentration of power, and the development of corporate pluralism. Reform-mongering and problem-solving have become important features of government because most voters wanted it so. Democratic politicians in the twentieth century have interpreted the mood of the voters correctly in furthering popular measures whose complexity has led to more elaborate problems and, as I have argued at length, weakened upward control over policy formulation and implementation. In this way the responsiveness of elected representatives to voters' pressures has led to a diminution of accountability. In the last resort, the proper functioning of democracy must depend on the electorate feeling, at least to some degree, that it is part of the country's political life and that it has some responsibility to concern itself with the effect of the implementation of majority demands on democratic processes and national well-being.

An authoritative statement about the relationship between accountability and democracy is impossible for reasons already given. Total accountability between elections would make any government unviable. Therefore we are left with the problem of determining how much unaccountability is acceptable before democracy is endangered; or how much accountability is needed to ensure a thriving democracy. Clearly this will vary between one situation and another. Accountability will be greater where there is much freedom of information, as in the United States and Sweden, and where processes of investigation and supervision are open to the public, possibly on television. Where parliaments have more power over governments, either because of constitutional provisions or because of multi-party legislatures, there is also likely to be more accountability. One might reasonably argue that upward control must include the chance to query minor decisions *post hoc* and to debate major issues before policy is finalized. Variations here will depend on political cultures. Where local government has vitality, as in Scandinavia, participation in a national debate over proposed policies may be much greater, though the 'remiss' system may reinforce pressure group consultation, rather than popular discussion. Undoubtedly higher standards of education are likely to produce democratically aware electorates more anxious to control governments. Attempts to improve accountability would therefore, be concerned with providing greater freedom of information; and with educating citizens to a higher level of democratic consciousness; as well as with constitutional change to give legislatures greater powers and weaken executives.

A good deal of the argument in this book has been based on impressions of how ordinary democratic citizens response to political procedures, decisions, and leadership. Much of the evidence stems from personal experience and observation and, more importantly, sample surveys and works such as Robert Lane's *Political Ideology*. It is not possible, however, to say with any precision how democratic electorates perceive democracy. Do they know what it is? Do they know how it works? To what degree is it associated in their minds with the reward system and/or all those other familiar institutional practices in their own country which may or may not be democratic? Are they familiar with the institutions of, and the points of access to, the decision-making system? Are they aware of the importance of the rule of law and observance of the constitutional conventions? Do they know the rules of the game? Do they react against attacks on democratic values?

No simple single answer can be given to these questions. In general it appears that democratic publics are fairly satisfied with their political instititions and procedures, though in their minds they may see 'democracy' as a term covering all the decision-making systems of their societies. Hence it is not easy to say whether it is the democratic regime which is seen as legitimate.[12] In Britain, for instance, it might be the presence of the monarchy which persuades many to accord legitimacy. Those who are familiar with questionnaires will realize how difficult it would be to put the question to the public. Long experience of talking to ordinary

---

[12] For a discussion of this point see F. Bealey, How, When, and Why does Democracy Collapse? Thoughts on Threats to its Stability. Paper given to the Workshop at Barcelona, March 1985.

citizens in several well-established democracies, as well as the results of opinion polls, leads me to guess that the rights of free expression are strongly valued, though taken too much for granted; that the voting right is often implemented as a civic duty without much feeling that it makes any difference; that the idea of governments responsible to the electorate is mostly only a concrete reality at election times; and that the rule of law is not often viewed as of importance to democracy, though people may accept it for other reasons. Different groups put their own interpretations on democracy. With trade unions the perception tends to be majoritarian and includes a strong emphasis on the right of association; with businessmen the accent is on minority rights and law and order; with intellectuals the priority is freedom of self-expression and creative activity. When its own cherished priority is under threat, a group may claim democracy is under threat. Radical governments that effect considerable changes are often perceived as menacing democracy, for example, the Labour governments between 1945 and 1951; or the Conservative governments between 1979 and 1987. Much of the hysterical language comes from those groups who feel their livelihood is menaced.

Whether democracy as a system is likely to be maintained is a question I have attempted to answer elsewhere.[13] *Coups d'état* by military men and foreign invasions are the two most common circumstances in which democracy has been terminated. Other democracies have collapsed through ethnic/linguistic conflict. All these factors have been operative in countries where democracy is very recent. In more established democracies, however, there are those who see the regime threatened by a legitimation crisis. Commentators on the left and right believe breakdown will come through economic failure destroying the legitimacy of democratic governments. The left sees the contradictions between the promises that governments have to make to maintain the capitalist system and their unsatisfactory performances in a world of inflation and depression. The failure of capitalism will be mirrored in the downfall of democracy, a structure maintained by the propaganda of the powerful capitalist state. This analysis is conditioned by the decline of socialism, as a popularly held set of ideas, over the last two decades. In Marxist terms the working class, instead of developing a higher form of consciousness, has actually degenerated by moving backwards and acquiring more widely a 'false'

[13] Ibid. See also Bibliographical note, 285, below.

consciousness. The right believe economic disaster will be the result of too much collectivism and welfarism, which will eventually result in public disorder because the masses, unwilling to support less public expenditure, will revolt against the harsh measures of monetarist retrenchment that are necessary. Both right and left views are postulated by analysts with little knowledge of ordinary democratic citizens, the vast majority of whom remain in the centre.

In all states, whatever their regimes, similar features can be found that characterize to a greater or lesser degree both the rulers and the ruled. Most ordinary citizens want as much unpredictability as possible removed from their lives; but they do not want to incur the costs of time involved in extensive political action. They are probably sceptical about the motives of those who participate in politics, especially those who become leaders; but the ruled are to some extent dependent on those who exercise power. Under democracy, however, dependence is qualified, and the somewhat arbitrary nature of governmental actions is mitigated by a certain amount of citizen control. Public contestation provides some opportunity to obtain information; but it obliges democratic citizens to relinquish some of their leisure. A minority may enjoy political activity and discussion, but most do not want to pay the price of informing themselves. Rulers everywhere do not enjoy criticism, and they want to conceal as far as possible information that may be used to their disadvantage. Furthermore, they want to stay in power as long as possible. Rulers in democracies, no less than anywhere else, harbour these sentiments; but unlike rulers in other regimes they find it very difficult to fulfil them. They will not be able to avoid criticism, they will not always find it easy to conceal information, and their stay in power is most unlikely to be lengthy.

Democracy, then, needs better politicians and better citizens. This would be true at any time. Is it especially a need in the late twentieth century? And have both leaders and voters deteriorated as practising democrats in recent decades? While it is quite impossible to respond authoritatively to these questions there are indications of cause for concern.

For example, the political culture of the major democracies will probably have changed in recent decades under the impact of some of the forces I have mentioned. Almond and Verba in their classic work,[14] concerned as they were with the future of democracy,

[14] G. A. Almond and S. Verba, *The Civic Culture* (Princeton, 1963).

confined their remarks to its evolution in the developed world. Any movement, they speculated would be to a higher form, that is from an Alienative or Apathetic political culture to an Allegiant one. They did not anticipate a tendency in the opposite direction. Yet there are contemporary trends which at least suggest that this is possible. The rather lower level of electoral participation in recent years might be one indication. This might be a sign of less subjective competence among the electorate—citizens feel they can do less to influence government in ways they want—and this might well be based on less information about political processes. I have given reasons above why this could be so. The division between the better educated and increasingly knowledgeable professional classes and the less well-informed masses might reflect a growing fragment-ation of political sub-cultures. A technocratic intelligentsia with greater knowledge and subjective competence becomes more politi-cally active (in single-issue pressure group politics, perhaps) at the same time as the less well-educated withdraw from political partici-pation. This scenario is not too far-fetched. In such a situation strains would develop between the new culture and new structures. The values and behaviour associated with pluralistic bargaining do not encourage political participation and probably discourage the growth of feelings of competence. Furthermore, it might be argued that there has been a weakening of the socializing agents which support the civil culture—that political culture which is congruent with democracy. For instance, the growing disintegration of family life imperils the transmission of cultural values; formal education, one can agree with Almond and Verba,[15] is not a powerful agent; and other socializing forces such as voluntary associations may be suffering from the same problems of membership withdrawal as political parties.

This analysis is at least feasible. It can hardly be denied that there must be a gap between the values and attitudes of a political culture associated with numerical democracy and the mixed polity as it has been described above. It is open to question how serious this is. Bargaining, for example, is very familiar and unlikely to be seen as illegitimate; and the decline in participation is of doubtful impor-tance. Explanations range from quite technical reasons to televi-sion.[16] The privatization of modern society does not necessarily lead

---

[15] Ibid. 502.
[16] For example J. H. Fenton, Comparative Study of the Relations Between Polit-ical Stability and Electoral Turnout in the UK and the US. Paper given at the ECPR

to atomization, even though it might obviate against collective action. The decline in popular interest in public affairs may only be temporary and it has not taken place in all the democracies. There is much evidence to support the view that ordinary citizens are becoming more confident and competent.[17] Agents like family and school may have been exaggerated as factors in *political* socialization.[18] In sum: it is not easy to evaluate how much the political cultures of the well-established democracies might be retrogressing from Allegiant to Apathetic. More research on public attitudes in the democracies would be needed before judgements could be made confidently. What is clear is that there has been socio-cultural change and changes in political structures and processes. Citizen 'orientations' (to use Almond and Verba's word) towards their democratic polities are likely, therefore, to be in some state of uncertainty. Suspicions in such circumstances may well be aroused.

I have argued that trust is an especially important value for the maintenance of democracy. Trust in the regime and its procedures is much more important than trust in politicians, but eventually if people begin to feel that all the politicians, and the rest of the state apparatus, are untrustworthy, the regime will be distrusted. Most human beings prefer to trust than to distrust; but trust is fragile. If trust is lost, it is difficult to regain. Distrust, as Luhmann says, 'has a tense, even frantic character'.[19] Simple micro-polities are likely, other things being equal, to arouse little distrust. But larger states with more complicated structures will need more effort to retain trust. Furthermore, where situations and people change, trust will be especially under strain. Luhmann argues also that highly differentiated and mobile systems need particularly high standards of trust.[20] Clearly the contemporary democratic states decision-making processes have become exceedingly complex, and as we have seen they can change quickly with the changing economic situation. It is easy, therefore, to come to the conclusion that a good deal of suspicion has been aroused by the proliferation of pluralistic bargaining in conjunction with the advance of technocracy. In

workshop at Barcelona, March 1985. Fenton argues that the lowering of the voting age to 18 accounts for much of the fall in electoral turnout.

[17] For example, there is much more pressure-group activity among under privileged groups.

[18] M. Rush and P. Althoff, *An Introduction to Political Sociology* (1971), 38. In pointing out this they quote M. K. Jennings and R. G. Niemie, The Transmission of Political Values from Parent to Child, *American Political Science Review*, 62 (1968), 169–84.   [19] N. Luhmann, *Trust* (Stuttgart, 1973), 71.   [20] Ibid. 28.

Britain successive governments' failed economic policies might also explain any increase in distrust of the democratic regime.

Fred Hirsch has written of certain social values as public goods whose presence makes society more pleasant.[21] Trust and tolerance, the two values basic to democracy, are clearly of this nature and, as he suggests, can be regarded as public goods. Secondary democratic values emanating from trust and tolerance are a belief in decency, or fair play; good manners and civility even to political opponents; civic courage; and a feeling that one can pursue a normal private life without too much arbitrary intrusion from other citizens. All are part of the quality of democratic life. All these values are public goods: in order for them to be enjoyed a sort of collective rationality must reign. It is hard to resist the conclusion that democracy operates more successfully where there is caring and consideration for others' democratic rights. All citizens can contribute to, and benefit from, the appreciation of these values. Indeed, in the long run, citizen appreciation is the only way in which they can be safeguarded.

Yet, in the short and medium run, democratic values are particularly in the custody of the media and the politicians. However vigorous the partisanship it should remain within the limits of the rules of the game. The actions of the chief contenders and their attitudes to each other and towards the citizens set the tone in which political relationships are carried on. If political leaders come to regard the voters as credulous, stupid, and easily manipulable, and if they presume that their political adversaries are capable of subverting democracy and should be silenced, the democratic polity may be in danger. The partisanship of the media can accentuate these tendencies: trivialization of the debate by the media may result in democratic values being neglected.

Thus there are numerous opportunities in the contemporary democratic state for the regime to be imperilled. Indeed, some may wonder why it has survived so long. Perhaps many younger democratic citizens today are unable to envisage democracy being overthrown. The older generation will have no problem in imagining how this could happen. Insensitivity to undemocratic behaviour does not help. The price of preserving democracy is eternal

---

[21] F. Hirsch, The Ideological Underlay of Inflation, in F. Hirsch and J. H. Goldthorpe (eds.), *The Political Economy of Inflation* (1978), 274.

vigilance. This implies a continuous effort to understand how it operates in a changing world. More knowledge about society, more knowledge about the economy, and more knowledge about the polity are essential parts of such an exercise in comprehension. I hope that in a small way this book will be a modest contribution.

BIBLIOGRAPHICAL NOTE

WRITING a book of this kind must involve consulting numerous works. Between three and four hundred are referred to in the notes, and listing these would run to many pages. Furthermore, each chapter relates to one of the major areas of political science, and bibliographies of each could be hugely forbidding. Consequently I am limiting this note to works which themselves contain useful bibliographies, or which are not mentioned in the text but which are helpful background reading, or to a few which have been published since I completed the text. Let it be said at the outset that unless otherwise stated, place of publication was London.

Chapter 1 is not a conventional introduction to democratic theory. A good preliminary to the latter, illustrating the variety of approaches, is the collection of essays published by UNESCO, *Democracy in a World of Tensions* (Paris, 1951). A recent revival of an old argument is H. P. Kainz, *Democracy East and West* (1984). R. M. Christensen et al., *Ideologies and Modern Politics* (New York, 1975) provides a useful beginners' reading list about democracy and modern ideologies. J. A. Corry and J. E. Hodgetts, *Democratic Government and Politics* (3rd edn., Toronto, 1963) also includes a basic bibliography, though now it is considerably out of date. J. R. Pennock, *Democratic Political Theory* (Princeton, 1979) is a wide-ranging treatment of concepts, though its illustrative material is largely confined to the United States. The bibliography is good on the conceptual side. G. Sartori's new book, *The Theory of Democracy Revisited*, 2 vols. (1987) is bound to be important, though it has no bibliography. As far as the state is concerned, T. Skocpol, *States and Social Revolutions* (Cambridge, 1979) provides a massive bibliography with regard to the development of the pre-democratic state. P. Dunleavy and B. O'Leary, *Theories of the State: The Politics of Liberal Democracy* (1987) is a very different treatment from mine. They focus on the state as it is perceived in terms of contemporary political science models and there is a lengthy bibliography.

For enlightenment about representative democracy (Chapter 2) one must still turn to the classic works of A. L. Lowell and J. Bryce cited in the text. H. F. Pitkin *The Concept of Representation* (Berkeley and Los Angeles, 1967) is a basic work on the idea of representation. General works about legislatures are rare these days. K. C. Wheare (1968) remains the best short introduction. It has a bibliography. C. Schmitt, *The Crisis of Parliamentary Democracy*, trans. by E. Kennedy (1985, 1st German edn. 1926) relates to the decline of legislatures. The bibliography, from the original edition refers predominantly to German publications. H. Eulau and J. C. Wahlke,

The Politics of Representation (1978) has a useful, though US-oriented, bibliography. Other works are specific to countries. The United States is best served in this respect by J. L. Sundquist, *The Decline and Resurgence of Congress* (1981). L. C. Dodd and B. I. Oppenheimer, *Congress Reconsidered* (New York, 1977) lists the important studies of Congress in the 1960s and early 1970s. Britain and France seem badly provided for. Direct democracy is even less well covered by general works. J. M. Denquin, *Referendum et Plebiscite* (Paris, 1976) is the best bibliography on the European experience. With regard to accountability of governments there seems little of a general nature. G. Marshall, *Constitutional Conventions: The Rules and Forms of Political Accountability* (Oxford, 1986) is specific to Britain.

Chapter 3, by contrast, is bibliographically blessed. M. Albrow, *Bureaucracy* (1970) concludes with an extensive bibliography of both theoretical and empirical works. D. Beetham, *Max Weber and the Theory of Modern Politics* (1974) is a comprehensive treatment. A. Downs, *Inside Bureaucracy* (1966) initiated the wider approach. He provides a long bibliography. E. Page, *Political Authority and Bureaucratic Power* (Brighton, 1985) also has a very up-to-date bibliography. J. P. Olsen, *Organized Democracy* (Oslo, 1983) likewise contains an exhaustive bibliography with a salting of Scandinavian studies. With regard to planning, the best bibliography from the philosophic angle is in M. Cambis, *Planning Theory and Philosophy* (1979). At the ends of the chapters in A. Faludi, *Planning Theory* (Oxford, 1973) there are lists of numerous references. The role of the state apparatus in individual countries has useful bibliographic coverage in J. Hayward, *The One and Indivisible French Republic* (1973); and A. G. Jordan and J. J. Richardson, *British Politics and the Policy Process* (1987). For the United States there is a vast literature. Bibliographies can be found in M. Crenson, *The Federal Machine* (Baltimore, 1975); H. Seidman, *Politics, Position and Power* (2nd edn., 1976) and M. J. Boskin and A. Wildavsky, (eds.), *The Federal Budget: Economics and Politics* (1982).

Chapter 4 also has much bibliographic support. Inevitably most of the discussion relates to the contemporary extent of centralization rather than the state of local democracy. A good beginning is to read the very scholarly bibliographic essay in D. E. Ashford, *British Dogmatism and French Pragmatism* (1982). J. Gyford, *Local Politics in Britain* (1976) has a useful bibliography. French authors fight shy of bibliographies. On French local politics P. A. Gourevitch, *Paris and the Provinces* (Berkeley, 1980) has a short but helpful one with references also to Italy. In M. Kesselman, *The Ambiguous Consensus* (New York, 1967) the bibliography refers to earlier in the post-war period. American local politics is impossible to cover as a whole. C. R. Adrian and C. Press, *Governing Urban America* (3rd ed.

1968) include a list of periodicals and works on American cities. Much of the coverage of US local democracy, however, is in community studies. C. M. Bonjean, T. N. Clark, and R. Lineberry, *Community Politics* (1971) contains two long lists of these, one of them compiled by R. J. Pellegrin. Two works on decentralization with bibliographies are B. C. Smith, *Decentralisation* (1985) and L. Lundquist, *Means and Goals of Political Decentralisation* (Malmo, 1972) which includes references to the organizational literature.

The theme of equality can be approached from several sides. From the philosophic angle J. C. Rees, *Equality* (1971) is a brief introduction with a competent bibliography. E. S. Phelps (ed.), *Economic Justice* (1973) stretches his list of recommended reading from ethics to welfare economics. R. C. O. Matthews (ed.), *Economy and Democracy* (1985) has useful references at the ends of some essays, especially P. Jackson, Economy, Democracy and Bureaucracy. D. Mueller, *Public Choice* (1979) provides a wealth of reading on that topic. Among sociologists, G. Lenski's classic work, *Power and Privilege* (1963), is accompanied by a lengthy bibliography on inequality and power. A. Giddens, *The Class Structure of the Advanced Societies* (1973) is useful as a background to Chapters 6 and 7 also. It contains an excellent bibliography.

Perhaps the best approach to general reading for Chapter 6 would be the bibliography, set out country by country, at the end of R. A. Dahl (ed.), *Political Oppositions in Western Democracies* (Yale, 1966). The same author's *The Dilemmas of Pluralist Democracy* (Yale, 1982) gives a wide though short list of cited works. W. A. Kelso, *American Democratic Theory* (1978) is a more discursive work with a much more comprehensive bibliography. In J. La Palombara and M. Weiner, *Political Parties and Political Development* (2nd edn., 1972), Naomi E. Kies has compiled a lengthy bibliography on parties and party systems generally. H. Daalder and P. Mair (eds.), *Western European Party Systems* (1983) have produced a comprehensive list for Western European parties. R. T. McKenzie, *British Political Parties* (2nd revised edn. 1962) has a good bibliography on British parties. D. B. Truman, *The Governmental Process* (2nd edn., 1971) concludes with a survey of the literature on American pressure groups. G. K. Wilson, *Interest Groups in the United States* (Oxford, 1981) brings it up to date. On British pressure groups, J. J. Richardson and A. G. Jordan, *Governing Under Pressure* (1979) contains a bibliography on British pressure groups and the policy process. M. Moran, *Politics and Society in Britain* (1985) provides a useful reading list on the socio-economic background and political culture in the United Kingdom. A. R. Ball, *Modern Politics and Government* (3rd edn. 1983) is a useful summary with a basic bibliography referring to all aspects of political systems.

With reference to Chapter 7, W. Korpi, *The Democratic Class Struggle*

(1983) is a very contemporary account of the role of organized labour in a democracy. It is well supported by a long bibliography with much material from Scandinavian writers. K. von Beyme, *Challenge to Power* (1980) is an even more general account of the position of trade unions and contains a wide-ranging bibliography. E. Shorter and C. Tilley, *Strikes in France, 1830–1968* (Cambridge, 1974) has not only a lengthy bibliography on France but also on industrial relations elsewhere. H. Pelling, *A History of British Trade Unionism* (4th edn. 1987) brings the story of British trade unions up to the 1980s. Particularly strong on political activity, it includes a bibliographic essay of 17 pages. G. K. Wilson has not only produced one of the best recent assessments of American labour in *Unions in American National Politics* (1979) with a helpful bibliography but also the best recent general work on *Business and Politics* (1985). In the latter there are separate treatments of the United States, West Germany, Britain, France, and Japan, followed by an up-to-date bibliography. P. G. Cerny and M. A. Schain (eds.), *French Politics and Public Policy* (1980) deal with aspects of the political activity of French business. The debate on corporatism is perhaps best represented by P. Schmitter and G. Lehmbruch (eds.), *Trends Towards Corporatist Intermediation* (1979) and C. Crouch, *The Politics of Industrial Relations* (1979). Both books have useful bibliographies.

L. J. Edinger (ed.), *Political Leadership in Industrialized Societies* (New York, 1967) contains easily the best bibliography for Chapter 8's contents. D. D. Searing assisted in its compilation. It is exhaustive, dealing with élites at both national and sub-national level; and providing biographies of individual politicians and studies of them from a psychological angle. Inevitably much of the literature is concerned with the American presidency. In J. M. Burns, *Leadership* (New York, 1978) there is a lengthy discussion of the sources used. J. D. Barber, *The Presidential Character* (Englewood Cliffs, 1979) has a very long bibliography appended. B. M. Bass, *Leadership, Psychology and Organisational Behaviour* (1960) provides a lengthy treatment of sources.

For the concluding chapter C. B. Macpherson, *The Life and Times of Liberal Democracy* (Oxford, 1977) is the best example of assuming liberalism and democracy are necessarily linked. Two other themes which emerge are the extent of media influence and the possibility of value change in directions harmful to democracy. With regard to the first, T. H. Qualter, *Opinion Control in the Democracies* (1985) contains an excellent bibliography. In the case of the second we confront the difficulties of assessing complex attitudes. Political psychology is an infant social science as yet. R. Inglehart, *The Silent Revolution* (Princeton, 1977) and A. Marsh, *Protest and Political Consciousness* (1977) deal with this topic. Both books have extensive bibliographies. The fears of anti-democratic attitudes emerging have been best exemplified in M. Crozier, S. P. Huntington, and

J. Watanuki, *The Crisis of Democracy* (New York, 1975). A long list of references about the crisis literature ends my article, Stability and Crisis: Fears about Threats to Democracy in *European Journal of Political Research*, 15 (1987) 687–715. A recent book on the British media is J. Seaton and B. Pimlott, *The Media in British Politics*, (1987).

Finally, it should be remembered that the books recommended in respect of Chapters 3, 4, 5, 6, 7, and 8 are each much more concerned with their respective sector of political life than with its implications for democracy.

INDEX